The Troubles
in Ballybogoin

The Troubles in Ballybogoin

MEMORY and IDENTITY
in NORTHERN IRELAND

William F. Kelleher Jr.

THE UNIVERSITY OF MICHIGAN PRESS
Ann Arbor

2006   2005   2004   2003   4   3   2   1

A CIP catalog record for this book is available from the British Library.

Library of Congress Cataloging-in-Publication Data

Kelleher, William F., 1950–
    The troubles in Ballybogoin : memory and identity in Northern Ireland /
William F. Kelleher, Jr.
        p.   cm.
    Includes bibliographical references and index.
    ISBN 0-472-11169-8 (Cloth : alk. paper)
        1. Northern Ireland—Social conditions—1969–   2. Northern
Ireland—History.   I. Title.
    HN398.N6 K445   2003
    306'.09416—dc21   2002156249

FOR
Jo, Susan,
AND *Kathleen*

Contents

Preface
and Acknowledgments

This book is about identity in Northern Ireland. In it, I delineate and interpret a number of sites where the work of identity formation takes place in and around Ballybogoin, a town in the western region of the province. Ballybogoin, a fictitious name, is a socially and politically divided place where Catholics slightly outnumber Protestants in the urban area but form a clear majority in the town's hinterland. Both town and country receive attention throughout this book.

The terms "Catholic" and "Protestant" designate political, not religious, communities in this text. Citizens in Ballybogoin refer to the broadest local group to which they belong and the group from which they differentiate themselves through these two categories. The rhetoric of religion certainly enters the politics of division in Ballybogoin, but political identities, not religious ones, constitute the major arena of struggle. "Protestant" translates into Ulster unionist and "Catholic" into Irish nationalist in this ethnography. I do not, as some social scientists do, use lowercase letters to spell these terms to index their meaning as political rather than religious entities. I maintain uppercase letters to remind the reader that these groupings are multiply formed. Religious discourses and economic discourses, among others, have worked to produce and reproduce the contested identities that concern this book, and the spellings deployed indicate that history.

The research that informs this work began in the mid-1980s and continued through 1999. I lived continuously in Ballybogoin from June 1984 until December 1985 and have returned for short-term visits to Ballybogoin and its outlying areas six times since.

I would have liked to be precise about the town's location, its name, its demographics, and its specific history because this book emphasizes the importance of the past and of the social context in understanding the everyday practices that make Ballybogoin's social identities and its political conundrums. I have been imprecise to protect the privacy of the people who taught me the complexities of life in the Ballybogoin region and for reasons of safety. Ballybogoin was a violent social space and is still a frightfully conflicted one. I promised anonymity to the many consultants who steered me through the area's complex social terrain, but I told them, as well, that total anonymity would be impossible if I told a story that would come to grips with their everyday lives. I do not use composite individuals, so people who know the area well will likely recognize persons described here. Readers familiar with Northern Ireland will likely recognize the actual place that is represented in these pages.

Ballybogoin's Irish nationalist people are the subject matter of this book. When I conceived this research, I had hoped this would not be the case. I planned to conduct fieldwork in two factories, a Protestant firm and a Catholic firm, to establish networks with what Ballybogoin people call "both sides of the house." I was not able to do this. I worked in a nationalist factory, one I have named the Drumcoo Glassworks, and did not get a chance to work in a unionist factory.

I developed ties with both communities but had the opportunity to engage Catholics to a far greater extent. I went to work with them, participated in their leisure time activities, and got to know Catholic families from a variety of places and in a multiplicity of relationships. I never became this familiar with the Protestant people from the area, but I did meet regularly with a relatively narrow network of the town's unionist citizens.

Irish nationalist citizens of the Ballybogoin area make their collective identities in constant negotiation with their unionist neighbors even when they do not speak to them. For Catholics, Protestants are an enduring presence however absent they may be from their immediate physical surroundings, homes, and neighborhoods. Protestants are in the same situation. Each constitutes the other as they go about the never-ending process of making their collective selves. This study registers this. Every site analyzed has both identities present, if not with concrete individuals then with beings of their social imaginations.

In the course of researching and writing this book I have incurred many debts. The greatest one is to the people of Ballybogoin. They welcomed me into their beleaguered social world and shared with me their considerable tragedies, their abilities to endure, and their wonderfully creative senses of humor. "Both sides of the house" left me with lessons of value that go far beyond what I can transmit in these pages.

The management of the Drumcoo Glassworks allowed me to conduct fieldwork in their offices and in their two factory sites. They opened up their archives and allowed me the freedom to explore whatever interested me in the production process. For this access and their generosity, I am extremely grateful. The workers at the glassworks, both white collar and blue collar, deserve my greatest thanks. They accorded me the wonderful hospitality for which they are renowned. They connected me to family and neighborhood networks, taught me about work and play in their divided social world, and extended kindness at every turn, as did their families and kin. No acts of exchange could reciprocate the debts I owe them and am still accruing after seventeen years.

The warmth and hospitality of many people in the Ballybogoin area made fieldwork remarkably easy to negotiate at certain times and very difficult at other times. Both Ulster unionists and Irish nationalists believed they suffered from negative representations at home and abroad, and they took it upon themselves to show me those aspects of themselves that differed from those stereotypes. The two groups understood, however, that the opposing political community often contradicted their stories. When one group or the other saw me with the other side, they often remarked on my absence from them and, at times, became suspicious of my intentions.

When I focused my attention on Protestants and let my relations in the Catholic community lapse for even a period of a week, I was accused of forgetting my friends and of ignoring my social obligations. The same was true, but less so, when my contacts with the Protestant community waned. Relatively less protest was made, I believe, because I was much less invested with the Protestants of Ballybogoin.

One interlocutor brought this to my attention one day at a drinking session in what was considered the most exclusively Protestant pub in the town, one that Catholic Irish nationalists did not patronize even though it was owned, as most pubs were, by a Roman Catholic. I asked this man, "Do any Catholics ever drink here?" He looked at me funnily and said, "Well, you're drinking here, aren't ye!" I was classified as an American, a stranger, in Ballybogoin but was labeled as leaning to the Roman Catholic, Irish nationalist side by both Protestants and Catholics, although people discounted that I could fathom the passions that possessed them. "You'd have t'have grown up here to really understand it," many people told me.

In these circumstances, and I believe it is impossible to get beyond this, I have produced only partial understandings, partial truths, of Ballybogoin's complicated social world. I did not establish a fully objective position. As Begoña Aretxaga writes in the introduction to her study of women in Belfast, "In Northern Ireland, as perhaps in all places, writing does not escape the arena of hotly contested political claims." Citing Max Weber, she reminds us that "partiality is the inevitable predicament of the social sciences" (Aretxaga 1997, 22). I produce partial perspectives throughout this ethnography and take full responsibility for it. I could never know it all.

A variety of colleagues and friends have constantly kept me in mind of that predicament as they have prodded me to improve upon the conceptualization and writing of this material. Aram A. Yengoyan, as a teacher and friend, was the first to do so, and his lessons at a variety of levels have been crucially important. In the planning stages of this project Joy Wolf, Yoshinobu Ota, Lindsay French, and David B. Edwards were important interlocutors. The Institute of Irish Studies at Queens University, Belfast, provided an intellectual home for me in the academic year prior to starting fieldwork. The director of the institute, Ronald H. Buchanan, advised me on the Ballybogoin area and connected me to it through his network of former students. I thank the Horace H. Rackham School of Graduate Studies at the University of Michigan for the Queens University Exchange Fellowship that enabled me to spend an academic year in Belfast.

The Social Science Research Council supported the first phase of the field research for this study through its Fellowship Program for Western Europe. Sponsored by the American Council of Learned Societies, funds for the program were provided by the Ford Foundation, the William and Flora Hewlett Foundation, and the National Endowment for the Humanities. A National Endowment for the Humanities Summer Fellowship allowed me to return to the field in 1992. A William and Flora Hewlett Foundation Summer International Research Grant enabled me to conduct research on the Irish border in 1996. I am grateful for a leave and a research fellowship from the Center for Advanced Study at the University of Illinois.

The collegial network at the University of Illinois has deepened my interdisciplinary resources and helped me to sort out some of the material in this book. The Unit for Criticism and Interpretive Theory provided me a forum with which to try out some of the ideas that appear here. The Department of Anthropology has been a source of welcomed criticism and intellectual excitement for me over the past several years. Matti Bunzl, Alma Gottlieb, Janet Keller, F. K. Lehman, Steve Leigh, Martin Manalansan, Andrew Orta, Arlene Torres, and Norman Whitten have been sources of intellectual encouragement. The department's sociocultural anthropology workshop gave me an opportunity to present some of my later thinking on this project. So Jin Park and Edward M. Bruner offered particularly insightful criticism on that occasion. Brenda Farnell and Charles R. Varela read chapters of the manuscript and offered particularly apt suggestions. Alejandro Lugo read a variety of chapters and offered persistent criticism and collegial advice. He has been a source of intellectual excitement and comradeship. I have been most fortunate to have Nancy Abelmann as a colleague and friend in my years at the University of Illinois. Nancy has read most of this book at one time or another and several parts of it in their different stages. I have come to expect insightful criticism, friendly encouragement, and helpful suggestions from her.

For comments and suggestions on drafts of chapters, I thank the members of the Anthropology of Europe Workshop at the University of Chicago, particularly Daphne Berdahl and James Fernandez. Yoshinobu Ota read chapter 6 and applied his astute theoretical insights to its problems. Begoña Aretxaga and Marilyn Cohen read the entire manuscript, lent insightful criticisms, and proposed suggestions for reorganization that were very helpful. Susan Whitlock at the University of Michigan Press offered appreciated guidance and encouragement.

I am grateful to the Grand Orange Lodge of Ireland for permission to reprint several long passages from *Orangeism: A New Historical Appreciation* (Belfast: Grand Orange Lodge of Ireland, 1969). A slightly different version of chapter 7 was published as "Putting Masculinity to Work on a Northern Ireland Shopfloor," in Marilyn Cohen and Nancy J.

Curtin, eds., *Reclaiming Gender: Transgressive Identities in Modern Ireland* (New York: St. Martin's Press, 1999), 123–41, copyright © Marilyn Cohen and Nancy J. Curtin. I gratefully acknowledge Palgrave and St. Martin's Press for permission to reprint this revised version of that paper. Steve Holland of the University of Illinois Department of Anthropology constructed the maps. I am grateful for his facility with this work.

I first considered pursuing a career in anthropology when I met Monique Girard and David Stark in Mexico during the summer of 1973. Trying to understand cultural difference alongside them was exciting, stimulating, and fun. Conversations with them now remain so, and the original title for this book, now the title of the introduction, was culled in exchanges with them. David came up with the title as the three of us talked about the themes of the book, and it still best captures the overall thrust of the ethnography in these pages. The introduction reproduces, in part, some of the ideas we played with that afternoon. I am thankful for their encouragement, creativity, and intellectual integrity. As this book demonstrates, my borrowings from David's work have considerably improved mine.

My family has been a source of encouragement through the years. The late Marjorie Mitchell Kelleher, my mother, showed me the value of intellectual pursuit early on and encouraged any such endeavors. Bill Kelleher, my dad, has been a foundation of emotional support. My sisters Nancy Kelleher and Joan Kelleher visited me in the field with their husbands, Bob Connolly and Paul Casey. Their interest in Northern Ireland has been gratifying. I thank my brother, Dennis, for his interest and support. I am grateful to Joan and Paul for last minute help collecting references.

I owe my greatest personal debt to Jo Thomas. Since I met Jo in the field and marveled at her energetic and insightful reporting on the conflict in Northern Ireland, she has had to live with this project. She has covered for me when deadlines loomed and has had to endure the absences of mind that accompanied them. She applied her keen copyediting eye to the entire manuscript and gracefully forced me to confront its excesses and superficialities. Susan and Kathleen Kelleher, our daughters, have had to forbear this project over the long haul as well. Susan's artistic sensibilities and Kathleen's humor have been constant sources of pleasure and joy during the ups and downs of writing. I dedicate this book to the three of them.

Introduction

Telling Identities and the Work
of Memory in Northern Ireland

I remember the baker O'Donnell blushing as usual, telling me:

> Ye know what they say about Ballybogoin, Bill. "When ye pull down
> yer zip to piss off'a Elizabeth Street, they're talkin' about it up on the
> square before it touches the ground."[1]

Back then, in 1985, in the context of a conversation aroused by my surprise at how much of my recent private life the baker and several of his
friends knew, this enunciation indicated that I should not be bothered
by the local knowledge accumulating about me, that stories moved fast
and furiously in Ballybogoin, and that there would be, as one of my
interlocutors said, "no harm done" by them.

   Now, writing here, having put this statement in a frozen position far
away from that pub just off Ballybogoin Square where it was uttered, a
place patronized at different times by members of the Irish Republican
Army (IRA) and their declared enemy, the British security forces, a
place where local Catholics said "we watch ourselves," I give this conversation piece a different meaning.[2] There and then I was taught how
to "watch myself," especially how to guard my words; how to disen-
gage myself, by subtle deflections and inflections, from conversations
going too far; how to play the game by telling partial truths; how to tell

"wee white ones" (little lies) and not get caught out; how to read and interpret the language and body movements of others; and how to relate words, bodies, and worlds.

Here and now I remember representations of the type of talk that we discussed in the pub that night and reflect upon the anthropological texts that have inscribed Ireland, particularly that of Nancy Scheper-Hughes. She writes:

> Yes, the Irish lie and lie they do with admirable touches of wit and ingenuity. Add to the normal defensiveness of the peasant, a folk Catholic moral code that is quite "soft" on lying, and a lack of toler-ance for *overt* acts of aggression, and you have a very strong propen-sity to "cod" (sometimes rather cruelly) the outsider. Beyond cross-checking information, the only safeguard the fieldworker has against "converting the lies of peasants into scientific data" (as one critic of the participant-observation method commented) is simply getting to know the villagers well enough to read the nonverbal cues that signal evasiveness or lying. (Scheper-Hughes 1982, 12)

In Scheper-Hughes's view, the talk of those Ballybogoin Catholics could not be relied upon. She submitted speakers to her gaze, read them, and distinguished between truth and lying. She realized the world must be read yet readily provided the last word. For Scheper-Hughes, it was the eye of the ethnographer that constituted the ethnographic ground, and she could discern a lie. Arriving on terra firma, she peopled it with com-posite individuals, a scriptural method that provoked this response from a village reader of Scheper-Hughes's text.

> Nonsense! You know us for better than that. You think we didn't, each of us, sit down poring over every page until we had recognized the bits and pieces of ourselves strewn about here and there. You turned us into amputees with hooks for fingers and some other black-guard's heart beating inside our own chest. How do you think I felt reading my words come out of some Tom-O or Pat-O or some publi-can's mouth. Recognize ourselves, indeed! I've gone on to memorize some of my best lines. (Scheper-Hughes 1982, 10)[3]

Talk, truth, and lying pose problems for the ethnography of modern Ireland. So do places like the other major component of the baker's utterance, "the square." Often, anthropologists depict such town centers as functional/historical wholes and emphasize their role in the "development" and integration of local economies and public spheres. The organizational pull of towns, especially their nuclei, places like the square, receives emphasis. Development occurs, and center domesticates periphery. Commercial functions change, but they persist and often dominate description.

Through the ethnography in this book I try to trip up these two representations of the "other": the Irish "other" as liar, a trope of a colonizing narrative, and the "other" as ordered from center to periphery, an element of a modernizing, teleological one. I disagree with Scheper-Hughes's contention that the ethnographer's sole or primary job is to differentiate between the true and not true. Instead, I shall argue that the so-called lies must be taken into ethnographic accounts, that their effects ought to be tracked. I prefer to follow the lead of Zora Neale Hurston, who perceives the difficulties of both teller and ethnographer in revealing "that which the soul lives by" (1979, 83), the words that make up worlds.

Hurston understands that the fibs and fabulations that the dominated construct are part and parcel of social relations. She discusses the proclivity of African Americans in 1920s and 1930s Florida to tell more powerfully positioned whites what they believed those people wanted to hear. Hurston calls these practices "a featherbed resistance." From her threshold position, the inside/outside position of the ethnographer that Hurston's writing never lets us forget, she imagines the desire that works these so-called lies. She represents her consultants' wishes with these words: "I'll put this play toy in his hand, and he will seize it and go away. Then I'll say my say and sing my song" (1979, 83).

Hurston alludes to the fact that words, signifiers, can deflect the definitions and practices of the dominant and make the places of the powerful subject to resistance. Hurston represents what Michel de Certeau theorizes when he questions the depiction of central places as social centers of gravity. De Certeau differentiates between places and spaces and describes how people make one into the other. In de Certeau's terms, places are the sites of power, the territories marked out and controlled by subjects of will and power who make them their own.[4] Spaces are those same places submitted to the practices of everyday life—speech, the discourses of family, neighborhood, and community—that consume the places and disorder the assumed order. De Certeau calls such cultural practices "tactics." They utilize time and open up the possibility of resistance (see de Certeau 1984, 29–42).

Ballybogoin Catholics, almost all of whom called themselves Irish nationalists, juxtaposed such spaces and places, and its people articulated them, joined the differences, and disarticulated them through stories and their moving bodies, signifiers in their social world.[5] For example, Elizabeth Street, the place invoked by the blushing baker, served as a site that transported and transformed meanings. Elizabeth Street connected the Catholic, Irish nationalist, residential side of Ballybogoin, its west side, to Irish Street, the Catholic commercial street that led into the square, a place that inscribed order. The residential units on both sides of Elizabeth Street were razed in 1984 to make way for a proposed commercial development, a project whose plans, never mind concrete structures, failed to appear until the late 1990s. The muddy, unpaved lots that remained functioned as parking lots for the Catholics who left their cars there in crisscrossed patterns and made the easy walk from this disorder to Irish Street or on to the square. On these journeys, from Catholic, Irish nationalist residences to the square, both space and time came into coalition. To the west, Elizabeth Street's pedestrian path ended at the gateway to an old manse, "the big house" Ballybogoin Catholics called it. At this juncture Drumcoo Road veered off to the northwest and led to the Catholic housing estates and out toward "the hill country" identified by many contemporary Catholic townspeople as their ancestral home places. The names of these "wee places," anglicized on British maps over 150 years ago and represented in less detail in early-seventeenth-century ones, memorialized the loss of a living language. They also provided an index to what Irish nationalists perceived as their social and political positioning in both their colonial past and their present: the position of excluded outsider.

These social spaces—Cornamucklagh, round hill of the piggeries; Culnagor, hill back of the cranes or herons; Knocknaclogha, the stony hill; Munderrydoe, the bog of the black oak wood; Aughagranna, the ugly or bushy field—were populated in the majority if not wholly by Catholics. They signified not only the poor terrain local Irish nationalists and their ancestors have inhabited but also the events—the sixteenth-century Elizabethan Conquest of Ireland and the seventeenth-century plantation settlement—that led to their settling in those hills. In

4

making these places organized by the colonial state into spaces, in vivifying these written places in speech, Catholics in these localities said of their more richly situated, lowland, Protestant neighbors, "They got the land, we got the view." Then they would add, "We were pushed here over three hundred years ago."

In similar ways, spatial stories made Ballybogoin, one of the first provincial towns created by the seventeenth-century early modern, colonial state, into a people's place. A lord who oversaw the area for the English Crown at the end of that century named Elizabeth Street after his daughter. It served as a passageway between the square (the site of managing the "other"—the descendants of the natives) and "bandit country" (the home of the "other") to its west. But Elizabeth Street domesticated the natives incompletely. The Stewart family, who accumulated its wealth in the area's nineteenth- and twentieth-century linen industry, owned "the big house" at Elizabeth Street's western end. Catholics remembered that family, its discriminatory employment practices, and the exclusively Protestant ownership of that industry, through stories of Margaret, the last Stewart heir to people the place.

Margaret's story was told to me by a group of Catholics who grew up on Irish Street in the 1940s and 1950s. They were trying to tell me what life was like then for Catholics before the civil rights movement and the start of the long-enduring political violence that had marked their lives in more recent years. They remembered that Margaret used to make her daily trip to the square by walking smack dab in the middle of Elizabeth and Irish Streets. Sturdy and staunch, she stared straight ahead, they recalled, not looking either left or right. If a vehicle of any sort trailed her, that car would have to wait. She would not step into the shuck, the gutter that flowed with the refuse from the sidewalk sweepings of these entirely Catholic thoroughfares, nor would she walk on the "pavements," the sidewalks on which these people's homes and shops abutted. She certainly would not talk.

In this Catholic, Irish nationalist story, Margaret's territorial practices represented the whole—the state, the Protestant people, and its institutions. She bore a metonymic relation to that whole, but, more important for the purposes here, the story indicated that these streets were made into the social spaces of the natives, as does a second story attached to memories of Margaret.

Margaret's family's will stipulated that "the big house" be sold only to a Protestant. When Margaret died, her heirs intended to carry that desire out. The trouble was that the Protestant man to whom they sold the place did not intend to keep it. A local Catholic, "part businessman, part gangster, a man who will stick the arm into ye," Catholics said, had arranged for a Protestant business associate from the Republic of Ireland to make the purchase and then sell it to him. When the heirs had their estate sale, this Catholic man, well known in the area, walked in, announced he was the new homeowner, and said he would buy everything in the place. The inheritors were stunned.

Irish Street is an uphill climb from Elizabeth Street, and when Margaret reached the top, she was at the square (see map 1). Running perpendicular to its center and running due west is Scots Street, duly named by His Lordship to mark a space for the Scots dissenters who came in the seventeenth century to populate the planned settler colony. This street entered the square from the west. Both Catholics and Protestants shopped and drank in establishments on this street. To the southeast lay Church Street, named by the lord because some of the town's Protestant churches were located on it. Both Catholics and Protestants bestowed their custom on its shops during the daytime. At night, most Catholics did not dare to go there. Only Protestants patronized its Catholic-owned pubs. To the northwest lay Irish Street. Named by the lord and designated as the place for the descendants of the natives, only Catholics shopped and, besides the rare exception, drank in Irish street establishments.

Robert Street, named by the lord after himself, exited to the north. At the corner of Robert Street and the square stood a deserted hotel, previously owned by Catholics. It was the only edifice on the square owned by that "side of the house" until the 1960s, when Catholics purchased one other building.[6] Carved onto the outside window of that hotel were the initials TB. Catholics said Tom Barry, a famous IRA fighter of the 1920s who went on the run for a number of years, had stayed in the hotel while the police and army searched for him. He left his mark there before his escape, people said. He and his exploits were sometimes sung in the pubs on Irish Street.

Like the Catholic-owned pub on Scots Street where the baker uttered the sentences that are the point of departure for this introduction, a place that local Catholics told me had been bombed twenty-eight times since 1971, the square was a place where people watched themselves. It was also a space where people were watched: a control zone.

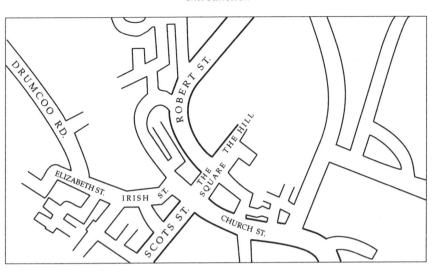

Ballybogoin Town Square

Drivers could only enter the town's center via one of two roads, and you could not leave your car parked in the few spaces available. Too many car bombs had gone off in emptied vehicles. In the mid-1980s a police car or two usually sat in the square, and heavily armed police sentries manned the checkpoints at the two entries. Yet, for the Catholics, this did not necessarily mean that this territory was under another's control. Their storytelling tactics, some may call them lies, transformed this ground and, if we adhere to de Certeau's terms, made these places into their social spaces.

No Catholic political or religious demonstration had ever penetrated the square. It was considered the place of both the Protestant community and the local state. In the 1960s, a local movement for social justice, entirely Catholic, had tried to organize homeless mothers to march into it, but they were stopped by what one participant remembered as "Orangemen who were off from their lunch hours and spat on us." A few years later, the nonviolent Northern Ireland Civil Rights Association (NICRA), a primarily Catholic group, tried to march into it, but the combination of a police barricade and the rumored threat of a loyalist paramilitary attack kept them on the town's outskirts.[7]

At the east end of the square stands a memorial to local men who

died in the twentieth century's two great wars and to British state struggles in Ireland to keep the island British. It is the ritual center of the
local state and its Ulster unionist community. Behind this, farther up the
hill, stands the outdated police barracks, over a hundred years old but
still used. It was rumored to house a variety of security force members
in the 1980s. A light brown, oddly designed building, it looks out of
place among the gray sandstone buildings of Ballybogoin town. Local
Irish nationalists said, "It's a mistake. It was intended for Bengal, but
the plans were mixed up in the colonial office and Bengal got Ballybogoin's building, while Ballybogoin got Bengal's." Official historians and
the Protestant people called this story "a lie."

Behind the old police barracks is the modern British army lookout
post, cameras clearly visible, high above the square. Local Catholics
believe that under the ground on which these two military edifices lie
are the remains of Hugh O'Neill's fort.

O'Neill was the last Gaelic leader to oversee the Ballybogoin area.
The rule of his lineage ended when he fled Ireland in 1607. O'Neill's
Gaelic forces had fallen to Elizabeth I's armies, and he had submitted to
Lord Mountjoy, the lord deputy of Ireland in 1603. The prolonged
negotiations for a settlement failed: O'Neill and his associates were
declared traitors and their lands forfeited. They fled to Spain, and
O'Neill died in Rome in 1616.[8] Ballybogoin's Irish nationalist people
remembered him when they dreamed of the future. Their talk had it
that when Ireland becomes "free," they would erect a historical park at
the top of the hill, excavate the old fort and the older druid one that,
they believe, is under that one, and tell their history, Irish history.

Ballybogoin's Irish nationalists said that under those forts are the
tunnels that their Gaelic forebears used to escape the Elizabethan forces
back in that sixteenth-century war. Outgunned by the English soldiers,
O'Neill's men would incinerate the fort, and a few of those fighters
would stay back as decoys. Once Elizabeth's troops charged, O'Neill's
men would escape through the underground tunnels dug for these
maneuvers and join their comrades, who would attack the English army
from the rear. No one knew, however, if those tunnels really existed.
They were said to exit underneath the headquarters of the local Ulster
Defense Regiment (the UDR), the almost entirely Protestant, locally
recruited unit of the British army whose regional headquarters was
located less than a mile from the top of the square. Someday, when they

became free, many local Catholics believed, their real history would finally be known.

In 1985, however, local Catholics adjusted to living in their fictions, worlds made significant through narratives, not merely made up. They negotiated their social relations through them as they made history. Departing from de Certeau's terms, their talk and their movements through the local landscape transformed the square and the ordered spaces of the town into their own places, interrelational terrains that transformed subordinated subjects into active agents. In deciphering the square, they took up local discourses of Irish nationalism, a powerful agency in contemporary Northern Ireland, and these practices, for better or for worse, made historical agents out of them.

The agency of Irish nationalism did not rule, however. Ulster unionism and British nationalism, more highly institutionalized and powerful social forces, ones organized by the state, entered this social space. Catholics, like Protestants, were made objects in the town, interpellated not only by the forces of the state but also by the force of their own communities' ideologies. Dependent on the relations of time, space, and place, the ground changed under their feet.

Positioned subjects, the spaces of Ballybogoin people changed as they stood still. As the context was transformed, so were their political subjectivities. Violence had much to do with this phenomenon and contributed to this unsteadiness as it solidified the boundaries that divided people on a variety of levels. Actions by the state, the soldiers, and police cemented these internal borders. This book reaches for those forms of writing that can both convey this complexity and undermine the discourses, nationalist and statist, that conceal it.

"The Northern Ireland Problem":
The Problems of This Book

The armed conflict in Northern Ireland was waged continuously from 1969 until 1994, when the first IRA cease-fire took hold.[9] That cessation of IRA violence was broken in 1996. In August 1998 "the real IRA," a renegade group of Irish republican militants who disagreed with both the IRA's termination of its war against the British state and the participation of Sinn Féin, the IRA's political allies, in peace negotiations with the British government, committed the worst atrocity of nearly three decades of fighting, the Omagh bombing. Protestant paramilitary groups have killed Catholics throughout the years of the peace process, but in 2001, as I write this introduction, a relative peace persists. The signs of military occupation—patrolling soldiers, strategic fortifications, checkpoints at the international border, control zones, surveillance cameras, and the cruising of armored vehicles—have decreased enormously. Struggles over a devolved Northern Ireland government that the main antagonists—the British state, the Ulster unionists, and the Irish nationalists—have put in place continue. In 2001 the square in Ballybogoin is a less daunting social space than it was in 1985.

Many of the people consulted in the research that has led to this book called the war they lived with for thirty years "the troubles." The vast majority of them wholeheartedly support the peace process, but they wonder if their troubles are over. As one local woman, Mary, told me in 1998, "The peace process may be making some things worse."

The "things" to which Mary referred were the social relationships that intersected her life and the boundaries that enclosed them, especially, but not only, the dividing line between Catholics and Protestants. The partial and tentative peace enabled her to confront some of these enclosures in new ways during the latter half of the 1990s. Those encounters, however, have sometimes led to new social injuries and different sources of pain as she has tried to negotiate social action with people to whom she would not have spoken in the past. Still, like many of Northern Ireland's people, Mary, a Catholic and an ardent Irish nationalist, has decided to struggle on, to engage those troubled relationships that surround her and, indeed, that she, like all Northern Ireland's citizens, helped make.

This book examines the boundaries that enclosed those relationships and people's struggles with them in and around Ballybogoin, a town situated in Ireland's borderland region. It lies less than fifteen miles from the contested international border between two nation-states—the United Kingdom of Great Britain and Northern Ireland, of which it is a part, and the Republic of Ireland to its south, the state to which the vast majority of local Irish nationalists desired to belong.[10] The bulk of the book considers lived events in the mid-1980s, a time of violent conflict in the area, but episodes from the 1990s are interspersed in it. The book elaborates upon the themes presented in the ethnographic vignette that opens this chapter, a story that introduces the social spaces of Ballybogoin's geographical center and some of the practices that constitute its version of "the Northern Ireland problem." The Ballybogoin area possesses a particular history and a specific set of social relations that differentiate it from other areas of Northern Ireland. This book keeps those differences in the foreground.

Telling

The baker's utterance that opens this introduction points to talk as a valued practice among Ballybogoin's Catholics. Irish nationalists in the area, people like the baker and his friends, talked about talk. They classified it, reflected upon its affects in their divided social world, measured the speed with which it produced effects, and evaluated it. They recognized that they forged connections among themselves and others through talk, that they used it to entertain each other, and that they made memories through it. In the pub that night, those men taught me about talk and how to account for it. When they told me not to worry about the talk building up about me, they were informing me that I, too, was part, albeit an anomalous one, of the portrait they painted of themselves through stories and song. That night the baker and his mates taught me talk's function in making their troubled social world interesting, thought provoking, and fun.

They also tutored me to articulate talk with caution. When they told me that they watched themselves in their everyday lives, they presented me examples from which I could learn about the dangers of social practices. They taught me not only which Protestant and Catholic neighborhoods were safe to enter and which Protestant and Catholic people were dangerous to talk with but also how to read situations and to know when to talk, when to keep silent, and when to extricate myself from social interaction. They instructed me how to tell and reminded me of an utterance commonly used in Northern Ireland: "Whatever you say, say nothing."

Among the first people I met in Ballybogoin, this group of young Catholic men had introduced me to the town and its social life seven months before this meeting. Natives of the town and employed in it, they frequented its pubs and had learned through talk about me that I had widened my networks in the weeks prior to this meeting. People reported to them that they saw me being frisked by the Northern Ireland police, the Royal Ulster Constabulary (RUC), along the motorway. Someone had informed them that I was with people from the town who were known republicans, people who supported the IRA and likely were affiliated with that secret organization (a fact I did not know), and they wanted to let me know that I could put myself in danger. They told me over and over again, "Watch yourself." And often, after that evening, these men would leave me with the same warning. They said "watch yourself" rather than "good-bye" as we parted.

This practice of watching yourself, these young Catholic men understood, was related not only to observing and being aware of one's self but also the selves of others. Watching yourself concerned making self/other relationships, making identities, and it proved to be a complicated differentiation process in Ballybogoin. Northern Ireland people have a name for the initial stages of this awareness and the practices of it: they call it "telling." Telling, a practice carried out by both Catholics and Protestants, refers to reading the bodies of strangers to tell whether they are Catholic or Protestant.[11] Ballybogoin Catholics said their interpretations were correct over 90 percent of the time, and they got a lot of practice at it in their town, one with a slight majority of Catholics.

In Ballybogoin, telling constituted a continual everyday social action that affected interactions and the making of social relations. Through it Catholics and Protestants discerned whether strangers encountered were from their own "side of the house." If they were perceived as different, no sign of recognition would emerge from an encounter. If they were interpreted as a member of the same side, communication might take place. A nod of the head or information about the weather might pass between strangers. In the course of such exchanges, identifications might have been established beyond the reading of bodies. People might have solidified their identities through verbal exchanges, and, in the process, they made "to tell" a polysemous verb, one that indexed watching and observation as well as talking and participation.

Telling who you were and interpreting others to discover who they were shaped the construction of identity in Ballybogoin. Statements such as "this is who I am," "I am," or "who are you?"—whether made through bodily movement such as Margaret's walks to the square or through language—absorbed the past that was signified by the spaces that contextualized these utterances. Identifying statements were insep-

arable from Ballybogoin's beleaguered history: they were not of immediate fact but were historical and biographical, and they still are. As
these stories of the town show, identification processes were intimately
tied to who occupied the spaces of power that enabled the telling of narratives that gave people senses of place and personhood.

The stories retold about O'Neill's fort and the lack of local knowledge about it revealed that a struggle existed over who told Ballybogoin's history. Many local nationalists said that their true story had
been kept from them by the actions of the British state and their Protestant neighbors. These local Catholics represented British state actions as
having displaced them in space and in time. The stories tied to the hills
and the fort's hidden history exemplified this. They articulated a criticism of the state and connected to nationalist dreams. Local Irish
nationalists hoped the future would allow them to explore their past
unfettered by British institutions so, among other things, they could better know themselves.

Who told identifying narratives? Who revealed what kind of people
Ballybogoin Catholics and Protestants were? Who gave instructions for
and formally organized those tellings? Who could tell their stories and
who could not? These were and are questions of immense import in the
town's life and for this book.

How people told who the people they encountered were also featured prominently in the daily performances that made Ballybogoin's
social world. The practice of telling placed emphasis on bodies as social
signifiers in Northern Ireland, and such embodiments, especially moving ones, figured prominently in how people told who they and others
were. Margaret's posturing and her determined movement typified the
bodies Catholics perceived as Protestant.

In the Catholic, Irish nationalist memories of those townspeople
who told me about her, Margaret stood straight and did not become
distracted. Set on her goal, she proceeded to her destination and
avoided any possible detour. Her straight-line path enabled her to avoid
matter out of place and the contaminating touch.[12] Margaret made
boundaries as she proceeded: she avoided the dirt in the shuck and the
metaphoric dirt, the Catholic sidewalk sweepers. Margaret kept her
body equidistant from the two shucks.[13] In the stories, nothing disturbs
that equipoise. Stronger forces, the cars that trail her, could not move
her aside. Catholics, for the most part, traveled on Irish Street, Mar-

garet's itinerary in this story, and that street, like all of the spaces around the square, was morally and politically significant. Those spaces provided the contexts that made those bodies meaningful.

Figures like Margaret referenced Irish nationalist identities in Ballybogoin. In the 1980s, Catholics pointed to their most significant collective others, local Protestants and the British (represented locally by functionaries of the security state), to answer the question, "How do you tell who you are?" Margaret, in the juxtaposition of stories that forms the introductory tale, bears a metonymic relationship to Ballybogoin unionists.

Catholics told who they were through stories that compared themselves to figures like Margaret, narratives of comparative worth. Early in my research, I asked one Catholic, Irish nationalist, middle-class woman, "How do you tell who is Catholic?" She responded, "Their men are bigger and stand straighter. They are more handsome. Catholic men aren't as big, and they slouch and look at the ground. Catholic women are prettier than theirs. Their women are big and strong." Catholics in the Ballybogoin area told who Protestants were through the reading of moving bodies, and these interpretations were often gendered. Catholics, in a variety of tellings, including their own, were feminized.[14] They identified themselves as such through the presentation of their bodies and through the stories, jokes, and songs they shared with each other. This book considers these three moments of telling throughout its pages: who tells identities (who tells who people are?); how people tell if someone is self or other through the contextualized reading of bodily and linguistic signs; and how people tell who they are as an act of telling, a communicative act like the telling of narratives, that relates identity. It reflects upon two additional forms of telling as well. It considers how an anthropologist tells what is going on, how, in this case, I learned to make sense of these actions. And it heeds questions concerning how I tell this complex story. What do I include and exclude from this ethnographic telling? How do I write it to transmit its complexity? I do not tell all.

To tell the tales of learning in the field and writing it up requires a move away from realist ethnography, a form of writing "that seeks to represent the reality of a whole world or form of life" (Marcus and Fischer 1986, 23). In recent years, realist ethnographies have come under criticism for objectifying cultures and for representing them as overly bounded wholes without differences within.[15] Such ethnographies have been called to account for presenting ethnographers as omniscient observers, but anthropologists have addressed this criticism with a variety of theoretical and textual innovations that attempt to represent the differentiation inside cultures. Many have depicted the cultural practices and social forces that make difference, and the decentering, global processes that articulate to the local settings typically focused upon by anthropologists.

George E. Marcus classifies these experiments as modernist because they problematize the perspective of the ethnographer, the observer, as they question the textual representations the observer makes of the observed, the people studied (see Marcus 1991). Modernist ethnographies often remake the observer by demonstrating the dialogic processes in the field through which ethnographers produce knowledge and by reflecting on the analytical categories and writing practices they use as they deploy them in their texts. Modernist ethnographers often remake the observed by reorganizing the spatial and temporal dimensions of their studies, a move they accomplish by juxtaposing different spaces and different temporalities in their writing.

These ethnographers, for example, have studied different places within a location to illustrate how people produce different identities from one space to another. Feminist anthropologists studying a wide range of geographic areas have contributed most significantly to this development as they have depicted the gendering of social space and the struggles of women to shatter the silences that have prevented them from telling their stories and asserting their particular senses of self.[16]

Both modernist and feminist ethnographers have moved away from realist ethnographies that represent cultures as determined by historically produced structures. They have shifted the sense of the temporal away from the realist representation that figures the contemporary ethnographic site as determined by grand historical trajectories such as the transition to modernity or the development of the postcolonial nation-state (Marcus 1991, 316). Instead, they juxtapose past and present, often representing histories not as determinants of an essential identity but as producers of signs that people use in contemporary social action.[17]

The opening juxtaposition of this introduction illustrates both the difficulties of realist ethnography and the methods of a modernist one.

Scheper-Hughes writes the characters in her realist work on mental illness in rural Ireland as composite individuals. This practice indicates that she privileges structures as her objects of analysis. The individuals she creates are justified because they are judged to typify the people that the structures, which in her case study are family and psychic ones, produce. This representation, then, abstracts people from space and time while it renders structures as agents: they produce typical individuals.[18]

The modernist ethnographic representation I begin with enfolds Scheper-Hughes's statements and the people with whom she consulted in order to foreground the multiple practices of telling that form the subject matter of this ethnography.[19] This beginning tries to evoke the question of who tells. It attempts to put the baker's utterance into complex spatial and temporal relationships, including the history of anthropological representations of "the Irish" that have often focused on their talk and their sensitivity to representations about them, particularly those made by outsiders. Adding the response of one of Scheper-Hughes's informants reacting to her award-winning book invites associations among that person's outrage at being bodily deformed by an ethnographic description, the disfiguring of physical space by British colonial inscriptions of Ballybogoin, and the contests over representation that have been an enduring social struggle in Ireland. It tries to relate the baker's perception about the speed of gossip to the need for Catholics to watch themselves not only with regard to the British security forces, local Protestants, and those on their own "side of the house" who may be dangerous but also with regard to a visiting ethnographer.

Many Ballybogoin area Catholics told me that they watched me and subjected me to the kind of inspection that Scheper-Hughes applied to her informants. They, at different times, said, "I've tried to catch you out" or "We've tried to catch you out." They tried to discover me lying and wanted to discern if I was the interlocutor I claimed to be. In time, they believed that I was. With trust established, they taught me how to tell "wee white ones" and to play a language game in which they tried to pull the wool over my eyes while I strove to recognize the fibs and return some of my own. Such practices created social networks and cultural intimacy in Ballybogoin's politically divided world. When it comes to Ballybogoin, ethnographers, for intellectual, moral, and political reasons, must watch themselves both during fieldwork and in the act of writing.

Identities

We live in a time and space in which borders, both literal and figurative, exist everywhere. . . . A border maps limits; it keeps people in and out of an area; it marks the ending of a safe zone and the beginning of an unsafe zone. To confront a border and, more so, to cross a border presumes great risk. In general people fear and are afraid to cross borders. (Morales 1996, 23)

People associate different social spaces with distinct identities in Ballybogoin, and they produce those differences through the invocation of complexly related historical signs. The story of Margaret and that of the fort(s) exemplify how Ballybogoin Catholics used physical spaces to "reinscribe, relocate, reactivate and resignify" the past (Bhabha 1996, 59). Through such retrospection, Ballybogoin's marginalized Catholic citizens mapped out their social terrain, emplotted social action, and worked through the present. They connected those memories to the future and its possibilities.

Sometimes the futures perceived and the actions taken were (and still are) utopian. Utopias "present society itself in a perfected form, or else society turned upside down" (Foucault 1986, 24), and they are unreal places. The many bombings that marked Ballybogoin serve as signs that "People cling to the dream of utopia and fail to recognize that they create and live in heterotopia" (Morales 1996, 23). Those bombings were done in the name of perfection, creating either a British or an Irish homogeneity. Violent acts—whether the bombings of the IRA, the sectarian assassinations of local Catholics by the loyalist paramilitary groups, or the ambushes of the British army that sometimes took the lives of innocent civilians—abort the creation and possibility of heterotopias, real places. In heterotopias, a number of possible social orders coexist, and people may transform a social order by interweaving fragments of established orders to make heterogeneous ones. In heterotopias, people transgress boundaries.

Although relatively rare because of the violence that kept people in their places in the 1980s, the transgression of even Ballybogoin's most heavily marked social border, the one between Catholics and Protestants, did sometimes take place. One day in a mixed pub on Scots Street, some Catholic and Protestant businessmen told me the stories of the forts and the barracks at the top of the square. They brought that history up because they were speculating the possibility of an economic boom should the troubles ever end. They imagined that when the British army left, they would be able to accrue knowledge about O'Neill's fort and the secret tunnels. Yet, they were not so interested in knowing "the truth" about that history and connecting the armed struggle to it as their "republican-minded" fellow townspeople were. Instead, they desired to sell that history.

These businessmen desired to market two histories, the Irish history that belonged to the Catholics and the British history that belonged to the Protestants. They asked me, "Do you think we could sell it to the Yanks?" They laughed at the possibility of selling the two histories together, uniting the high-tech British surveillance center, the barracks intended for Bengal, and the Gaelic and Druid forts buried below them. This dreamed up business venture, one that provoked a Rabelaisian laughter, signified the possibility that these Protestant and Catholic small businessmen could make a new history, one that recognized their mutual constitution of each other.[20] The buried and marginalized histories of the Irish were central to the controlling identities of the Ulster unionists and the British state, and, in turn, those identities of will and power were central to Irish nationalists, their sense of displacement, and the need to fight back.

In Ballybogoin, Catholic identities were constituted in relation to Protestants, and Protestant ones were made in relation to Catholics. This book tells identities by examining the considerable social border that divides these two groups but does not hold that studying it will get to the bottom of the identity question in this Northern Ireland town. Other social borders besides that between Irish nationalists and Ulster unionists are explored in this book. The Ballybogoin area, a region that extends to an international border that brings with it the territorializing machinery of the British state, is characterized by an everyday life "crisscrossed by border zones, pockets and eruptions of all kinds" (Rosaldo 1989, 207). These other borders within the Ballybogoin region's social space include those revolving around place, "race," class, and gender. Each will be explored at a number of different sites in the chapters that follow.

Ballybogoin's Ulster unionists and Irish nationalists, despite that they had been mired in political violence for nearly thirty years and appear to possess identities that correspond to those made in their seventeenth-century encounters, negotiated their identities through everyday practices in the varied social spaces they occupied. Those identities may become fixed at moments, but they always concern "questions of using the resources of history, language and culture in the process of becoming rather than being" (Hall 1996b, 4).[21] People articulate those cultural resources differently in different locations at different historical moments. So, the concept of identity I use in this book focuses attention on problems of "who we are" in relationship to representation, its uses, its history, and the memories of it in specific locations and at particular historical moments. In particular, it examines how Catholics have been represented and tries to discern how the effects of those representations influence Ballybogoin Catholics' struggles over the divisions and visions of their social world.

A strategic and positional concept of identity, then, one that works against the stable concept of the self that conceives it as moving through history unchanged, grounds this ethnography. This does not mean that I reject notions of cultural coherence and systems of cultural meaning. I try to trace "the powerful institutional nodes" (Sewell 1999, 55) that organize cultural difference and give it coherence, especially the state. Ballybogoin's Roman Catholic community, "the natives," as many of its members called themselves from time to time, reproduced itself through one set of social and cultural institutions and took advantage of the services of a state that it saw as alien. The Protestant community, "the planters" or "the settlers," as they sometimes called themselves, made its way through a different set of organizations and pointed to the state as an embodiment of its enlightened ways and as a justification of its privileged position.[22]

These naming practices—"natives" versus "planters" or "natives" versus "settlers"—and the contrary orientations to the state that they implied indexed different narratives of the past and clashing claims upon the future. Many Catholics proclaimed that they inhabited the land first and, on the basis of the value that distinction created for them, they demanded the right to national self-determination. They desired to be part of an Irish nation-state.

The Protestants, through a variety of cultural events, particularly through Orange Order marches and associated celebrations, declared that they brought rational social arrangements to the area, made the landscape productive, and set the region on the road to modernity. Their ancestors, Protestants say, put British institutions in place. They first established the modern state and developed civil society. Protestants used those historical facts to justify their right to keep the northeast corner of Ireland, the area in which they are the majority, part of the British nation-state, the United Kingdom of Great Britain and Northern Ireland.

These two firsts, "native" as first occupant and "planter" as first maker of modernity and civil society, have functioned as crude indexical signs.[23] In the tired binary of the colonizer and the colonized, they have reproduced stereotypes that oversimplify Ballybogoin's divisions, obscuring their complexity and variety. "Native," "planter," and "settler" are not useful categories for social analysis, but in Northern Ireland they, as colonial categories, have exerted social force. They have effected at least two fairly coherent cultural orders so ethnographers must track them.

In the Ballybogoin region, the categories colonizer, "planter," and colonized, "native," produced the dominant narrative in which ancestors of local Protestants were the makers of modern industrial society while the more traditional Catholics resisted modernity through violence.[24] The British state as an authoritative cultural and political actor has much to do with the development of this dominant form and the cultural hierarchies it produced. State practices, particularly their production of representations, were dispersed into the sites of cultural and material contest presented in this book, and they will be treated here as working "to give a certain focus to the production and consumption of meaning" (Sewell 1999, 57) in Ballybogoin's social spaces.

By analyzing such state practices, this book addresses what Alejandro Lugo calls culture's "double life," its existence as "the simultaneous play of order and disorder, coherence and incoherence, chaos and antichaos, contestation and shareability, practice and structure, culture and history, culture and capitalism, and, finally, patterns and borderlands" (Lugo 1997, 59–60). It tracks the state's efforts to sustain coherence and the practices of Catholics that both mimic the state's social and cultural forms and contest them. The book pays attention to practices of representation and systems of representation at a variety of levels and through a number of sites—the western region of Northern Ireland, the town in its relationship to its hinterland, the ritual spaces of the Orange Order, Ballybogoin's town square, the space of ethno-graphic writing, a factory shop floor, and a picket line.

Telling identities requires a complex set of processes for Ballybogoin people. It requires that people understand that past events are effective in the present, that they are "not really past" (Boyarin 1994, 2). This does not mean that people live in the past. It suggests, instead, that contemporary people in Ballybogoin, and I do not understand them in this book as "traditional" persons, use the meanings of the past to organize the present while they deploy present meanings to organize the past. Ballybogoin's Irish nationalists and Ulster unionists use the past to represent themselves, to speak for their named social groups. When they do this work of representation "they attempt to create alliances," and when Irish nationalists question the state they try "to alter the contours of the cognitive maps on which society is represented"(Stark and Bruszt 1998, 193).[25]

The British map that Irish nationalists encounter is very powerful. The Northern Ireland state and the subjects it has saturated have invested enormously in it, and fashioning new associative ties in the province, as this book shows, is a difficult and prodigious undertaking. The knowledge entailed in established modes of telling identities articulated to matters of life and death. Transformations of them engender great risk.

This book attempts to show the interplay of cultural practices, the continuation of old associative ties in Ballybogoin and its region, the transformation of some social relations, and the difficulty, although not impossibility, of crossing those internal and invisible borders that constitute Ballybogoin's version of the Northern Ireland troubles.

I

Mapping Moves

If this was Beirut we would just take you out into the yard and shoot you. You're not going to walk out of here, but if you do then someday you'll get what's coming to you. We mean to get you, you murdering little bastard. You don't come from Newry. You're from Camlough and your mother's from Crossmaglen. You're a murderer from south Armagh. We don't give a fuck what goes on in the mountains and bogs of South Armagh, or who you Provos kill out there in your gaelic shitholes, but you're not going to bring it into Newry, Warrenpoint and Rostrevor like you've done; you're not going to bring it into civilization.

Eamon Collins, Killing Rage (1997)

Eamon Collins was an IRA intelligence officer who joined the Provisional IRA in 1979, was expelled from it in 1987, and, many people surmise, was murdered by members of it in 1999. Responsible for organizing a number of brutal murders and bombings in the 1980s, he was questioned by detectives from the RUC on several occasions. The quote in the epigraph represents his memory of one such interrogation. The RUC was investigating the murder of a Roman Catholic whom Collins had mistakenly identified as a member of the security forces, and an RUC detective uttered this statement, Collins remembers, as he presented the possible results of Collins's refusal to cooperate.

As he interrogated Collins, the RUC man drew boundaries between safe and civilized spaces, Protestant and British ones, and dangerous and uncivilized spaces, Catholic and Irish nationalist ones. He valued

those spaces differently, and he drew lines at which the actions he associated with "gaelic" spaces must stop. His rhetoric demarcated sites
that coincided with the division of Northern Ireland made by a line provided by nature, the River Bann. Camlough and Crossmaglen, the
places he associated with Collins, were west of the river. Newry, Warrenpoint, and Rostrevor, the places he associated with himself, were
east of it. Ballybogoin, too, lies west of the River Bann. Map 2 shows
the island of Ireland divided into its four provinces and thirty-two counties. Map 3 features the six counties of Ulster that were made into
Northern Ireland in 1921. Colonizing and decolonizing meanings
adhere to these maps and the territories they represent.

Geography and Space

The River Bann nearly bisects Northern Ireland. It flows from the
North Atlantic and enters the northern coastline at County Londonderry, an official name not recognized by Catholics, who refer to it as
County Derry. The word "London" was prefixed to the Irish Gaelic
name for the monastic settlement in the area when the London Company established a plantation there in the seventeenth century.
Catholics do not use this colonial appellation.[1]

For a considerable distance, the River Bann forms the border
between the counties of Londonderry and Antrim until it empties into
Lough Neagh (see map 3). The river flows south from the lough into
County Armagh, sweeps through the loyalist stronghold of Portadown,
then turns into the Newry canal. There it divides rural south Armagh, a
notorious Irish republican terrain and Collins's home area, from south
Down, the area of Newry, Rostrevor, and Warrenpoint, until it enters
into Carlingford Lough, along the north central east coast of the island.

Three counties lie to the west of the River Bann: County Tyrone,
County Londonderry, and County Fermanagh. The river splits County
Armagh, and to the east lie County Antrim and County Down. The
counties east of the river have a different demography than those to its
west. The eastern region has greater population densities. Historically,
it has had many more people employed in manufacturing.

A map of industrial employment produced by the Royal Irish Academy in 1979 represents this clearly. Colorful circles indicating the number of persons employed in manufacturing in 1971, the period when

The Island of Ireland: Its four provinces and thirty-two counties

The six Ulster counties that comprise Northern Ireland

Northern Ireland's troubles accelerated, nearly cover Counties Antrim, Down, and north Armagh (Royal Irish Academy 1979, 69–71). The only dull brown spaces within those three counties, those indexing the lack of industry, occur in north Antrim, the Moyle District, and south Armagh/south Down, the Newry and Mourne District, the two districts in those three counties that had a majority Roman Catholic population.

Dull brown spaces highlight the lack of industry in Counties Tyrone, Fermanagh, and Londonderry, which splits one of its industrial conurbations, the city that Protestants call Londonderry and Catholics call Derry, with the Republic of Ireland. Textile and clothing manufactures, older industries, dominated manufacturing employment west of the Bann. Although these declining industries formed the largest single manufacturing sector east of the Bann in the 1970s, only in Armagh did such jobs form the majority, just over 50 percent.

Representations: Geography and Identity

Roman Catholics formed the majority population west of the Bann. In elections, they have voted for parties that identified themselves as Irish nationalist. Some of those parties supported violence in the name of the nationalist cause, although the Social Democratic and Labour Party (SDLP), the majority Catholic party, did not. In the 1980s some groups of Protestants from east of the river named that region "Wobland" according to a 1984 report in the *Irish Times* (McEldowney 1984). This pejorative name, one not taken up widely in the east of the Bann vernacular, referred to the political sentiments of the west's citizens and the region's economic plight. Several locations within the region had unemployment rates nearing 40 percent at the time. Voters in Fermanagh and South Tyrone had elected Bobby Sands, the IRA's commanding officer in the H-blocks of Northern Ireland's highest security prison and the leader of their hunger strike, as their region's member of Parliament (MP) at Westminster in 1981.[2]

Historically, the area west of the River Bann had less manufacturing industry than the area east of the Bann, and its Catholic citizens were assumed to be less disciplined because of their relative lack of industrial employment. When I told Catholic, Irish nationalists from Belfast that I was studying an effort to build a new industry in this less developed area, I was often asked, "Can they find any good workers out there?"[3]

People living east of the river often referred to the western area as "bandit country" in the 1980s. Such cultural codes inscribed national popular mappings of Northern Ireland. The March 1984 *Irish Times* article addressed this culturally configured political economic division.

In this article, entitled "The New Partition of Ireland," Eugene McEldowney, the reporter, writes:

There's a new word beginning to creep into the political lexicon of Northern Ireland. It's used mainly in the eastern part, and mostly in Unionist circles when there are no Catholics present.

The word has definite derogatory undertones, and perhaps in its own way, underlines the defeatism felt by those who use it.

The word is Wobland—and it is shorthand for what is perhaps the most significant development taking place in the North today.

Wobland means West of the Bann land, and it is used to some extent in the same patronizing way that Northern Yankees used to refer to Dixie in the Reconstruction days after the American Civil War.

The big difference is that this is happening now, before any civil war, real or imagined, takes place on this island.

Wobland is important to the political viability of Northern Ireland because, possibly for the first time since the State was set up, most of the people in the area are voting against the Government.

GROWING

A large, and possibly growing, number of them are also voting against the very existence of the Northern State altogether.

Wobland is Fermanagh, Tyrone and Derry. It has a majority of Catholic voters and the majority is increasing. It is growing because, despite the gerrymanders and discrimination practiced by successive Unionist governments, the Catholics have stayed and bred, perhaps not like rabbits as some people would have it, at least faster than the Protestants.

And if that sounds sectarian, that is how life is down in Lisnaskea and Newtownbutler.

The Catholic majority is growing also, because Protestants are beginning to desert the frontier posts assigned to them by the generals behind the lines. They are moving to Belfast, and towards the golden triangle of Portrush, Ballymena and Coleraine. (McEldowney 1984, 13)

In 1984, when I announced my plans to do ethnographic work in this western region, an anthropologist who knew Northern Ireland told me that nothing happened "out there." When I protested he said, "yes, a lot happens up here," as he undulated his fingers over the back of his head. One Belfast social scientist told me that "those people out there" had high rates of spina bifida and passed it on to their children. In the eugenic discourse this man deployed that population lacked genetic diversity. At another juncture, a Belfast supporter of Sinn Féin told me that "those people out there" were not political, not progressive. "They're Fianna Fail with guns," he said, indicating that they were atavistic, backward Irish republicans, unlike the forward-looking Belfast activists with whom he partially identified.

These statements demonstrated that a transition narrative marked Northern Ireland social space. Transition narratives, which Dipesh Chakrabarty, writing about India, believes are "shared by imperialist and nationalist imaginations," work to marginalize populations as they figure them as lack, as those who "fail to measure up to the 'secular' ideals of citizenship" (Chakrabarty 1992, 7). The category "wobland," the industrial maps, and the fragments of everyday discourse uttered by the people who represented the Ballybogoin area to me as passive and backward figured this area through such a narrative. They positioned its residents as lesser.

On several occasions, Sinn Féin members from Ballybogoin's hinterland described to me the dismissive way their comrades from Belfast treated them when they tried to organize the area during the mid-1980s. They said these urban leaders did not recognize their particular political and economic situations. This lack of acknowledgment was remembered as one reason why some Ballybogoin area republicans quietly resigned from the party. Such positionings and the discourses that accompanied them devalued the differences in the western region and distanced the spaces of the dominant from the subordinate. But, in this case, complication abounded. Some Irish nationalist republicans from the east, descendants of the natives who identified with those dispossessed in the long ago past, deployed representations culled from the transition narrative to differentiate and distance themselves from their fellow Irish nationalists in Northern Ireland's west. For this reason, Frankenburg and Mani's understanding of the postcolonial applies to this discourse and its 1980s moment, a time when ambiguity marks "the post," a moment when some colonizing processes have ended, others have transformed, while still others have remained intact (Frankenberg and Mani 1996, 276).

This specific understanding of the postcolonial does not indicate a disavowal of "the conviction" that the Northern Ireland problem "is, above all, a colonial crisis" (Deane 1990, 6), but it complicates that belief.[4] It holds that both decolonizing and colonizing processes occurred simultaneously in the past and do so today. This concept of the postcolonial maintains that cultural processes of colonialism continue, and it enables the specific cultural practices of Ballybogoin's everyday life to be articulated to colonial history and the continuing, imperialist practices of the British state.

Following Irish cultural critic Declan Kiberd, I understand imperialism and colonialism to be intimately related. Imperialism "is a term used to describe the seizure of land from its owners and the consequent subjugation by military force and cultural programming," which entails "the description, mapping and ecological transformation of the occupied territory." Colonialism describes the settling of the land seized by imperialism "for the purpose of appropriating its wealth and for the promotion of the occupiers' trade and culture" (Kiberd 1996, 5).

Acts of cultural resistance that challenge the military conquests, cultural impositions, or redrawn maps and social borders of colonial formations are understood as decolonizing practices. As such they are postcolonial: they engage in struggle with colonizing processes, transforming some and eradicating others while leaving many intact (see Kiberd 1996, 6). The postcolonial, then, includes native acts of cultural resistance to the technologies of colonial rule as those tools are being implemented.[5] It does not necessarily imply the period after colonizing states have abandoned their colonies, but it may refer to such historical conjunctures because the cultural programming that imperial formations require endures long after colonizing states depart once-conquered lands.

This coupling of colonizing and decolonizing processes enables a view of colonial identity formation that transforms the binary of the colonizer and the colonized. It requires specific historical, geographic, social, cultural, and political economic analyses that demonstrate the interrelations of those who seized the land and those whose social worlds were remapped by such colonizing actions.[6] It opens up the possibility that colonial forms of knowledge and its accompanying discourses could be taken up by the colonized in acts of resistance or accommodation and used in the remaking of their social order or vice versa.[7] It takes the position that both the colonizer and colonized constituted each other and that the hybrid cultural forms they often produced endure long after colonial rule ends.[8] From this perspective, then, the struggles around colonization/decolonization, as well as the memories and legacies of them, form an axis, one among many, through which social relations and subjectivities get shaped in both colonized and formerly colonized societies.[9]

In contemporary Ballybogoin, this colonizing/decolonizing axis works on a variety of levels and across social and cultural differences. It influences how people locate themselves in their social worlds and how they form relationships with others. For example, the stories of Margaret and the stratigraphic representation of the British and Irish forts in the introduction as well as the quotation from the RUC officer that opens this chapter show the value for the state and its unionist citizens of controlling social space. The maps re-presented and the newspaper account of "Wobland" demonstrate that many northern Ireland people attribute value to space, and their evaluations cannot be so easily described as the opposition between Protestant settler and Catholic native.

The region east of the Bann is modern, industrial, orderly, and valued; the west is partially industrialized, disorderly, and less valued. The social scientists who believe that nothing happens "out there" and that the gene pool prevents development position people west of the Bann as passive and restricted. The Belfast Sinn Féin supporter who took up this discourse connected the people "out there" to an urban, socialist nationalism that Ballybogoin nationalists did not take up, and he rendered them backward, devaluing them in terms of the hegemonic discourse of modernity and its progressive sense of time. His representations differed from the unionists, however, because he did not articulate their backwardness to other colonizing discourses. He positioned people "out there" as nonmodern, not other, but those location practices had effects on Ballybogoin party members' senses of belonging to Sinn Féin.

Such wrangles over space and its representations have a long history in the area west of the Bann. They marked Ireland during the Elizabethan Conquest and its aftermath, when the colonial state reconfigured Ulster's social space. Ballybogoin people remembered that history when they repeated, "They got the land, we got the view." They reproduced a social memory of the early-seventeenth-century events associated with Charles Blount, Lord Mountjoy. When Mountjoy was appointed lord deputy of Ireland in 1600, discourses representing the Irish as a population of savages, beasts, and vermin prevailed. How to dispose of the Irish was a topic of debate among colonial administrators. Proposals had circulated in 1599 for transferring the Irish as a whole "to provide a helot class in England," and Mountjoy himself desired "to make Ireland 'a razed table' upon which the Elizabethan state could transcribe a neat pattern" (Foster 1988, 35). Mountjoy wanted to remap Ireland and inscribe it anew. In 1600 Richard Bartlett, who was beheaded by Irish warriors in the course of his work, began making maps of Ulster (see Ó Tuathail 1996, 1–15).

These early modern state projects indexed a transformation in power/knowledge relations between the English and the Irish. Gearóid Ó Tuathail, citing Michel Foucault, interprets this shift as an epistemic move from the preclassical episteme in which knowledge was organized around "resemblance, affinity and similarity" to a classical one "that inscribed the 'Irish' as irreducibly and permanently inferior" (Ó Tuathail 1996, 6). Hugh O'Neill, the earl of Tyrone, whose fort people sometimes remembered when they imagined the future in 1980s Ballybogoin, embodied this shift. O'Neill went to school in England, addressed the queen in Latin, and in 1591 married Mabel Bagenal, whose brother, Sir Henry, was marshal of the Elizabethan army in Ireland. Four years later, O'Neill defeated Bagenal at Clontibret and was declared a traitor.[10] Although a culturally hybrid character who mixed English and Irish cultural practices, he, the territory he controlled, and his followers became an other against whom the English fashioned themselves as early modern subjects in the late sixteenth and early seventeenth centuries (see Cairns and Richards 1988, 1–21; esp. Hadfield and Maley 1993, 1–23). Ireland was often punned as "Land of Ire" and represented as a woman, a virgin in need of husbandry, in British representations at that time. The native Irish were "inadequate suitors for their own land" (Hadfield and Maley 1993, 4). British colonial rule represented itself as the able-bodied filler of that gap.

Throughout the Elizabethan Conquest the English attempted to map Ireland, but their cartographic efforts met with difficulties. "English mapping," David J. Baker writes, "was not a one-sided affair, but a

complex attempt to create coherence in a space populated by antagonistic and elusive 'others'" who, in battle and beyond it, could not be
located. Ireland was marked by cultural borders, and its landscape was
confusing and "its inhabitants incomprehensible" to the cartographers
and those who used their maps (Baker 1993, 79–80). The English could
not make sense of Irish territory during the battles that raged during the
last half of the sixteenth century. They were unable to demarcate it
because Irish disorder kept entering the spaces they believed they had
ordered. The recalcitrance of the Irish to mapping was the reason why
the "razed table" became Mountjoy's hope at century's end.

In 1602, Mountjoy destroyed crops in the Ballybogoin region, dispersed its inhabitants, and destroyed the coronation stone where successive O'Neill leaders underwent investiture. In 1603, upon his surrender, Hugh O'Neill accepted an arrangement that permitted him to
retain his traditional title to territory under English law, but the
arrangement did not endure. The new English lord deputy, Sir Arthur
Chichester, and the Irish attorney general, Sir John Davies, challenged
O'Neill's legal agreement. O'Neill and the other Gaelic leaders, their
power lost and their rights abrogated, fled to Spain in 1607. This event
has become known as "the Flight of the Earls" (Bardon 1992, 75–125).
In the dominant Protestant narrative around Ballybogoin, one partially
reproduced in a variety of local histories, textbooks, and classic works
on Irish history, that flight was a move for progress, for modernity.[11]

Geography and Memory

Nearly four centuries later, Ulster unionists and Irish nationalists
recalled these colonial struggles in their daily lives. During the mid-
1980s Ballybogoin and its hinterland were the sites of an intensive IRA
assassination campaign. In response, the British security forces carried
out several controversial killings in the area. Irish nationalists remembered the violence of the Elizabethan Conquest as they represented the
violence of the 1980s in Ballybogoin not so much with monuments,
parades, or even storytelling but in the bodily practices and sensory perceptions of "both sides of the house."

Allen Feldman has elucidated this interrelation among violent political acts, memory, and embodiment in his ethnographic work with both
British loyalist and Irish republican fighters in the unionist/loyalist and

Irish nationalist/republican ghettoes of Belfast.[12] Building upon Edward Said's classification of geography as the imperial methodology, Feldman demonstrates that the ghettoization instituted to implement colonial agendas in Belfast used "geographical control to constrain and rationalize social and therefore bodily and perceptual contact" between Protestant unionist and Catholic nationalist populations (Feldman 1997, 34).[13] In this setting, travel between strange neighborhoods could be dangerous, and it was essential to be able to recognize bodies in and out of their proper places, to be able to identify them as Protestant or Catholic, as one traveled through social space. The eye became the privileged organ of perception.

This "ocular strategy of ghettoization," as Feldman names it, has continued in Northern Ireland during the last thirty years of ongoing political violence, through the practice of telling that was described in the introduction. Telling requires the reading and typifying of bodies through a visual imaginary, and it marks others as strangers or friends, as victims and possible aggressors, or as coreligionists and possible colleagues and defenders (see Burton 1978, 1979; Feldman 1991, 1997).

At times, telling can be as simple as asking job applicants where they went to school. At other times, it can be as imprecise as defining specific spaces with specific types of politicized bodies, such as neighborhoods that are Protestant or Catholic, Ulster unionist or Irish nationalist. Loyalist assassins of the Ulster Volunteer Force (UVF), for example, would travel to a Roman Catholic neighborhood, select a pedestrian at random, usually a male, and kill him because they perceived all bodies moving through that space as Irish nationalist.[14]

Now and then, these paramilitaries and those of the IRA mistakenly killed a member of their own population. Such errors, Feldman notes, reveal the imaginary dimension of telling that organizes victims and aggressors into stylized embodiments. These stylizations articulate to the "high contrast categories" of Irish politics—colonizer/colonized, unionist/Irish nationalist, loyalist/republican—and the spatial backgrounds of these marked individuals identify people as self or other (Feldman 1997, 34–36).

Feldman holds that ideological objects in Northern Ireland are made through typifying practices analogous to the imaginary practice of telling and that people evaluate political acts or statements, whether they be ideological arguments or acts of violence, through a lens provided by the imagination of prior events or practices. Violence, its embodiments, and typologies function as collective memory. Feldman writes, "contemporary political acts of insult and injury are proposed and popularly received as reenactments, replications, analogies, and echoes of earlier acts in a linear trajectory that eventually recedes toward an elusive historical horizon line of first injury, first assault, and first death dating back to the Cromwellian Plantation if not earlier" (1997, 35).

In the Ballybogoin area during the mid-1980s such invocations of the past were common. With the signs of the forts and the place names of marginalized Catholic spaces readily available, historical horizons before Cromwell's incursion into Ireland were often retrieved. The IRA assassinated several security force members in the town and its vicinity during those years and justified those acts by referring to the victims as "legitimate targets" because they worked for the British state. They remembered that political entity as having established itself in the area through violence and declared it illegitimate. The IRA also killed some Roman Catholic businessmen in the area who did contract work for the state. They too were labeled "legitimate targets," and several local republicans told me, "History shows violence is the only thing the Brits understand."

When an act of nationalist violence was committed, a prior violent act by the British was often cited as justification in the everyday talk of Ballybogoin's pubs and clubs. Even people who did not believe violence was a legitimate political method uttered these justifications. Most Catholics knew these narratives and might repeat them to maintain social ties even though they were ambivalent about them. Irish nationalist people who strongly disagreed with the assassination campaign remained silent in such settings. They were regarded as people who were "deep as a well," and their associates were not sure how to read them.

For the most part in the 1980s, the IRA's support community did not retrieve memories from the long ago past to justify IRA actions. They pointed to the controversial "shoot to kill policy" that the British army and the RUC carried out in the area west of the Bann at that time. The security forces reported that these killings occurred as the police or army attempted either to intercept IRA volunteers picking up and moving weapons or to foil a military action by the IRA. But many Catholics believed that the security forces shot suspects on sight instead of trying to arrest them. This practice led to the deaths of unarmed IRA members and civilians who happened to be in the wrong place at the wrong time (see Asmal 1985; Thomas 1985, 1986).

In my first month of fieldwork the IRA murdered two men in Bally-bogoin, off-duty Protestant members of the UDR, the locally organized, part-time, almost entirely Protestant fighting force that supplemented the British army in Northern Ireland. The UDR was a regiment much reviled by Catholics, and the IRA justified the murders of these UDR men simply because they were in a British military unit, a fighting force that, from their perspective, had done injury to the Irish for centuries and still did.

In Ballybogoin, the IRA's support community, the minority of the Catholic townspeople who called themselves Irish republicans, applauded this violent act. They believed that UDR men like these had perpetrated similar killings, and they had stories to prove it. It was not unusual to hear yelps of victory at the factory where I worked when workers heard on the news that the IRA had carried out such a murder. Such justifications and emotive responses absorbed acts like these killings into a "mimetic temporal schema" (Feldman 1997, 36) that con-textualized them as repetitions of analogous, prior acts perpetrated by the other side.

Feldman calls this justificatory schema "the historiography of excuse" (1997, 36). Through it, prior violent acts provide extenuating circumstances to contemporary ones and become typified, a representa-tion that renders acts of violence immediately ascertainable as to cause and consequence, "undifferentiated as to their concrete human conse-quences," and excusable because they are taken up into idealizing cul-tural codes that render the bodily and environmental harm done, what-ever its brutality, as already a representation, a reenactment of what happened previously (Feldman 1997, 33–36).

Introductory Tours: Moving Stories

These processes of political objectification did not go entirely unrecog-nized by Irish nationalist people in Ballybogoin. A variety of people questioned the violence of this locally hegemonic form of representing political deaths. I learned this early in my fieldwork, within weeks after the murders of those two UDR men, when Kathleen McDuffy, a Roman Catholic in the town, a woman who described herself as religious and Irish nationalist, introduced me to the town and the villages around it. Kathleen had some sympathies for the cause of Irish republicanism but generally supported the moderate Irish nationalist SDLP rather than Sinn Féin. She could not bring herself to support violence.

Kind and hospitable, Mrs. McDuffy met me early on in my stay and wanted to teach me about the area's history and "how to go about the town and the country." Mrs. McDuffy drove me around the Ballybogoin region and told me how to negotiate the RUC-operated checkpoints that controlled traffic in and out of Ballybogoin's town square. She warned me not to leave my car in that space because many cars with bombs in them had been left there since 1969 and it was illegal to park a car and leave it.

She told me that people had to drive their automobiles to a car park on the square's periphery and walk to the shops. She pointed out the parking lot where Catholics likely left their cars, the westernmost one, and where Protestants left theirs, the one to the southeast. She let me know that many bombings had occurred in the town as she pointed out which buildings had been built anew and which had been repaired in their aftermath. She considered Ballybogoin to be "the most bombed town in Northern Ireland," "town" as distinguished from "city," until the late 1970s or the early 1980s, when another town surpassed it.[15]

She pointed out to me, and others repeated it, that these bombings were not by any means the work of the IRA alone. Loyalist groups had carried out bombings in the town, including the most deadly one, a no-warning bomb that had killed some Catholics drinking in a "nationalist pub." She believed many loyalist bombings had been organized by Protestant business people in the town who wanted their premises renovated and used the insurance available for bomb damage to get that new work done, an abuse of the British political system that Ulster unionists believed only Irish nationalists perpetrated.

Mrs. McDuffy indicated to me the housing estates that were inhabited by Protestants and those by Catholics. She warned me about entering those that were dangerous. She marked all the Protestant working-class estates as ominous social spaces, and she noted that a stranger like me entering the most beleaguered Catholic working-class housing development could be unsafe as well. She remarked that if I got to know the people there then I would be all right inside that neighborhood, an opinion that differed from many middle-class Catholics in the town who told me never to enter that place.

After touring the town Mrs. McDuffy took me to the countryside, to the surrounding villages from where her ancestors had come. She taught me the geography of these settlements, all of which were to the west of the town, in the "hill country," as she named it, to which she said Catholics were dispersed at the time of the late-sixteenth-century conquest and during the seventeenth-century plantation. Teaching me the landscape, she specified not only the villages where the ancestors of her mother and father had lived before moving to the town several generations earlier but also the townlands, the small land divisions that evolved from the *ballyboes* of Gaelic society, the territories on which a group of families worked the land prior to the plantation (Robinson 1984, xiii).

Mrs. McDuffy identified strongly with Ballybogoin, the town where her family had made successes of themselves, but she affiliated herself to the relatively infertile and poor-quality townlands to which she believed her ancestors had been exiled. Solidly middle class, Mrs. McDuffy nonetheless identified with the Catholics who lived in these marginal agricultural areas and their relatives who moved to the town several generations earlier, many of whose descendants lived in the Catholic estate she noted as dangerous. She and they shared the powerful narrative of dispossession that Catholics in this area told, retold, and used to emplot their lives.[16]

After showing me around the hill country, Mrs. McDuffy drove from the mountains and headed east. We did not descend the road to Ballybogoin on which we had come but went down into the region's rich agricultural valleys on a more northeasterly thoroughfare. As we descended, Mrs. McDuffy pointed out the changing house structures to me. There were a greater percentage of large two-story houses as we left the hill country, and those belonged to Protestants, she said. She advised me that if I ever needed help traveling those roads, I should look for it at the smaller, newer, one-story houses. Catholics lived in those poorer, more disheveled domiciles, she held, and they would most definitely come to my aid if I ever needed it. As we traveled down, those one-story abodes dwindled until they were marked by their absence. Mrs. McDuffy remarked on the size of the fields in these lowlands, their relative flatness, and their suitability for agriculture and grazing. "The Protestants got the good land," she said as she took me to a site from which she could teach me the history behind this social fact.

Nestled in a grove of trees in this lowland area, an idyllic space, stood an old church with an old cemetery alongside it. Mrs. McDuffy stopped there and showed me a story displayed in a glass case erected at the start of the pathway to the church.[17] The narrative summarized the church's early modern history. It mentioned that the original church building had been constructed as a Roman Catholic one, but, near the beginning of the seventeenth century, at the end of the Elizabethan Conquest, that building had been appropriated by the Church of Ireland, the Episcopal church established in Ireland and affiliated with the Church of England.

The Church of Ireland added to the architecture of this formerly Roman Catholic edifice by raising a new portal through which congregants could enter. Those early plantation settlers extended the entry outward, creating a large foyer and a new door. Around this new threshold the colonial builders mortared pieces of the O'Neill coronation stone that Mountjoy, the Crown's lord deputy, had broken to pieces in 1602. Mrs. McDuffy pointed out these jagged, irregular, off-colored bits of stone to me. She lamented that there was little worth seeing at the original coronation site and took me into the church to show me how the planters had modified and subverted its spatial organization.

After a quick tour of its interior, Mrs. McDuffy escorted me to the small cemetery on the church's west side, where she tried to decipher the washed away gravestones. She had studied these objects before and emphasized their age and the Irish language inscriptions on them. She showed me dates but stopped at a particular grave, one with a story attached. It marked the remains of a Roman Catholic priest who was native to the area and died after the Elizabethan Conquest and the establishment of the plantation. Mrs. McDuffy told me the story of that priest's desire to be buried at his home church and the difficulty his family and friends had carrying out his will.

The priest died far to the southeast, in the Dublin area, she believed, and, at the time of his death, priests and the honoring of them were suspect throughout the colony of Ireland, particularly in Ulster. Getting him home proved a demanding task, according to Mrs. McDuffy. His supporters and family members disguised him as a peasant and put him in a simple wooden casket, she told me. They then transported him secretly for the long journey home. They carried him through the countryside at night when they could, and during the day they staged local funerals to move him through towns and villages. "He had more funerals than any Irishman who ever lived," she joked, but he made it back and was buried in the place he wished to lie.

After touring me around the Ballybogoin area for several hours, Mrs. McDuffy took me back to her home. Her teenage sons and husband, Sean, were there, and I sat in the parlor with Sean as she put together some tea for us. He asked what I thought of the tour, and I told him that the still functioning Church of Ireland that we visited was surprising. The building's history made it an interesting tourist site, I noted, although it was not marked on the various Northern Ireland tour guides I had seen. He told me that it would not be because "it gets too close to the way things are around here."

Sean said that history was the reason for the ongoing troubles. He believed, however, that it did not justify them, and he remembered the killing of those two Protestant, UDR men that took place several weeks before. He informed me that he agreed that the history between England and Ireland and between local Protestants and Catholics was a terrible one, that Britain and local Protestants had oppressed Catholics, and that the security forces had dealt with local Catholics unfairly, even oppressively. He believed that some members of the UDR had terrorized Catholics in the earlier days of the troubles, in the 1970s particularly. Still, he iterated, he saw no cause and no justification to murder those men.

Sean said it used to be that the IRA killed policemen and UDR members who had harassed Catholics, but that had changed. "Now they kill anybody they can," he uttered, and he questioned the morality of such acts. He reaffirmed that the history perpetrated on the Irish, like the history I had learned that day on my tour around Ballybogoin, was horrific, and he understood that such historical events were used to rationalize and normalize killings such as those of the local UDR men. He worried about that, about those justifications, about the historical practices entailed in excuse making. He told me that those particular UDR men "had done nothing to nobody as far as I know." He knew them by sight. He had patronized their place of work, and they had provided him services. One of them had carried supplies he purchased out to his car one time, and as a result of that encounter Sean perceived him as "a man who would do no harm to nobody." He believed these men had joined the UDR not for sectarian reasons, not because they hated Catholics, but because they needed money for their families.

At the same time as he deconstructed the IRA's legitimization of these local killings, Mr. McDuffy found a full-fledged condemnation of this act and others like it difficult. He damned the act but not necessarily the agents of it. He did so by remembering local IRA fighters who had died in action or had been convicted of violent crimes. He recalled the story of two men who had blown themselves up with several bags of explosives they were moving one evening when they got home from work.

He described these men as hard-working, good men, as many Ballybogoin Catholics did when they told this often-narrated story. Such men, the storytellers said, never would have been involved with such crimes in a properly functioning society. Sean had known them as children and thought them to be good people despite their hardships growing up. He told of other IRA members who had grown up in families who suffered because of acts of discrimination by the unionist government that ruled Northern Ireland from 1922 until direct rule by the British Parliament in Westminster that took over the government of Northern Ireland in March 1972.

Mr. McDuffy told of one family that had produced convicted IRA members. The extended family lived together in a small rented house. "The children used to sleep in shifts," Sean said, "and the mother used to try to get them to sleep standing up to make room for all of them!" Although their needs were great, they were unable to get family housing from the Ballybogoin District Council, Sean believed, because they were Catholic. Before the Parliament at Westminster took control of local government functions, he said, such discrimination was the rule.

Sean said that many IRA members were produced by injustices, but he was not certain. He worried about the direction the IRA had taken, because it was not directed at those who could be specified as unjust. He worried that the history of long ago, whose local version I had learned that day, was behind the shootings of local security force members and individuals, both Catholic and Protestant, who did any work for the security state, such as building security walls or putting plumbing in police stations. He agonized over the possibility that he might be lured into Feldman's "historiography of excuse," that he might rationalize these killings as reenactments of prior events and forget the specific time, place, and circumstance of those human beings killed, maimed, and injured.

Sean's fears of typifying others in terms of this perceptual apparatus become understandable when placed in the context of an event that occurred several weeks after this discussion. Mr. and Mrs. McDuffy took me for a scenic drive beyond the Ballybogoin region, up into a different "high country" than I had seen on my first tour. After climbing several hills, we stopped at a point with hills and valleys all around. An RUC station stood there with a wall, a barbed wire fence on top, and several thick rows of sandbags in front. The road had large speed bumps to prevent high-speed driving around that point, and the scene reminded Mr. and Mrs. McDuffy of a story.

Several years earlier, they said, they had been driving this road with their sons, observing the growing number of security instruments that had attached to the station, from thickening walls, to a greater and greater number of surveillance cameras, to higher speed bumps, to more and more sandbags. They registered these changes each time they drove by. Then one day this concatenation of bricks, mortar, tarmac, sand, and high technology was almost gone. The IRA had bombed it. As they drove past shortly after, the boys, their parents remembered, "laughed and laughed for miles, so they did." They found this penetration of state space very funny, as did Mr. and Mrs. McDuffy, who accompanied this story with slight laughter. They never said if anyone was injured. They did remark upon the alacrity with which the state rebuilt the station, a site ready for reenactment.

When Kathleen McDuffy had finished making tea the day of that first tour, she asked Sean to call the boys for tea. Sean finished our conversation about the UDR men before they arrived. "I'm afraid of forgetting that they're human beings. I go to mass every day, and I pray. I pray that we don't forget that."

Different Settings, Alternative Mappings

Sean feared the objectification and typification of his Protestant fellow townspeople, although he understood it. He reflected upon the terms through which the IRA and its local support community represented political killings, but, as the laughter over the bombing of the police station shows, these categories were articulated to spatial practices and spatial stories, to social memory and embodiments of history (see de Certeau 1984, 91–130).

Sean found it difficult to distance himself fully from Feldman's "historiography of excuse," although that was his desire, and he did not engage his dilemma publicly. There were no institutions of civil society available for him to articulate his concerns. No political party met locally for any regular discussion of social problems. The organizations affiliated with Sean's Roman Catholic parish did not address such issues. The one group that might have engaged Sean's moral and political worries was composed of college- and university-educated teachers and Catholic business leaders. Sean was placed outside this group and did not attempt to participate in it. He dealt with his predicament in his home and in his prayers, his most intimate private spaces. Yet, Sean's statements demonstrated that possibilities for transformation existed. The subtle changes he introduced to that common moral discourse, "the historiography of excuse," offered possible signs for the transformations of political subjectivity and, perhaps, of political organization.[18]

Even if such statements were taken up by others and became public, agentic discourses, these complex moral quandaries would be difficult to resolve. Practices of everyday life were linked to the discourses that constituted "the historiography of excuse." Such practices were repeated in a variety of social spaces and made local explanations for violence appear a natural cultural artifact.[19] The ethnicized landscape and the dominant perceptual apparatus of the persons that moved through it, the focus on the eye and watching, made a powerful combination of hegemonic social forms that countered the transformative possibilities indexed by Sean's discussion. Even in the local Roman Catholic churches such discourses of excuse did not get addressed. When priests offered criticism of them from Ballybogoin area pulpits in the 1970s and early 1980s, "republican-minded" individuals shouted protests and walked out of Sunday mass.

The Ballybogoin region's politicized landscape was experienced from different perspectives, however, as it produced different subject positions. Three additional introductory tours to the Ballybogoin region demonstrate this. They illustrate the enigma surrounding the forgetting and remembering of "the historiography of excuse" that Sean faced.

Colm Muldoon, an unskilled Irish nationalist worker at the Drum-coo Glassworks, worried that I was getting a prejudiced view of the area because people from Ballybogoin itself, the urban district, had been showing me around, taking me to the pubs they dominated and to their Gaelic football matches. Loyal to his locality, just a few miles from the Ballybogoin town square, Colm wanted to acquaint me with his valued places. He brought me to where he lived, the last Catholic enclave before reaching the predominantly Protestant lowland area that Mrs. McDuffy had introduced to me.

Several Protestant farming families lived down the road from Colm. He knew their surnames, but he did not recognize them by their first names, even the young men his own age. He knew the specific households from which each person came because he had passed by them and observed them on the roads all his life. He did not know them personally, he said, "because I don't talk to them."

People who knew Colm did not read this lack of talk as a sign of bigotry. He often drank at the one pub where working-class Protestants and Catholics of several generations congregated in Ballybogoin. He had played rugby for a while, a sport considered Protestant by Catholics in Ballybogoin, and he traveled to Scotland with local rugby club members, primarily young Protestant men, to support regional and Irish national teams. When I worked at the factory he wanted to make sure that I met Protestants around the town. Politically, he supported the SDLP. He told me he had never voted for Sinn Féin, but he did not denigrate or condemn them or their supporters.

One night as we crawled around the town's pubs with a group of his fellow glassworkers, we discussed Irish nationalist politics seriously. He told me, "I could not vote for Sinn Féin, but I know what they're trying to do." When I asked him what that was, Colm replied, "See, out our way the Protestants have all the land, and that's not right." And later on in the conversation he added, "They and the Brits have the power, but we will win because we always outwit them."

Colm was against violence, but he believed that wrongs had to be righted. Those seventeenth-century injustices, the escheated lands of the plantation, appeared to him to be the preeminent injustice. Colm had a reputation as a man of wit. He could quickly respond to remarks made to him or about him, and his company was looked for when his fellow workers wanted a good time. On the Friday and Saturday nights of drinking and dancing in which he and his workmates partook, he was a chief source of story and song. He would often be mocked for his idio-syncrasies but came back with humorous rejoinders when made the object of ridicule. People appreciated him for that.

Colm was particularly adept at negotiating the police checkpoints and roadblocks that he and his mates encountered when they went to the Chinese take-away after the pubs closed. He knew some RUC men from his travels to rugby matches and felt he understood that category of persons and could exchange verbal ripostes with them if anything untoward was said to one of his companions. He could have some *craic* (the Irish word for wit in conversation, pronounced "crack") with the police, not defer to them but outwit them.[20] Colm was confident that he could displace the angrier reactions aroused in his friends by routine police procedures, the occasional frisking and the repeated questioning about their departures and destinations. Like his mates, Colm did not like these interrogations, but he knew how to handle the police through wit not anger. He believed he always came out on top when he had verbal exchanges with the RUC.

The day Colm toured me around his neighborhood he told me he saw the Ballybogoin townspeople as somewhat rude, a belief that stemmed from the rivalry between his rural Gaelic Athletic Association football club and the town's. He measured his team's accomplishments by their victories over the town's team, a group that had a much bigger population from which to choose their players. This rivalry had led to fights at matches and some enduring personal animosities between Colm and his Ballybogoin Irish nationalist neighbors.

Colm told me that the workers from the town would not possibly recognize and represent his townland and those surrounding it ade-quately. He was right. No one from the town had showed me the places he did in their introductory tours. He brought me to new and different houses to which he attached stories. Colm showed me one that was built by a young Catholic man who had made himself into a success through hard work. His modern home was on the top of a hill, on use-less farmland his grandfather, who had migrated back and forth to Scotland over the years to work, had given him. That young man had earned the money to build the house by working in West Africa for a British construction firm. Colm took me to see several other houses, one of which had been built by a locksmith who had worked in the United

States and was about to return because his Jamaican-born wife was lonely in the nearly all-white environment of Northern Ireland.

Colm brought me to see the big new homes of a local builder and a plumbing contractor. Catholics in his area were making successes of themselves, and he was proud of that. He showed me the land in the Catholic areas and compared them to the neighboring Protestant holdings. Protestants won this comparative contest.

As we got to the rural Protestant neighborhood adjacent to his, we encountered a funeral procession. There were many cars heading down the lane to the Protestant cemetery, so Colm backed up and took a different route. He took pride in his knowledge of local lanes and roadways, and we ended up near the Church of Ireland site Kathleen McDuffy had shown me. When we saw that steeple on the horizon, I asked Colm if he knew the story of that church and the O'Neill coronation stone. He did not, so I told him. When I asked him if he wanted to get out and see it, he said something to the effect that he did not want anyone to recognize him, to see him out of his place. He did not want to walk through the area, a space he had only driven through in the past. We went straight to his home for tea.

Ian McCumber, like Mrs. McDuffy, was from the town. A Protestant, Ian had gone to the local Protestant grammar school and worked at a Ballybogoin industrial company, one that was known as "a Protestant firm." Ian's company employed a few Catholics, and Ian was friendly with them. He brought me to his place of work and showed me around. He took me to a state school, what local Catholics called "the Protestant grammar," and toured me through the grounds. He brought me to the old linen mills in the area and showed me some of the tiny, saltbox-shaped houses in which workers in those mills lived, where older, retired working-class couples still did. He wanted me to know, as he put it, "the hard lives we had."

Ian brought me to a nineteenth- and twentieth-century industrial area in the town that Mrs. McDuffy had told me about but to which she had not taken me. She had said, "it's a black place," meaning that the people there hated Catholics. Ian knew that reputation, told me it was partially true, but qualified it with some stories of individuals he knew who lived there. He did not make comments about security measures and the activities of the police, UDR, and army as we drove around, nor did he reiterate stories about bombings. Neither did Colm.

For our final two stops Ian took me out to the area around that same Church of Ireland with the pieces of the O'Neill coronation stone. On the way, we came across several UDR roadblocks. Ian knew some of the part-time soldiers manning them, waved, and rolled down the window to shout a greeting as we were signaled through. We drove in and out of Colm's area, but Ian did not comment on that terrain. He went beyond that territory to two historic, rural industrial sites. The first was located in a village that Mr. and Mrs. McDuffy, along with many other Catholics, warned me to stay out of. They referred to this rural village in the same way they referred to the industrial neighborhood in the town: "it's a black hole." They described the people living there as "bitter" and antagonistic to Catholics. "No Catholic would ever be allowed to live there," one Catholic woman reported. They told me that it would be a dangerous place for any stranger.

This village possessed plantation architecture. Its stone buildings were well preserved, and its streets and lanes were remarkably neat and clean. Ian pointed me to the architecture of an old mill and residences for workers, and he contrasted those worker residences to those in the town that he believed were inferior. To him, such architecture signified that some mill owners and early industrialists treated their workers well, just as he believed he was well treated in the firm that employed him. He favored the architecture of this village to that of his hometown of Ballybogoin.

The final site we visited that day was an early linen mill preserved by the state-run historic preservation body. It was a marked tourist site and well maintained. Ian toured me through the stone building and described the production process to me. He emphasized the hard labor that had gone into this aspect of linen manufacturing. Like Colm, whom Ian knew from the rugby club, Ian worried that I got a biased view of Ballybogoin and its hinterland from the Irish nationalist people. As we drove back to his house for tea, he asked me if I had previously seen the sites he had shown me. I told him that I had not, and he responded, "We'll set you straight."

Ronan McShane also wanted to set me straight about the Ballybogoin region. He, too, believed I would not get the full story from the Ballybogoin Irish nationalist people with whom he associated me. He wanted me to tour his small town, another rival of Ballybogoin located in the bigger town's hinterland, and get a sense of the way things were in his home place. He insisted that I did not have a full picture of life in the area, that his home place was different.

I had met Ronan while I was doing some research on programs combating unemployment in this "economic blackspot," a term used to mark the Ballybogoin area because of its joblessness. He worked in one of the area's employment "schemes," a word used locally to describe government-backed attempts to deal with economic problems, specifically ones that gave jobs, however temporary, to the unemployed, especially young people. This training program was located in an abandoned factory building in an evacuated industrial site that formed a borderland area within the town of Ballybogoin, one separating exclusively Protestant and exclusively Catholic neighborhoods.

Ronan was a man of many skills. He could turn his hand to most manual trades and had some artistic abilities. He taught general carpentry, and he tried to develop craft skills in his students that went beyond the basic requirements of the courses he taught. Ronan was a dedicated Irish republican. He had spent several years in the Maze prison, in the H-blocks, among the Irish republican prisoners whom the state classified as political, and he made this autobiographical fact known shortly after I met him. I was surprised that he talked so openly about his political past and his experiences in prison with the mixed Protestant and Catholic group of students and staff at the center when we all took a tea break. He made his republican identity public and was proud to do so in a variety of social spaces.

Ronan wanted to show me how the politics that articulated to his autobiography were embodied in his town. A few weeks later, after meeting him on occasion in a Ballybogoin pub, we arranged to meet for a tour. We met at his fastidiously neat home in a working-class housing estate. Ronan took me for a walk around the estate and gave me a sense of the kinship networks that were in place there. He told me who was related to whom. He then drove me around the town, showing me abandoned factory buildings, the new Roman Catholic parish hall, the football pitch of the Gaelic Athletic Association with its pro-Irish republican inscriptions painted all around, and the ever-expanding RUC station that hovered over the center of town, whose traffic pattern had been rearranged for security reasons. He told me a few stories about the owners of the town's commercial premises. Catholics owned most of the town's enterprises and formed a solid majority. Our tour of the town was short. Ronan was more interested in bringing me to the surrounding countryside.

Ronan took me in the direction of the solidly Protestant industrial village to which Ian had introduced me. As we drove there, he told me, "the SAS [Special Air Services] might be watching us," a statement often uttered by Irish republicans as they took me through sparsely populated rural townlands or border zones. When we got to the outskirts of the village, Ronan stopped to show me the spot where he and his colleagues were arrested by the RUC after they tried to carry out an IRA military operation that was foiled by the British army back in the 1970s. He described with technical precision the action they had plotted, what went wrong with the explosives, how they tried to get away, and why and where they were apprehended.

After viewing this site, we drove a little farther down the road, a straight one that ran through the flat country and provided travelers with good views on both sides. Ronan told me that this road had often been used for IRA operations in the past. After a short drive, we veered off this thoroughfare a bit, went down a narrow, tree-lined lane, and stopped at a field, one on which a close relative of Ronan had been killed in a controversial shooting a little over a year before.

We got out of the car, and Ronan had me stand in the spot right next to the driver's side door. He told me to watch him as he jogged across to the other side of the field. He stood next to a grove of trees and yelled across, asking if I could see him clearly. I said that I could. Then he came back to explain what had happened at that small field.

The IRA had an arms dump at one end of the field, he said. His relative and another man had gone to move the weapons. However, before they got to the spot, they were shot dead by a unit of the SAS, the crack unit of the British army that was lying in wait. Ronan believed that the men who were killed were unarmed. He admitted they were IRA members, but he maintained this double killing was an act of state terror in which the orders were "shoot to kill" and "take no prisoners." He believed the soldiers could see the two unarmed men clearly from where they shot, where I stood that day.

At the time there was a growing list of security force engagements that were marked by army ambushes of both unarmed and armed people, sometimes members of the IRA and other times not. To Ronan, this was a campaign in which the security state was hunting IRA members.

This thought was provoked by a Northern Ireland unionist politician who said, "Two swallows do not a summer make," after this particular killing. In Ronan's view, that statement indexed a desire for repetitions of acts like this SAS one.

We ended our tour, Ronan's moving story, with a visit to the Irish republican plot in Ronan's parish cemetery. He showed me the graves of IRA members and picked up the debris blowing around them. We went back to his home for tea when we were done.

"Workin' Work and Workin' Moves"

"Workin' work and workin' moves" was a phrase used by Seamus McRory, the shop steward for the skilled glassworkers in the glass-blowing shop of the Drumcoo Glassworks. I first heard him use this term when he was joking with the managing director of the firm, Nicholas Dolan, in a nationalist pub just after a meeting between management and the skilled glassblowers over a one-day labor dispute. Dolan had just introduced me to Seamus, who, he had warned earlier, might not speak to me because of his general militancy on both labor and political matters. The opposite occurred. Seamus joked with Dolan and me. When Dolan sarcastically said, "you boys need to learn to work," Seamus replied that all the men who survived Dolan's firings were men who "worked work, not them ones who worked moves."

At other junctures in the next year and a half, Seamus said that Catholics in the area had to do both, "work work and work moves." It was a phrase he had coined to represent the workers as their spokesperson, but he extended it to describe the general condition of Ballybogoin area Catholics. To "work work" meant to be disciplined. It indicated disciplining the body, and, I was to learn later, Seamus's glassblowing team exemplified it. They kept their heads down at the factory and worked very quickly, almost in a unified motion. They watched the clock constantly and measured, themselves, how long it took to make particular items of glassware. They always tried to produce more, to prove themselves and what they called "our inventions," the procedures they introduced to speed up production. Disciplining the body, following rules, "keeping the head down," "watching yourself" while watching the clock, and yielding to authority were the practices entailed in "workin' work" at the Drumcoo Glassworks.

Seamus, a Catholic and a strong supporter of Sinn Féin, believed that Protestants were more likely "to work work" than were Catholics. They succumbed to authority more readily, in his view, and you could see that on their bodies. You could recognize them, he believed, because they stood erect and looked straight ahead when they walked. Many of them dressed more neatly, and they talked less often. "They have no *craic* and no culture," he often said.

"Workin' moves" differed. Seamus said that Dolan had fired those workers who "had worked moves" at the Drumcoo Glassworks. In the factory context, to "work moves" meant to subvert rules, to question institutional authority, sometimes for no reason, to attempt to get something for nothing, to be dishonest, or to steal from the company. But, as "workin' work" did, "workin' moves" articulated different meanings in different contexts.

"Workin' moves" also described practices that Seamus felt Catholics, by necessity, had to produce. They had to try to manipulate situations to their advantage in an institutional context that, he believed, excluded or marginalized them. While he castigated workers who stole from his "nationalist" company, he exhibited some appreciation for those workers around the area who "did the double," who worked at a job and registered for unemployment benefits simultaneously. He thought the generally low-paying jobs open to Catholics required such deception. He classified practices of outwitting authority, like Colm's engagement with the RUC men at security checkpoints and roadblocks, as "workin' moves."

Seamus lived in a border area and loved to regale people with stories about trickery in the border zones around his home. These included stories of smuggling in the 1950s and 1960s, when sugar was illegally brought back and forth across the border, and in the 1980s, when Catholic farmers around his home place herded cattle across the border in the dead of night to make profits on fluctuating exchange rates or varying market conditions.

Such tales also extended to the IRA, who evaded the police and circumvented the British army's border checkpoints, hiding arms and explosives in truckloads of hay and other vehicles carrying sundry agricultural supplies. "Workin' moves," in Seamus's usage, extended to IRA acts such as the bombing of the RUC station that created laughter among the McDuffy boys, who seemed to be aroused by the IRA's outwitting all that visible state power. Tricking and outwitting "the Brits" was a common narrative form used in Ballybogoin to frame acts of Irish challenge to the British state. The stories of O'Neill's fort, Tom Barry (TB) and his inscription on the square, and Colm's interaction with the police demonstrated this.

These stories became entangled with each other in Ballybogoin, and violent acts, such as the bombing of that highly fortified RUC station, were added to them. Tricking the state and the displacement of it through wit or violence, however temporary, were remembered through stories that were often the source of laughter. Acts of terror, like tales of trickery, turned the world upside down and were utopian moves: many Irish nationalists, particularly Irish republicans, did not perceive such violence as affecting real places. The trickery was focused upon and remembered, while the victims of violence were forgotten.

Seamus classified the maneuvers leading to IRA attacks that entered into and disturbed exclusionary state spaces and the witty relational practices with the security forces, such as Colm Muldoon's, as "workin' moves." These tactics of the marginalized displaced the powers at the center and were sources of laughter. Seamus did not categorize the people who carried out the acts of violence as men and women who "worked moves," however. People like Ronan McShane were people who "worked work." They were "hard men" and had to maintain control at all times.

Republicans like Ronan and Seamus would hardly speak to soldiers and policemen at checkpoints: jokes and sarcasm were out of the question for them. Ronan gave one-word answers to the security forces if he gave any at all when he was stopped at roadblocks. Republicans like Ronan and Seamus would keep silent after answering the basic and often repeated questions about where they were going and from where they were coming. Often, they would not answer at all.

Such everyday practices required self-discipline, control of the body, "workin' work." They required silence in the face of the provocation that may have erupted in these tense encounters. Ronan and Seamus were brought to interrogation centers during the mid-1980s, and they told me they had kept silent as the Special Branch of the RUC vigorously questioned them. This brand of "workin' work" was highly valued in the Irish republican support community.

Seamus McRory was the only person I encountered during fieldwork who regularly referred to situations as "workin' work" or "workin' moves." I heard him use these phrases often at the Drumcoo Glassworks and occasionally in other settings. I had no doubt that his interlocutors understood what he meant when he used them. They nodded their assent or added material that corresponded to his message. I understand "workin' work and workin' moves" to represent everyday Irish nationalist practices not because of their wide use around Ballybogoin but because they describe a split subjectivity that I find key in making sense of Ballybogoin area Irish nationalists.

In my translation, Seamus's "workin' work" describes the modern, the practices that make a modern subject. This term describes activities, not categories of people, but in Seamus's understanding, Protestants, members of the security forces, English people, and certain elements of the local Catholic middle class, including some members of the Drumcoo Glassworks management, were totally subjected to such practices. Most Catholics, as he described them at various times, were subjected to them, but never totally, although Irish republicans had to subject themselves to the disciplines associated with "workin' work" more often than most. He used to say, "We have to work work and work moves."

I translate Seamus's "workin' moves" as indexing practices that are modern and nonmodern, ones that are not "traditional" as we commonly understand the term.[21] These were not resurrections or direct continuations of the past but ones that were marginalized by the ideologies of the modern nation-state and its preferred modes of cultural organization.[22] From the perspective developed in this book, people who work moves are neither modern nor traditional, but contemporary (see Lloyd 1997). They differ because they move through different spaces, not because they exist in separate times or perpetuate past historical practices without creatively articulating them to the present. Their spaces and their connection to the dominant ones surrounding them require examination: their modernity is a colonial one, and that difference makes a difference.[23] Catholic people in 1980s Ballybogoin knew they were watched, and they watched themselves. Their consciousness was double (see DuBois 1903, 1–4).

Moving Maps and Finding Directions

These four introductory tours function as moving stories, and they index the embodiment of history. As these people move through their social spaces, they make the structures that, in turn, make them. Their practices made the ethnicized landscape into the real, making them fields for particular types of action. Each of these four people moved through social space differently, but each of them paid heed to boundaries that could be connected to seventeenth-century events. As these people moved through their home places, they brought the past into the present not only by telling stories but also by their bodily movements and the everyday practice of telling.

Telling has a double sense that relates to the complicated relationship of history and memory, a connection that anthropologist Tim Ingold addresses when he writes of the duality marking the difference between commemoration and memorization (see Ingold 1996, 201–5). History writing and commemoration resemble each other because both represent past events. Historical writings, dramas, the erecting of cenotaphs, and the reciting of oral narratives separate the past from the present. The experience of the past so commemorated cannot be reproduced and made authentic. Too much history has intervened between that past time and the time of writing or commemoration, so people who perform that past history, whether it is a historian writing a past event or a group of marchers reenacting one, have been transformed by the intervening history.

Ingold holds, however, that another form of remembering exists where this distance between then and now is not so clear. This different memory forms practical consciousness.[24] It informs social action, but the agents of the action do not remark upon it. Memory here involves repetition and embodiment and constitutes the skill-deploying faculty that people use to make their way through everyday life. Such repetitions, forms of sociocultural practice, not only take place in time and space, they form it (Ingold 1996, 202–3). They make different experiences of time, different temporalities.

Ingold illustrates this point further by discussing the dual meanings of narration or telling. Telling stories entails the telling of past or fictional events for the speaker and the education of the senses for the listener. It has a dual function. More relevant here, telling possesses a dual meaning. It has the sense of narration where the past is placed elsewhere as the object of a story told in the present while it also refers to the perception of an astute observer for whom "past experience provides the very foundation, through practice and training, for present skills" (Ingold 1996, 203). Telling, in this second sense, references moving into situations, interpreting them, and responding to them without reflection. Such practices bring space and time together, and Ballybogoin's telling is a practical one in this sense.

Nancy D. Munn has studied space and time relations in the Massim region of Papua New Guinea, and her work sheds light on this process. People on Gawa, the island Munn studied, evaluated acts in terms of their relative capacity to extend or expand what she calls "intersubjective spacetime—a spacetime of self-other relationships formed in and through acts and practices" (Munn 1986, 9). Practices such as food hospitality were valued differently than the exchange of Kula items that Malinowski made famous, because Kula exchange expanded intersubjective space-time to a greater degree. Kula exchanges mapped out who was where in the interisland network, and the exchanges of arm shells and necklaces with stories attached functioned to move the mind with social force. Kula exchanges expanded the actor's time and space to a greater extent than acts that exchanged food, for example. The more highly valued Kula objects created longer memories than food sharing did and mandated traveling over greater spatial distances, a touring that made Kula partners renowned and valued.

Kula exchanges, then, had subjective effects, remembering being an important one, and they influenced future actions. Munn writes, "in certain crucial cases, Gawans emphasize the importance of remembering as the means by which acts occurring at a given time (or spatiotemporal locus) may be projected forward and their capacities retained so that they may yield desired outcomes at a later time" (1986, 9–10). Acts like this displace the present, make it past, and establish the ground for the future. The past enters one's subjectivity and becomes a part of one's self-organization.

This point can be applied to the Ballybogoin area and articulated to the theoretical positions developing in this book. Think of those four tours retold in this chapter. Those spatial stories narrated the articulation of space and time by Kathleen McDuffy, Colm Muldoon, Ian McUmber, and Ronan McShane. They demonstrated the construction of different, yet patterned, intersubjective space-times.

Each of these persons possessed a different mapping of the Ballybogoin area, but they conducted most of their lives within recognized boundaries. When they transgressed them they did so differently, but they all brought space and time together as they moved. All four people observed boundaries more multiple than Protestant versus Catholic, native versus settler, colonizer versus colonized. They mapped their social world through their moving bodies. Those moves were acts of memorization, forms of practical consciousness, and they elicited narration. As these four people taught me how to move through their social spaces, they told stories that connected those present-day movements to the recent and long ago pasts. In narrating their stories they objectified the past and distanced themselves from it as they celebrated or regretted past events.

Simultaneously, however, they enacted that past. They utilized the past experience that has been carried on for generations to perceive the invisible boundaries around physical sites and human bodies. This historical consciousness, which Ballybogoin Catholics believed stems from the Elizabethan Conquest, provided the foundation for the skills needed to negotiate Ballybogoin's complex social world. These four people wanted to teach me those faculties as they told me the stories of their home places, but those lessons of the everyday were not pedagogical. They were practical. I learned them by observing and developing patterns of movement, not by being lectured. I, as a stranger, however, could transgress those established patterns and cross boundaries that "the natives" from "both sides of the house" could not.

These mapping movements recognized differences within each "side of the house," but the routine ways these four people traveled through space maintained the political binary, either in articulated narratives like Kathleen McDuffy's or in the moving of their bodies through the ethnicized landscape that they reproduced as it reproduced them. Such movement has historical meaning. It is an iterative product, reproduced over time and in space, and those repetitive acts that make it "are built into the bodily *modus operandi*" (Ingold 1996, 203).[25]

The competencies deployed in these tours were ones articulated to the colonial past, the imperial geography that divided planter and native. They connected not only to the contact avoidance and ocular strategy incurred by current political violence, that is, competencies concerning the dimension of space, but also to the narration of stories and talking to or remaining silent with others, that is, competencies concerning the dimension of time.

These tours narrated and constituted intersubjective space-times, ones that did not simply follow Protestant and Catholic divisions but were articulated to the interweaving of colonizing and decolonizing processes that adhere to Frankenberg and Mani's understanding of the postcolonial. People located themselves through colonization/decolonization. Colonizing practices rank order social formations, and, in the Ballybogoin region, the town center and the lowland agricultural spaces were valued by the state and were associated with Protestants in patterns consonant with seventeenth-century mappings. Catholics felt out of place in Protestant and state spaces. The boundaries they observed got materialized in a variety of ways: whether a space is populated by people wearing uniforms or not, whether a house is two stories or one story, whether or not you and your neighbor know each other's first names, whether one's movements through space are "Protestant" or "Catholic," whether you park your car east or west of the town square, whether you talk or do not.

These materializations of everyday life exhibit a memorization of the colonial past for Catholics, and penetrations of exclusionary spaces were often understood as reenactments of past efforts to decolonize. Colm Muldoon carried out decolonizing acts by "workin' moves." He valued outwitting his Protestant neighbors and the police through indirect means, and his practices articulated to those stories told about O'Neill's warriors at the fort. He tried to get the last laugh and upend the hierarchy that put Protestant policemen and UDR soldiers in control of the spaces through which he moved. Ronan McShane confronted the security forces head on and let his position be known through a directness associated with "workin' work." Ronan identified with and valued the fighting men of the past, as the tour of the death spaces of his fallen comrades and the cemetery indicated. He understood himself as living the militant nationalist tradition of decolonizing struggle.

Ian McCumber did not recognize the colonial past in the introductory tour he gave me. The well-preserved industrial sites to which he brought me demonstrated his identity with and positive valuation of the modern, the industrial history of Ballybogoin. For him, the moment of plantation and the ensuing industrialization of the area marked local history's beginning, but his was an identification made in ambivalence. When I asked him what he thought about the category "Wobland," he interpreted it as a sign of betrayal. He responded, "It sounds like they're getting ready to sell us down the road." He read "Wobland" as a sign that he might be marginalized by unionists east of the Bann, that he might be excluded from an entity he cherished.

Local Irish nationalists whom I queried about "Wobland" had a different response. Several reacted by looking away, pausing, and making statements like this one made by a middle-class man: "It sounds like they think we are an African tribe or something." Catholics read this signifier to represent them as other, a colonized one. Both responses indicated that each group west of the Bann was aware that a dominant geographic discourse divided their respective "sides of the house." East and west of the Bann were markers of difference within each group. The unity of the two sides of the Protestant/Catholic binary could not be assumed.

These tours show that the everyday practices of Catholic, Irish nationalists subdivided the divisions in their ethnicized landscape of Protestant versus Catholic. People constructed those subdivisions as neighborhoods, in Arjun Appadurai's sense, as places, ones staked out in physical space, that "imply a relational consciousness of other neighborhoods, but they act at the same time as autonomous neighborhoods of interpretation, value, and material practice" (1996, 186). Such neighborhoods proliferate in the Ballybogoin area. For example, Colm Muldoon separated his townland and those neighborhoods that joined together to establish his Gaelic Athletic Association football club not only from the Protestant neighborhoods next to his but also from those of Catholic Ballybogoin, where he conducted a good part of his work and recreational life. He highly valued those practices that made his home place appear markedly different, especially the *craic,* the wit in conversation that brought people together in his locale. The stories he told and the conversations in which he participated made his home place. They distinguished him, and he identified those forms of cultural practice, as most Catholics in the area did, as those that his "side of the house" possessed.

These valued practices differed from those ocular strategies involved in telling, the reading of bodies and the scopic regime that organized bodies and political spaces in Northern Ireland, ones that the state arranged with most social force. If those strategies privileged the eye and contributed to the form of remembering and forgetting that marked "the historiography of excuse," then the practices of building apparently autonomous neighborhoods for Catholics valued the mouth. They valued talk and storytelling, drinking in pubs, and singing, the means of exchange in these Irish nationalist locales that created shared memories and the notion of a shared space.

Talk indexed a different embodiment than that of the ocular strategy. Oral practice countered the positioning of others through telling that so pervaded the spaces of everyday life. The stories and verbal games that made these troubled spaces into places articulated differences, linked them together, as they enacted desire (as they related one person to another). Such practices are highly valued among Catholics, not only because they constructed "community" but also because they expanded spatiotemporal relations in the context of their having to endure both an ethnicized landscape where silence reigned and a nation-state that attempted to saturate their everyday lives and reduce their spaces to relate. In these home places, these subdivisions of acute division, talk enabled members to locate themselves, to render their spaces meaningful and make them into their own places.

These efforts show that place-making practices are not natural but are contingent. Social and political processes effect them, and in this case they are colonial. As the preceding stories about space and place show, such processes may be profoundly connected not only to space but also to time and the organization and movement of bodies. Colm Muldoon did not want to visit the old, colonized Roman Catholic church because he did not want to be perceived as being out of place, even though he was close to home. Ronan McShane wanted to differentiate himself from such Catholic acts. He said SDLP supporters were like him and his colleagues, "except we won't lie down no more." Ronan wanted to make his incursions into exclusionary spaces public and direct.

Both men's practices articulated to the colonial past, and that past was not only background: it entered social action. Its meanings were present in telling and in the practical consciousness that guided their bodies through space. These practices indexed the fact that colonialism remains a social force in Northern Ireland. Its discourses are taken up in representations of the contemporary social world, and people emplot social actions through the narratives associated with them. Past meanings remain, although they, of course, are articulated to the social and political world differently than they were. The people who deploy them are contemporary, not traditional, but they often use "tradition" to blind themselves to the complex cultural and political differences and similarities that surround them, ones that the binary of the colonizer and the colonized, lived through the telling associated with memorization and the foundation for the practical skill of moving through social space, makes them, too often, forget. Their modernity, although colonial, is mixed.

2

Dividing Space
& Making "Race"

"Race consciousness," Zora Neale Hurston wrote, "is a deadly explosive on the tongues of men." In 1973 I was amazed to hear a member of the House of Lords describe the differences between Irish Protestants and Catholics in terms of their "distinct and clearly definable differences of race." "You mean to say that you can tell them apart?" I asked incredulously. "Of course," responded the lord. "Any Englishman can."

Henry Louis Gates Jr. (1985)

In Ballybogoin on the last Sunday in May 1984, eleven-year-old Patrick, a Roman Catholic, knocked at the door of my one-room cottage that stood adjacent to his home. He uttered, "it's a blistr'n hot day," as he entered the door, but he, like most Ballybogoin people, was glad of it. "I'd rather it than the blustr'y days," the windy, rain-chilled days common in Irish summers, he said.

Despite the good weather, boredom had the better of Patrick. It was a typical north of Ireland, Presbyterian, Sabbatarian Sunday, "the longest day of the week" many young people in Ballybogoin called it. Patrick's "ma and da" were visiting his "grannies," aunts, uncles, and cousins in "the hill country" to the west of the town, and he chose to stay home. He told me, "I just called for a chat," so I offered him a chair.[1]

[I had been writing at my little dining table desk when Patrick "called." Having just returned from a long walk around Ballybogoin, I was jotting down thoughts on the Sunday sermon I had heard at St. Columbanus's Roman Catholic Church that morning. The local campaigns for the upcoming European parliamentary elections were under way, and the candidates had passed through the town the day before. I was also thinking about the signs of social and cultural renewal beginning to appear in the Protestant neighborhoods throughout the area, the way they reconfigured those social spaces and, it appeared, transformed the people who resided in them.

Writing now, I realize that the symbolic revivification that took place was tied to the elections. The posters of the two unionist parties, those who wanted to maintain the union of Northern Ireland with Great Britain and had an almost exclusively Protestant membership, had red, white, and blue Union Jacks and "Ulster is British" imprinted upon them. The aura of patriotism they evoked seemed to spur a premature preparation for what many Protestants in the town referred to as "the glorious twelfth," the Twelfth of July, the annually celebrated "national holiday" in which unionists and loyalists remembered and ritually celebrated the victory of King William of Orange over King James II, the Pretender, and his Irish supporters at the 1690 Battle of the Boyne, a historical site now in the Republic of Ireland.

Already people in the Protestant neighborhoods were tidying up their streets for what one Protestant shopkeeper told me was "our day." They painted their "pavements" (curbstones) red, white, and blue; assiduously swept and washed their sidewalks; and hoisted the Ulster flag along with the Union Jack from their homes and places of work.[2] The fife and drum bands, what Ballybogoin's Catholic nationalists called "kick the Pope bands," could be heard during the evenings. One of the main roads out of the town, near the entrance to a large, exclusively Protestant housing estate, had a six-line jingle written across its entire width. It recalled the Protestant might of 1690 and reminded people that the Ulster Volunteer Force (UVF), a Protestant paramilitary unit, could muster the same strength in 1984, should the situation warrant it. Many Catholic nationalists read these signs as triumphalist and exclusionary. Patrick's parents, among other Catholics with whom I spoke, interpreted these acts to signify that "the Protestants are in high dough," a phrase they repeated often during those days. They warned me, as they did their children, to stay out of the Protestant territories demarcated by British symbols. Patrick's older brother and I stopped playing tennis in the town's one public court, on the Protestant east side of town, because of his mother's worry. This national holiday and its symbols signified danger for many local Catholics.

Although Catholic neighborhoods did not respond with tit-for-tat symbolic acts, the signifiers that one nationalist party displayed, in its electoral campaign, elicited outraged and derisive responses from Protestant unionists. Sinn Féin had designed campaign posters whose green, orange, and white stripes replicated the Irish tricolor, the flag of the Republic of Ireland. "A Nation Once Again," a popular Irish nationalist song and a statement anathema to Protestant cultural knowledge, adorned these posters along with a photograph and the name of the Sinn Féin candidate, Danny Morrisson. Many local Ulster unionists and Ulster loyalists said that this "nation," reputed by Irish nationalists to have existed in times long ago, lived only in the nationalist imagination. Unionists were infuriated when Irish republicans invoked this cultural product as a political weapon meant to justify the usurpation of what many among them believed to be a right given by God and justified by natural law: a state tied to Great Britain. Local Protestants and unionist political leaders who appeared on Northern Ireland's media derided these allusions to a long-ago Irish nation by asking, "When did it ever exist?" The question simmered in the media for the entire election season.

The status of the Irish nation was an issue in those 1984 elections, in part because the New Ireland Forum had convened that year in Dublin, the capital of the Republic of Ireland. It was a series of presentations, representations, and discussions initiated by the major Irish nationalist party in Northern Ireland, the SDLP, and the government of the Republic of Ireland. It addressed the relations between the Republic of Ireland and the United Kingdom, particularly as they articulated to the political status of Northern Ireland.

The constitutional nationalist parties from all parts of Ireland put forth policy proposals and imagined new sets of relations among the islands of Great Britain and Ireland.[3] Irish nationalist rhetoric, at times, marked the deliberations, and some Irish nationalist participants queried the naturalness of the Northern Ireland state. They maintained that the Government of Ireland Act of 1920 that partitioned the island of Ireland did not "accept the democratically expressed wishes of the Irish people" and "had created an artificial 'system in the North of supremacy of the unionist tradition over the nationalist tradition'" (McGarry and O'Leary 1995, 28).

The subject of democracy and British acts against it informed the recommendations put forward by the New Ireland Forum. Prime Minister Margaret Thatcher of Britain rejected outright any possibility that such proposals might be instituted, a position that greatly relieved Northern Ireland's unionists (see Lee 1989, 674–87). In November 1985, however, Prime Minister Thatcher sundered that solace when she signed the Anglo-Irish Agreement. The first clause of this document guaranteed unionists that Northern Ireland would remain British as long as the majority of citizens within Northern Ireland desired it, but the second clause nullified that commitment from the unionist perspective. The second clause stipulated the determination of both the London and the Dublin governments to make "all efforts" to find agreement among the islands and its peoples on the administration of Northern Ireland.

To unionists, this spelled betrayal because it included a foreign, sovereign state in their governance. Unionists believed the agreement subverted the nation-state of the United Kingdom and its democratic institutions. Although the Dublin government's "consultative role" was relatively powerless, it signified a profound transformation of the political order in unionist understandings. Outrage ensued. "Margaret Thatcher has murdered democracy in Ulster" became a refrain from a wide variety of unionist positions. A funeral for democracy, draped caskets and all, was held in the center of Belfast a few weeks after the agreement's signing. On radio call-in shows the unionists, like many I talked to personally, expressed outrage and hurt that they, the majority, had not been consulted. Margaret Thatcher and her government had denied "natural justice," they said. She broke "the natural law." The themes of the responses I collected in Ballybogoin revolved around the following statements: "She's sold us down the road." "They let us down." "We're the backbone of this place, and look what's been done to us. This is the worst thing that's ever happened to Northern Ireland."

Ballybogoin's Irish nationalists gave the agreement faint praise. They told me, "Ach, it'll put a little life into the old place." "It seems a damp squib to me, like." "It's nothing but a security agreement, but it's better than nothing."

The constitutional Irish nationalist parties of the Republic of Ireland and Northern Ireland, the majority of the United Kingdom's Parliament at Westminster, as well as politicians throughout Europe and the United States praised the agreement. They concentrated on the rhetoric of this political construction. Northern Ireland people focused on what was happening on "the ground," in their social and cultural spaces. Protestant unionists believed that with the Anglo-Irish Agreement the British state betrayed Northern Ireland's loyalty to the United Kingdom and the liberal individualism that it entailed. They felt that "the natural law," the British tradition in the classic liberal sense of John Locke and John Stuart Mill, was being removed from under their feet. And this loss, they believed, was being put into place to accommodate an artificial entity, the nation of Ireland.

Unionists discussed the Anglo-Irish Agreement, in part, by opposing nature and artifact. By this logic, since Irish nationalists derived their political aspirations from an artificial entity, those desires deserved no recognition. For many unionists, individual subjects freely making choices constituted the basis of natural law, and the British state's enactment of the Anglo-Irish Agreement transgressed that state of nature. Since the unionists had not been consulted, the Anglo-Irish Agreement denied that freedom of choice, an element of nature.[4]

Natural or not, nation or not, Ballybogoin's Irish nationalists did not mark off their territory with any religious or political symbols as their unionist neighbors did in May 1984. The last remaining graffiti memorializing Bobby Sands and the nine other Irish Republican hunger strikers who died in 1981 while protesting their loss of political prisoner status had washed off the boundary walls of one of the town's large Catholic housing estates. In faded black paint, along dull gray walls, the graffiti "Don't let them die" and "Bobby Sands MP" had marked this estate's main entry when I first visited Ballybogoin in late 1983. Both signified important dimensions of Irish nationalist political sentiment. "Don't let them die" was directed to Prime Minister Thatcher and left no doubt that many Ballybogoin Irish nationalists held her responsible for the ten deaths.[5] Many referred to Mrs. Thatcher as a murderer when they spoke with me. I read the "Bobby Sands MP" graffiti as a statement that proclaimed, "Like it or not, Bobby Sands represents us, and we in this housing estate are proud of it."

Sands won his seat as the representative to the Queen's Parliament in a suddenly called by-election when feelings were running high. Protestants were irate, and Catholics who opposed the hunger strike, mostly middle class, were mortified at the election results. Still, these slogans and graffiti lacked the triumphalism of the flags and the Union Jack red, white, and blue curbstones.[6] These annually regenerated, ritually extended symbols of loyalty to the British state marked and bounded social space.

To Catholics, the flags and curbstones were signifying practices that positioned them as subaltern. They dared not cross the boundaries marking off these territories this time of year. Catholic citizens were always warning me to be careful, to avoid those neighborhoods at night. "It's dangerous if you're a stranger about them places," many Catholics repeated. To Catholics these signifying acts seemed to state, "We, the Protestant people, are British and proud of it, and we have the power to enforce it." On the Twelfth of July Northern Ireland holiday, Ballybogoin Catholics left the province if they could. Most, especially in the year the regional Orange Order marchers convened in the town, took vacations in the Republic of Ireland, England, or elsewhere during the height of "the marching season." If they stayed home, they avoided the areas of celebration.

Although a few Protestants criticized these summer rituals, for most they were essential. These cultural practices were a way of asserting, "Our struggle for freedom has been long and hard and still goes on, but we, with eternal vigilance and no compromise, will endure." The phrases "Not an inch!" and "No surrender!" appeared on the walls of local unionist housing estates those summers to signify unionist resolve. To Irish nationalists, they also said, "No Trespassing" and "No Exit."

Catholics who called themselves "moderates," members of the SDLP, pleaded for a foundation upon which to talk to their neighbors across "the divide." Comparing himself to these moderates, Ronan McShane, as cited in the previous chapter, told me, "We're no different from them, except we won't lie down no more." His statement invoked the memory of a song hated by Irish nationalists, one with the refrain "Croppies lie down."[7]

> Poor Croppies, ye know that your sentence was come,
> When you heard the dread sound of the Protestant drum;
> In memory of William we hoisted his flag,

And soon the bright Orange put down the Green Rag.
Down, down, Croppies lie down!

In the summers of 1984, 1985, and 1986 only Protestants constructed such formal exclusionary markers in Ballybogoin. The town's poorest and reputedly toughest housing estate, the entirely Catholic Killybackey Road estate, pejoratively known as "the OK corral," had, like most other Irish nationalist housing estates, lots of graffiti berating the RUC and the British army while celebrating the IRA. But the residents placed no specific, boundary-making social signifiers around the complex's edge.

A large painting of one of the foremost nationalist symbols, the phoenix rising, covered one of its walls, but it did not face outward to the border of the estate. It turned inward to the estate from its isolated rear entrance. It addressed the residents, not outsiders. Coarsely daubed onto a windowless, soot-encrusted red-brick wall marking the end of a row of terraced houses, the bottom half of this mural was layered with thick black paint and the top half showed a large bird, splattered with that black paint, emerging from the black. "Out of the ashes of 1969 rose the provisional IRA," read the caption stretched above and around the barely distinguishable bird's head. No such splatters erased the unionist and loyalist murals in the Protestant estates. "The soldiers throw buckets of paint on it all the time," the people of the Killybackey Road told me when they explained the erasure of this sign that transformed their physical spaces into their neighborhood, their home place.[8]

With such political symbols surrounding them during the election campaign, few Ballybogoin people of any class demonstrated the Europeanization of middle-class culture that anthropologist Thomas M. Wilson reported around that period for County Meath in the Republic of Ireland (see Wilson 1988). On the contrary, north of Ireland issues dominated the discourse of the election. The issue in Ballybogoin, as usual in the 1980s, was Sinn Féin, the political wing of the Provisional Irish Republican Army. Since the time Bobby Sands was elected MP for Ballybogoin's parliamentary seat, Sinn Féin had contested elections there and was raising its percentage of the vote with each successive electoral attempt.

The British government, the two major unionist political parties—the establishment Ulster Unionist Party (UUP), which was popularly referred to as the Official Unionist Party in the 1980s, and the populist, more stringently loyalist Democratic Unionist Party (the DUP)—as well as the SDLP, for different reasons, wanted to stop Sinn Féin in its tracks. "Smash Sinn Féin" became the dominant slogan of the DUP during the 1984 elections for the European Parliament, while the SDLP, not wanting to lose votes to Sinn Féin, constantly harped on the problem of that party's impersonation at the polling booths, a strategy that they and both unionist parties were believed to practice. One Belfast man told me his grandmother voted eighteen times for an SDLP candidate in the early 1970s. She had been chauffeured around, given several changes of coat and hat, and cast votes for various dead people throughout her area.

Europe was hardly heard about during the campaign, except from John Hume, head of the SDLP and the leading nationalist politician. He was also a sitting European member of Parliament (MEP). He was reelected, but the big victor was the Reverend Ian Paisley, the leader of the DUP, who garnered more votes than any other candidate in all of Europe while speaking less about the European Community than any of his Northern Ireland counterparts. The Sinn Féin candidate, Danny Morrison, was the first runner-up, finishing fourth in the eight-candidate race in which the first three finishers won seats in the European Parliament. He received nearly the same percentage of the vote as his party had in the previous election. He got 13.3 percent, and there were no findings of any large-scale impersonation, although Irish nationalist voters had fun with all the rumors and innuendoes.[9]

I walked through the polls with several Catholic Ballybogoiners as they voted. When they met their fellow Irish nationalist townspeople, they would smile and say, "What about ye? Vote early and vote often now, Paddy." "Aye, vote early, vote often, Francie!" would come the laughing reply, and guffaws generally emanated from any Catholics within hearing distance. But that distance was never a great one because, knowing these remarks would offend Protestants, they tried to "keep them low." I did not observe any Catholic women say this, but I did see them join in the laughter. I saw no Protestant voters partake in such *craic*.]

Needless to say, I knew eleven-year-old Patrick would not be interested in either my field notes or my thoughts. Neither was I when I had the chance to speak with him. After some small talk about the weather,

Patrick told me how bored he was and that all but one friend, the next-door neighbor whom he had just seen from his bedroom window, were away. He added, though, that he did not play with that particular lad anymore. I asked him why not and he said, "Ach, it's a queer thing what a school can do to a lad!" I asked him what he meant, and he hesitated before informing me, "Aye, ye know, that secondary is one of the cheekiest schools in Northern Ireland." Telling him I did not know that (actually I did know local Catholics believed that, because Patrick's mother had told me about it just a few days before), and writing his words down all the while, I again asked him what he meant. He then told me that the boys were very bigoted there at the state, Protestant, school and that his friend must have learned to be bigoted, "black," too. Since that lad had started there the previous fall, he had not played with or talked to Patrick. "He's all the time cheeky to me, and he used to play basketball here near every day," Patrick said.

I asked Patrick if he had learned to be bigoted too. He said no, not like that, and he told me that teachers from his school and his ex-friend Steve's school had arranged a deal in which a teacher from St. Columbanus Roman Catholic School would exchange classes with a teacher from the Ballybogoin secondary, the next-door neighbor's "state school." It never worked out, he said, because those lads shouted and raised such a fuss that the teacher from the Roman Catholic school could never "get spakin'," but the state school teacher got along okay in his school.

He also told me what had happened recently to Michael (Mickey) McCann, a friend of his. Mickey lived across the street from "the Protestant secondary," which started and finished their school day a bit earlier than the Catholic secondary and grammar schools did. With staggered schedules, there was less of a chance that groups of Catholic and Protestant schoolboys would meet. One day, though, Mickey had a dentist's appointment scheduled before school let out, and he went home early. Unlucky for him, he walked by the secondary school, wearing his St. Columbanus school uniform, just as the students from the Protestant secondary got out. A group saw him and set upon him. "They knocked him about a bit, covered him in spittle and chased him right into his house," Patrick narrated. "Lucky for him, he didn't get really hurt. Our lads wouldn't do that."

Mickey and I had talked at length on a number of occasions. An engaging eleven-year-old, he was curious about the United States and wanted to hear all he could about it. In turn, he told me his "da" had died more than ten years earlier, when he was an infant. His father, a veteran policeman, answered a telephoned request to deliver a message to a family who lived out in the town's hinterland and had no phone. A close family member had died, and the police were asked to notify the rural household of the wake and funeral. When Mickey's father reached his destination, however, Provisional IRA gunmen set upon him. They shot him dead with a bullet through the head. The call was a decoy to kill an RUC man, any RUC man.

Mickey's "da" had joined the RUC in the late 1950s or early 1960s: Mickey did not remember. At that time, before the onset of "the troubles," so the stories Catholics tell went, there were few job opportunities for Catholics that would provide any semblance of a middle-class life. "They kept us out or only gave us the dirty jobs," many Catholics remembered. To get middle-class status, one had to emigrate to England or the United States, they said. Catholics who joined the police in those years wanted to stay home and make something of their lives. Ballybogoin's Irish nationalists numbered Mickey's "da," a well-liked man, among these.

Mickey's family belonged to Irish-Gaelic sporting and cultural organizations. These groups did not allow policemen to join. Mickey, too young at the time of his father's death to remember him, echoed his family: "I don't like the RUC, surely, but I loved me da."

After Patrick told me about the bigotry at the local secondary, I asked if he had learned any sectarian songs since starting at the Catholic grammar school. Blushing, he said that he had not, got up from his chair, and started moving toward the door. "Do you want to play some basketball?" he asked me. I said I would and followed him out. He had tactically placed the basketball at the doorstep. His ordeal was over, and at last he had found a companion with whom to shoot hoops.

> To recognize the moral tension, the ethical ambiguity, implicit in the encounter of anthropologist and informant, and to still be able to dissipate it through one's actions and one's attitudes, is what encounter demands of both parties if it is to be authentic, if it is actually to happen. And to discover that is to discover also something very complicated and not altogether clear about the nature of sincerity and insin-

cerity, genuineness and hypocrisy, honesty and self-deception. (Geertz 1968, 154–55)

Learning to Tell the Troubles

Almost two years later, I returned to Ballybogoin after a five-month stay in London. On my first weekend back, the Boston Celtics participated in a National Basketball Association playoff series in the United States that was televised on the British Independent Television Network. Patrick, excited, came running to my door to invite me to watch "the playoff match" at his house. Glad to see the Celtics, my hometown team, but more glad to have the chance to talk with Patrick, I left what I was doing and went with him. We conversed more than we watched the game. Patrick caught me up on all the news I had missed while I was away, especially the mortar bomb attack that the Provisional IRA had carried out on the UDR barracks next door to his school.

The IRA had ejected rockets from the back of a van, and they misfired. One had gone over the school wall into the regiment's grounds. Some had stayed on the van, and others had gone off in every direction. Luckily, no one was killed, but damage had been done to some St. Columbanus school property. The row of houses across the street from the school, all Catholic owned, lost every window. Patrick told me it happened when school was not in session, but people were pretty angry about it. He emphasized, though, that "the Catholic people are sickened by the carry on of the UDR and the Protestant politicians" and proceeded to tell me how the helicopters left the UDR base several times a day and made such a "deafening noise" that the students and teachers at St. Columbanus could not hear each other. He viewed this as a deliberate act of harassment by the state.

It was the first time I ever really heard Patrick talk about politics, and he added that he and his family could hardly watch the news anymore. They were all "sickened," he said, by the "constant crying of Paisley and the unionists over the Anglo-Irish Agreement" of November 1985. Patrick and his family felt the pact did nothing for the Catholics and did "no harm" to the Protestants. Patrick told me that he expected these troubles to last all his life. "They'll never end," he said, "and if the Brits leave, the Protestants will just fight in their place. The IRA won't stop." More serious than I had seen him before, he said he was "fed up with it all."

We sat quietly and watched the Celtics, who numbered Patrick among their fans not only because they were "the green machine" and had a shamrock and leprechaun for insignia, as Patrick well knew, but also because my sisters and brothers-in-law had visited Ballybogoin while I was there, had taken a liking to Patrick, and had sent him Larry Bird posters, Boston Celtics souvenirs, Nike basketball shoes, and a variety of Celtics and National Basketball Association paraphernalia. At thirteen, he was "all style," as the local people said: designer jeans with the cuffs rolled a little distance above the ankle, the latest Nikes (unavailable at the time in Ballybogoin), a Boston Celtics T-shirt, and a haircut with a bit of individual flair from one of the new, young, "modern" hairdressers in the area. In Boston he would have been considered a hip young teenager. In Ballybogoin, his style signified he was a middle-class Catholic, and most Protestants and Catholics would be able to tell what religion he was just by looking at him.

After a few moments of silence, a car pulled up outside. Patrick went to the window to see who it was, and he said, "It's a girl. Must be going to visit that English fella stayin' in the room next to yours." He stayed at the window, looking, and said "Ach, she's Protestant." "How do you know that?" I asked him. "I can tell by the blue jeans. You can only buy those at Dixon's, and not many Catholics'll shop there. Besides, she's blonde and big-boned and has one o' them short haircuts they give over at Robinson's."

I had known the physical codes for "telling," but, although I knew that people from each of the two main interpretive communities read who was who via certain dress codes, I did not know the specific brand names and designs that signified Protestant and Catholic until Patrick pointed out this middle-class consumption way of "telling" to me. Long before this encounter, both Protestants and Catholics had told me the physiological characteristics of the opposing side. Protestants informed me that Catholics were "dark," "skinny," "their dark eyes were close together," and "they always looked hungry." One Protestant woman with whom I worked in a voluntary program that served both communities shivered in a performance of fear as she described such a character to me. Catholics said, "Protestants are light," "many are blonde," "they have eyes close together," "often they have a wee dimple on the chin," "they are big-boned with large features, especially the women," "the men are handsome, the women are not," "they do not smile, and they would not talk til ye."

In their pubs and clubs Protestants often alluded to Catholics, primarily by mimicking the way they talked. Their renditions, which reminded me of the classic "stage Irishman," a caricature resembling American minstrels' representations of African Americans, consisted of rapid-fire talk, much of it nonsensical, full of non sequiturs and formal devices—terms of address, tag endings, and what Catholics call "sayings" (aphorisms). These Protestant performances effected an image of people who used language abundantly but not properly. Their mimicry seemed to index a border between Catholics and themselves on the basis of speech.

I did not witness Catholics engaging in any tit-for-tat *craic* like this in their pubs, although they did imitate the Reverend Ian Paisley for laughs on occasion. I do not recall any mimicry performed as a representation of the entire group—Protestants. When Irish nationalist people were "in good form" they often sang "the Sash," an important song of the Orange Order, the exclusively Protestant, secret society that organized most of the sectarian political ritual in the community.[10] All present would usually join in this singing. It was considered "great *craic*." Someone would just get up and sing the opening lines while others immediately joined in. They did not mimic the solemnity with which this song was accompanied in the unionist context, but they did not mark the singing with pejorative signs.

Colonialism, Race, and the Practices of Everyday Life

Prejudice is expressed as social signs, that is, as meaningful behaviors and actions that take place in ordinary social interaction. Social signs include but go well beyond language. Communication is thus a complex system of meaningful social action—that is, a semiotic system. Much of communication is politicized because the interpretations that count depend on who has power. (Urciuoli 1996, 1)

These episodes, from the beginning and end of my initial fieldwork, exhibit the social signs that make division and prejudice in Ballybogoin. They also attest to the politicization of communication to which Urciuoli refers, and they suggest, in the context of Northern Ireland, questions about the political nature of ethnographic writing. In Ballybogoin communication between "the two sides of the house" and the individuals living within it became problematic when concentration was placed upon relationships and not the content communicated.

In the cases described earlier, the concentration on form led to silence. Patrick and Stevie did not talk to each other. The boundary making, spatial practices of the state combined with those of the two major social groupings, Protestant and Catholic, focused attention on the form of communication, not the content communicated, as "telling" and the questioning by the RUC at checkpoints so clearly showed. None of the three sides communicated well with the others, if at all. Irish nationalists of all ages could not remember communicating with unionists through any form that was not orchestrated by "telling." This discordance, whose roots Catholics believed were in the seventeenth-century plantation and the colonial state that accompanied it, one that divided social space into areas of "settlers" and "natives," appeared to be a four-hundred-year-old condition in Ballybogoin.[11] Kathleen McDuffy, in the tour she gave me around Ballybogoin, represented it that way, but, four centuries old or not, it has received a modern-day jolt since the local civil rights movement started in Northern Ireland in the mid-1960s. In the aftermath of that suddenly stilled movement, politics in Northern Ireland devolved to violence.

Patrick and Stevie no longer talked. Their respective communities were in conflict. Patrick's parents remembered that their generation, the one that grew up just before the 1960s civil rights movement, spoke some to "the other side of the house," but there was not a great deal of *craic* to report in those exchanges. Patrick's and Stevie's cohorts did not even approach their parents' paltry level of across-the-divide talk. Like Patrick and Stevie, young Protestants and Catholics in the Ballybogoin area marked each other by silence in the 1980s. Patrick's schoolmates who lived in the western areas of Ballybogoin's rural district reported that they rode on the bus to the Ballybogoin Square with the few Protestant schoolchildren who lived in their area every day for several years and never spoke to them. Patrick added cheekiness to his description of Stevie. Both, by the time I left their town, were extremely conscious of style. The majority of Ballybogoin adolescents could not afford to purchase the elements of this mode of dress, and Patrick (I do not know about Stevie) had become expert at reading "Protestant styles."

"Telling," the name they gave to this constructing and deconstructing activity, was communication on the level of relationship, form, not content, and it was disturbed communication. Studies with an interest in deciphering the relationships leading to certain mental illnesses such as schizophrenia have shown that, when the content levels, the reports, the everyday communications among people, are discordant, then the relationships between those communicating "are characterized by a constant struggle about the nature of the relationship, with the content aspect of communication becoming less and less important" (Watzlawack, Beavin, and Jackson 1967, 52).

What Catholics and Protestants have to say to one another is less important than the form those messages take. Telling was one example of this concentration on form, and the territorializing of Protestant living spaces during the summer marching season was another. A historical product, the marches and signs that marked Protestant territory began to be constructed in the late eighteenth century and grew, in the context of Catholic challenges to them, throughout the nineteenth century.[12] A nearly two-hundred-year-old ritual phenomenon, these social practices of marching and boundary setting, an honored "tradition" among many segments of the unionist communities, indicated that problems with the form of communication, a focus on relationship not content, were likely very old ones in Ballybogoin.[13]

These struggles over form, whether in ritual, popular art, or everyday interaction, constituted historical struggles while the struggles themselves produced and reproduced the problematic forms. Telling in Northern Ireland, the most pervasive of these forms of struggle in everyday life, intruded into the ways people held and carried their bodies—the pattern of postures, both systematically and individually produced, that Pierre Bourdieu calls "body hexis"—as well as the ways they pronounced their words (Bourdieu 1977, 87).[14]

In Ballybogoin and other areas of Northern Ireland, stories about the pronunciation of the letter *h* were told to me over and over again in the 1980s. During the 1981 IRA and INLA (Irish National Liberation Army) hunger strikes, as the stories went, it was common for Catholics, when approaching a group of Protestants, to be accosted by a question that took variations on the form "Where is Bobby Sands on hunger strike?" When the Catholics who were being questioned responded with "the H-blocks," those questioning them could tell by the person's pronunciation of the letter *h* whether that person was Roman Catholic or not. Protestants and Catholics pronounced the letter *h* differently, and that difference could carry consequences. Some of the identified Catholics reported getting beaten up. Others reported getting chased out of the section of the town square where these encounters often occurred. All Irish nationalists who experienced such events, or said they did, believed that the Protestants who judged their pronunciations perceived their pronunciation of *h* not only to be different but also to be wrong. Their talk constituted speech events that were laughed at.

Such judgments were the product of a historically colonized society. The legacies of colonialism have produced the segregated institutions and residential areas that have led to these different speech communities. In these pronunciation stories, unionist people took up a discourse of colonial difference. The Irish nationalists they encountered during the hunger strikes, unable to speak properly from this unionist/loyalist perspective, were forcibly evicted from public space. Such forms of communication kept the subjectivity of colonialism, the meanings of colonizer and colonized, alive around Ballybogoin. Telling functioned as a distancing mechanism, and deciphering its effects around Ballybogoin may answer the questions that Frankenberg and Mani ask in their discussion of postcoloniality.

> In what senses are we now situated "after" "coloniality" in the sense of "coloniality" being "over and done with"? What about "the colonial" is over and for whom? This is not a rhetorical but a genuine question, for it seems to us that in relation to colonialism, some things are over, others are transformed, and still others apparently are unreconstructed. (Frankenberg and Mani 1996, 276)

In 1980s Ballybogoin telling told that colonial relations continued. It constituted a significant part of the struggle over social and political identity that has characterized anticolonial and other struggles, the ability to name, attain voice, and form a group. Telling was a struggle over classification, and it helped to sustain a discourse that had its roots in colonial power. Both Protestants and Catholics constructed themselves through it. Through it, Catholics were not only marked but also painted as dangerous. The differing treatment they received at roadblocks and military checkpoints indexed this, as did their understanding that their movement through social space was restricted. Catholic, Irish nationalists were "told" in order to be controlled in these situations.

By concentrating on form, not content, telling focused upon names, categories, and classifications, on who was whom in the society, on what people were to call each other, and whether or not they should talk to one another. Were they British, Irish, native, or settler? Was he "black," a bigoted descendant of "the settlers"? Was he "a waster," a descendant of the "lazy natives"? Telling formed, in part, a contest over who defined whom.

Often written off as irrational or archaic, problems like these can reveal much about history, power, subjectivity, and culture. They resemble those struggles over names and language that women and blacks have experienced in U.S. society: struggles over racial terminologies, struggles over terms of address, struggles over classification schemes at the workplace such as the 1970s women's movement for comparable worth. All these give credence to the statement of Luc Boltanski and Pierre Bourdieu that "To possess the name is to feel the right to claim the things normally associated with those words, and the corresponding material and symbolic profits" (1977, 61).[15] Telling is about "possessing the name"—the name of the nation and citizenship—and the rights associated with it.

Labeled as marginal, Ballybogoin Catholics struggled over the words that represented them. Calling themselves Irish and excluded from power throughout Northern Ireland's history, they did not accept either the state's definition of them or their Protestant neighbors'. Both groups focused on the form of communication because there rests a form of power, the power to name. Talk occurred infrequently between "the two sides of the house," and silence marked the relationship for a variety of reasons. One of them was certainly the fact that the two groups could not agree on the naming of the politico-cultural world around them.

People use forms of talk, languages, dialects, and accents to classify themselves much like they use national identifications, ethnic classifications, and class categories (Urciuoli 1996). They also use bodies to classify, as the history of exclusion against people of color in the United

States clearly shows (Omi and Winant 1994, 53–76). Bodies, moving bodies particularly, are signifiers and constitute important parts of semiotic systems (Farnell 1994, 1996). In Ballybogoin, bodies functioned as indexes: they worked to signify connection, causality, or coexistence (Peirce 1956; Keane 1997; Urciuoli 1996). They formed an important social aspect of meaning.

"Indexes are words, sounds, or grammatical elements that carry information about the speaker's identity or location," Bonnie Urciuoli writes (1996, 7), and I would like to add bodies to her list. Indexes are dependent: they depend on the perspective of the person doing the interpreting. The statement "That man over there is Protestant—I can tell by the way he walks and carries his umbrella" is understood only when the speaker's location is known.

Michael Silverstein (1976) elaborates upon indexicality by noting its presupposing and creative properties. A presupposing index indicates information that speakers and hearers in a social situation take for granted. A creative or performative index signposts social relations by making them explicit. It can stage new relations or set up terms for interaction. The experience of indexicality "must be understood in the context of who is unmarked (a typical member of a category) and who is marked (not typical)" (Urciuoli 1996, 8). In the United States the unmarked category "American," as Urciuoli reminds us, is white, Anglo, and middle class.

In Ballybogoin, deciphering the unmarked may be more demanding, since skin color does not enter the calculus of markedness. "Both sides of the house" have marked others. On the unionist side, the unmarked are the middle class, people who give the appearance of "workin' work." On the Irish nationalist side, the unmarked, typical persons seem to be members of the working class. "The ordinary five-eighth" is the term Ballybogoin Catholic people use to figure this typification, the average Catholic male, people who give the appearance of both "workin' work and workin' moves." For Protestants this ordinary, Catholic, working-class figure who works moves is unmarked: the Catholic person who works moves is typical. Catholics mark the middle-class "workin' work," Protestant figure as the ordinary member of that political/religious category, the typical Northern Ireland/British citizen.

The experience of indexicality became complicated in Ballybogoin's split society. Bodies as indexes created situations. They located others into those to be spoken to and those to be ignored. Performative, in Silverstein's sense, they set up the terms of interaction. The resulting interrelations, however, did not get played out on a level surface. Ballybogoin's social space tilted toward the Protestant side, and that made a world of difference. It made a racialized world or, at least, a world that leaned from an ethnicized to a racialized one.

Ethnicized discourses frame difference in cultural terms. Racialized discourses do so in natural terms, and often the "races" produced by racializing discourses are devalued by state institutions. Ethnicized discourses mark difference but view it as positive for the modern nation-state, while racialized discourses view difference as negative. The naturalizing filter developed in nineteenth-century transition narratives—the stories marking social Darwinism, the rise of capitalism, and the move from tradition to modernity—characterizes racializing discourse.[16] Such discourses are tied intimately to the nation-state. Brackette Williams addresses this esprit de corps when she notes that kinship precepts make possible the creation of races within modern Western nations:

> The nature of western derived precepts produces views of nature that are diverse in character and that conceptualize the consequences of interactions with it in a variety of ways. Ideas about the logical possibilities for the production and reproduction of racially defined substances shape the means by which nature gets into persons as tokens of types (e.g. races, nations, ethnics) through reckonings of shared historical events, both adverse and triumphant. From the standpoint of racial ideology, varied patterns of interaction with nature as climate, with forms of social adversity and of triumph socialize conceptions of the natural out of which groups as races produce the biogenetic substance of nationality. The flow of the substance is then directed by a code for conduct required to replenish and maintain the unity of substance. (Williams 1995, 230)

This flow of natural substance, in turn, requires the state to move it along. Nation-states organize the "code for conduct required to replenish and maintain the unity of substance" that makes the nation, that may make its citizens a "race." National narratives supply the cultural material to keep this substance flowing while, at the same time, bounding it. Nationalist ideologies substantiate this substance. They do so by saturating the field of subject formation "so that, for every individual, the idea of nationality, of political citizenship, becomes the central organizing term in relation to which other possible modes of sub-jectification—class or gender to cite only the most evident instances—are differentiated and subordinated" (Lloyd 1997, 182).

The practices—spatial, discursive, and bodily—described at the beginning of this chapter effected such a saturation, one that made nationality the central term of subjectification in Northern Ireland. Moreover, this saturation took on a racializing form: it produced an opposition between dominant (Protestant, unionist/loyalist, British nationalist) and subordinate (Catholic, Irish nationalist/Republican) in which the Irish nationalist group had little authority to manage its position in the British nation-state.[17] Over and over again, the unionist/loy-alist version of British nationalism was performed, and it put Irish nationalists in their place. Ballybogoin Catholics had little power to stake out a place of belonging. Urciuoli writes, "Racialized people are typified as human matter out of place: dirty, dangerous, unwilling, or unable to do their bit for the nation state," and "In these discourses lan-guage difference is routinely racialized, typified as an impediment to class mobility" (1996, 15–16).

In the summers of 1984, 1985, and 1986 the unionist/loyalist political community and the British state performed racializing practices in Bally-bogoin.[18] They instated structures that typified Catholics and rendered them as matter out of place.[19] Moving from the body to discourses of the nation, this racialized, othering process becomes clear. Unionist telling practices marked Irish nationalist accents as lesser, not proper, as the H-block stories clearly showed. Protestant townspeople represented their Catholic working-class bodies (and Protestant townspeople referenced such bodies in their descriptions of the signs through which they read Catholics) by the mouth, an open orifice. The descriptions of Catholics I collected from Protestants did not depict a disciplined, modern body that conveyed an optical strategy. They described Catholics as bearing eyes that were "close together" and that looked down.

In the pubs patronized by Protestants in Ballybogoin, Catholic talk and banter were continually mimicked. People would represent Catholic talk as nonsensical. Words would just be attached to one another without rhyme or reason in these performances. Such talk in the unionist pubs devalued Catholic, Irish nationalist verbal perfor-mances. In this "scopic regime," where the eye and watchfulness sig-

naled value, the Catholic organization of the senses around the mouth
was caricatured. That mimicry represented Catholic talk as a site of
unreason.

The state, through the practices of the military, and the unionist
political community, through its celebration of the Twelfth of July holiday, detoured Irish nationalist bodies moving through space. As the
stories of Ian, Colm, Seamus, and Kathleen in chapter 1 reveal, the state
organized Catholic and Protestant movements through security spaces
differently. This resulted from the war situation, of course, but the fact
remains that bodies were told and treated differently by the security
forces.

During the summers I lived in Ballybogoin, Irish nationalist movements were constrained by the Protestant marches. The only Catholic
marches I ever witnessed during the time I spent in Ballybogoin town
were the annual "cemetery Sunday" marches that, once a year, went
from St. Columbanus Church after Sunday mass to the Roman Catholic
cemetery on the western edge of town. The parade, which rimmed the
town, did not go anywhere near unionist spaces. It was a small, focused
gathering, relatively quiet, with few band members, and it had a religious function, honoring the Catholic dead. The priest carried a mon-
strance displaying the communion host, an object tied to a Roman
Catholic sacrament that indexed superstition and idolatry to many local
Protestants. Many Protestants believed such a nonmodern practice was
out of place in the spaces of modernity. As mentioned previously, no
Catholic group, political or religious, had ever organized a march,
parade, or ritual that gathered at the town square. That center was off-
limits to assemblies of Catholics.

No story of Irish nationalist Catholics' positioning as matter out of
place indexed race like that of spittle-daubed Mickey escaping into his
home. His racialized body could not move through his neighborhood at
certain times of the day. That body, the progeny of one recruited to and
murdered in the services of the state, was outcast by the state's unionist
support community.

The unionist discourses that represented both the election struggle
of 1984 (the election to the European Parliament) and the Anglo-Irish
Agreement of 1985 represented Irish nationalists as a counterfeit population. The DUP's slogan "Smash Sinn Féin" sought to limit that group
to a position outside the state and outside dialogue. Since Sinn Féin's

allies, the IRA, had engaged the state militarily for almost fifteen years and had killed many Protestants, such discourse was understandable. Nonetheless, it positioned Sinn Féin and its supporters outside political possibility.

The associated discourse about the artificiality of the Irish nation located Irish nationalists as an unreal group. Such a nation never existed, this discourse repeated. Again, this discourse was understandable, given what we know about nations as "imagined communities" (see Anderson 1983), but in 1985 the unionists and loyalists articulated that discourse to statements concerning nature, the natural way of living in the world. The Anglo-Irish Agreement was represented as transgressing nature's way. Irish nationalist desires therefore were not "natural," so this discourse placed all nationalists outside the realm of the political. Located outside the natural law, Irish nationalists did not emanate the signs indexing the natural predispositions required to claim membership in the state or, for that matter, to claim the right to create one.[20]

This discursive formation kept at bay an analogous narrative that could be applied to unionists themselves. The sharing of this naturalizing, liberal discourse was predicated on the reenactment of historical events that the Orange Order and other institutions of unionism organized each summer. In unionist terms, it depended on constructed (artificial) entities. This logic exemplifies Brackette Williams's position that "the nature of western-derived precepts produces views of nature that are diverse in character and that conceptualize the consequences of interactions with it in a variety of ways" (1994, 229–30). The resultant "nature" gets into people "through reckonings of shared historical events" like the commemorations of the 1690 Battle of the Boyne. From the unionist perspective, Protestant perseverance won the day in 1690, and their freedoms were restored at a time of danger. The repetitions in the 1980s made Ulster identities, and they were perceived as natural. Through those summertime rituals, unionists shared that substance of kinship and nation that made them strong. Mimicry made them men.[21] Protestant traditions of freedom and the "naturalness" of individual rationality were opposed to the hierarchy of Roman Catholicism and such ritual productions as the procession demonstrating the communion host on "cemetery Sunday."

The unionist discourses possessed power in Ballybogoin. Institutions—the Orange Order, the state, and the Apprentice Boys, another

Protestant "loyal order"—took these discourses up and became their agents. They, especially the state security forces, exerted considerable force in the social life of the 1980s. The political rituals of the Orange Order and the Apprentice Boys bolstered a sense of belonging among Protestants while symbolically marking the exclusion of Catholic, Irish nationalists.[22] Along with the discriminatory practices of state and business institutions, these rituals kept colonial meanings alive for the Catholics.

Race and Time

> I was responsible at the same time for my body, for my race, for my ancestors. I subjected myself to an objective examination. I discovered my blackness, my ethnic characteristics; and I was battered down by tom-toms, cannibalism, intellectual deficiency, fetishism, racial defects, slave-ships, and above all else, above all: "Sho' good eatin'." (Fanon 1967, 112)
>
> I am haunted by the human chimpanzees I saw along that hundred miles of horrible country. . . . to see white chimpanzees is dreadful: if they were black, one would not see it so much, but their skins, except where tanned by exposure, are as white as ours. (Charles Kingsley, quoted in Curtis 1968, 84)

Frantz Fanon writes of his black body being battered down by the narratives of cannibalism, slavery, and everyday commercialization ("Sho' good eatin'") that objectify him as other. Charles Kingsley batters down the Irish in this statement about his travels through Victorian Ireland. Fanon writes of the experience of being marginalized. Kingsley marginalizes the Irish. Fanon in "The Fact of Blackness," the essay in *Black Skin/White Masks* from which this passage comes, writes of the exclusion of the black man from the temporality of modernity, and the stories he invokes in the passage cited batter his body down into another time. Charles Kingsley batters down the Irish as prehuman.

Fanon writes what it means to be a member of the marginalized. He conjures what it is like, as Homi Bhabha writes, "To be amongst those whose very presence is both 'overlooked'—in the double sense of social surveillance and psychic disavowal—and, at the same time, overdetermined—psychically projected, made stereotypical and symptomatic"

(1994, 236). Kingsley disavows the Irish. They may belong to the same empire as he does, but they belong in another time. The Orange Order political rituals and unionist discourses of the 1980s performed a similar disavowal. They did not recognize Irish Catholics as beings with the same nature. Spatial and discursive practices indexed Irish nationalists as possessing a different temporality, a long-ago one that did not share the substance of British nationality/rationality.

Space and its rationalization were important in the organizing of Ballybogoin's 1980s social order. Rationalization signifies the organization of reality according to an ethic of means and ends, but it also means to give an excuse. In Ballybogoin, rationalization was used as an excuse for racialization. One could be read for the other, and the rationalization of time figured large in Ballybogoin. A comparison of Ian's tour and the other tours rendered in chapter 1 illustrates this. They constitute a story around the two firsts glossed over in that chapter—the fact that Catholics believe that their ancestors were in Ireland first and the contrasting Protestant belief that what is important is the fact that their ancestors established civil society first, in the seventeenth-century colonial plantation (see Deane 1990).

Ballybogoin, ordered into a plantation town in the first decade of the seventeenth century, suggests to the descendants of the planters today that they brought progress to the place, and the "natural justice" they believe is due them arises from this socially constructed fact. It signals their rationality, their "chosenness," in terms of the natural law they invoked in their 1980s political crises.

The natives, however, were excluded from this "natural justice," and that exclusion is reinforced today through the stereotypes used by Protestants to label Catholics. "They don't want to work." "They waste time." "They're wasters." "Their Catholic schools don't prepare them for technical jobs." These were some of the pat phrases that questions about the higher unemployment rate among Catholics elicited from Protestants. Time and their use of it, their "backwardness," and disaffiliation from progress defined Catholics in the prevailing, contemporary stereotypes that Protestants used. It was their temporality that truly made Catholics different in the hierarchical scheme.

Religion and work both entered these othering discourses. Roman Catholicism was viewed as hierarchical and nondemocratic, as antirational, and as the past. Protestants saw the comparatively unkempt

Catholic housing estates and their higher unemployment rates as signs of sloth. They understood Catholic adherence to what they regarded as a superstitious religion to be a sign of irrationality. To Ballybogoin's Protestant unionists, the belief of Roman Catholics in their priests indexed "backwardness." It worked to hold back progress, whose supporters are entitled to "natural justice."

Catholics see these socially constructed facts differently. From their point of view, the ragged appearance of their housing estates had to do with the inferior care given to those places by the state agencies that oversaw them. Also, in the stream of discrimination, Catholic housing was built on less amenable sites and was cheaply constructed. Catholics did not make the connection between Protestantism, individualism, and liberalism. In their view and in their accountings of their local history, they saw the Protestants as effacing their history and them, as Kathleen McDuffy's tour of that Church of Ireland building and the stories of O'Neill's fort showed. Catholics say they provide the *craic* in Ballybogoin because the Protestants will not talk. "Them Protestants took the land from us, the rightful owners," one man from the hill country west of Ballybogoin told me, "and now they won't talk til us." Each side's discourses struggled with identities whose significance was intimately tied to the past, to ideas of social justice associated with different accounts of the past, and to the question of whose temporality should be recognized today.

The two firsts evident in the different origin stories told by Ian and Kathleen as they moved me through the Ballybogoin area "are not nugatory distinctions," as Seamus Deane writes, "for it is from them that so much of the later history of strife and disagreement evolves. Priority is a claim to power" (1990, 17). The power under dispute in these two different origin stories, as Deane aptly points out, is the power to name nature. Ballybogoin's unionists and Irish nationalists fundamentally disagree over that naming, and their cultural struggles often revolve around it. Irish nationalists believe that the fact that their ancestors arrived and established communities on the island of Ireland first entitles them to name the nation and define its territory, the island of Ireland. Ulster unionists believe that their organization of rationality in the plantation settlement—the towns and private property that constituted it—instituted the rational predispositions that nature has assigned people. For them, time on the island begins with that early 1600s settlement, the time when Mountjoy wanted to make Ulster "a razed table" to see and know it all.

In Northern Ireland the two sides struggle violently to institute these distinctions. As the material in this book shows, people browbeat, physically and psychically maim, and kill to legitimate the distinctions of their "side of the house." The struggles over social distinctions, over narratives of origin, over space, over place, and over the positioning of bodies (telling and killing) in Ballybogoin were, in the 1980s, and are, today, products of imperialism. All these struggles constitute what Edward Said calls "the formidable difficulties of empire," ones that, he emphasizes, anthropologists ought to examine (1989, 225).

3

Writing Ireland

One way to think about intellectual activities and disciplines is to inquire about the organization of knowledge, to ask what counts as knowledge in a particular domain—and indeed the history of disciplines is in large measure a history of the organization of knowledge.

Jonathan Culler (1988)

Racialization practices exclude, and their combination of politicized semiotic systems and institutional power has become, in this period of decolonization, objects of struggle. Ethnographies have also become contested items in this period of predicament, and the struggle has given rise to concern with ethnography as persuasive fiction, as something both made and moral (Clifford 1988).

In Ireland these wrangles are acute, not only for the places such as Ballybogoin in the north of Ireland but also in the discussions between the people studied to the south of the island of Ireland's border and the anthropologists who study them, many of whom are from the United States.[1] Realist ethnographies have been discussed and debated in the national press in the Republic of Ireland, and the genre of American ethnographic writing on rural Ireland that prevailed at the time I started fieldwork came under public criticism. This anthropological genre, in the words of one Irish journalist,

focuses invariably on dysfunction—the stresses and strains of our rural culture in the problem areas of the west. It reaches for words

like "repression," "demoralisation," and "anomie." When the studies reach print they can be deeply upsetting to the people put under
the microscope. And the more vivid and perceptive the writing, the
more likely it is to hurt. (Viney 1983, 9)

These upsets deserve consideration at this postcolonial and reflexive
moment in sociocultural anthropology. Irish scholars and artists, like
other intellectuals in formerly colonized and colonized areas, have
directed themselves to rereading their home country's literary, historical, and political texts. Such reevaluations have the goal of reimagining
Ireland, of enabling "new writing, new politics, unblemished by Irish-
ness, but securely Irish" (Deane 1985, 58). It seems constructive for
anthropologists of Ireland, wherever they are based, to engage Irish
intellectuals in this project. Evaluations of past anthropological texts
and their effects on the world render a sense of anthropology's history
and its articulation to power.

In their discussions of place making and the anthropological tradition, Akhil Gupta and James Ferguson have suggested that the reflexivity demanded of anthropologists should be not only that which reflects
on the individual's personal biography and theoretical position but
also, and more important, that which contextualizes their ethnographic
writing in terms of the texts that have written the particular region
under study (Gupta and Ferguson 1997b, 25–40). Both the ethnographer
and the place studied have been written, and an engagement with past
writings can elucidate that process. A critical anthropology, then,
requires an examination of its organization of knowledge. This chapter
will relate this ethnography to a genre of anthropological writing of Ireland from the recent past that has dealt with topics discussed here: the
importance of talk in forming social relationships, the splitting of subjectivity, and Irish identity.

A feature of everyday life that has marked the Irish—talk and what
it means—has formed a considerable problem area in the anthropology
of Ireland. In his *Irish Times* article depicting the controversy surrounding ethnography in rural Ireland, "The Yank in the Corner: Why
the Ethics of Anthropology Are a Worry for Rural Ireland," Michael
Viney (1983) addressed this issue indirectly, but the artist assigned to
illustrate Viney's piece made the centrality of talk and silence perfectly
clear.

Three cartoons caricatured anthropologists and held up an Irish mirror to the U.S.-based ethnographers of rural Ireland. The most prominent cartoon depicts a barman beginning to hoist his pint of beer. A balding, giant man with a hooked nose and a half-smile, he is conversing with a little, round man who is staring into his pint. On the bench in front of the bar sits a tape recorder. An anthropologist, a young bespectacled man, leans back against the wall watching the conversationalists out of the corner of his eye. His arms are folded tightly across his chest, his legs are crossed, and a look of frustrated boredom marks his face. "He's lookin' bored out'a his tree," an Irish wit might say.

The second cartoon shows three people, two old men and a woman, sitting on a bench. The men, talking together, are wearing suit coats, knitted hats, and ties, the dress of the Irish countryman. They lean on canes. A woman, an anthropologist, has squirmed onto the end of the bench. Wearing knee-high boots and designer sunglasses, she looks straight ahead and writes on her notepad.

The third cartoon shows three men. Two are hard at work, the third watches. The workers have on "wellies," the knee-high boots that farmers and fishermen all over Ireland wear. The bigger, brawnier one, his sleeves rolled up, pulls at something that could be either a *currach,* an Irish fishing boat, or a fishing net. The smaller man, looking frightened, grabs a net while his companion seems to shout an order or a curse at him. The anthropologist looks on from a distance, standing tin-soldier erect. He has jowls, is overweight, and has a receding hairline. A pince-nez is balanced on his nose. He wears a wrinkled suit. His notebook lifted to his shoulder blade, he gazes at the two men with an expression of wonder. He is too far away to speak with them.

With these images of modern, scientific anthropologists as disengaged observers, gazers, and distanced "others," Viney opens his essay with a story that he says was told in a doctoral dissertation on rural Irish psychology "back in California."

The conversation in a quiet farmhouse kitchen in the West of Ireland was brought to a halt by a persistent and puzzling sound—a mechanical fluttering that seemed to come from a shoulder bag resting beside the young American visitor. The woman of the house made a joke of it: "Have you a bomb in there?" But the young American's face was already scarlet. His hidden recorder had just run out of tape. (Viney 1983, 9)

From this embarrassing moment, Viney writes a review highlighted with quotes, not only from a variety of anthropologists but also from community members in the places they studied. He converses with the several sides and shows how they contradict one another. Viney narrates the ethical problems involved when anthropologists divulge "the family secrets" they collect during fieldwork. Although he does not belabor the point, all the studies he addresses concern, in one form or another, the sexual practices of rural people and fit somewhere within the framework of psychological anthropology. The one sociologist included in the essay employed a strikingly similar paradigm.

Viney quotes from a paper by John C. Messenger, one of the prominent American, post–World War II ethnographers of rural Ireland. In his version of "the Irish problem," Messenger writes:

> Among the prominent traits of Irish basic personality are sexual repression, masochism, depression, conformism, ambivalence towards authority, secretiveness, envy and jealousy, indolence, dogmatism, verbal skills, and a feeling of inferiority. Each of these is linked, more or less, to the inordinate sensitivity of the Irish to what is said of them. (Viney 1983, 9)

Messenger, it seems, did not get the point made by the Irish cartoonist. He apparently never asked the people he studied what bothered them.[2] Like those anthropologists in the cartoons, he submitted his subjects to his gaze, and that was the end of the story. When interviewed by Viney, he held to his stereotypical categorizations and saw no need to reflect upon either his analytical categories or his literary form. Writes Viney:

> Some of what John Messenger calls the "Young Turks who are 'reinventing' anthropology" would argue for a community's "right" to discuss an anthropologist's interpretations of controversial issues with him before he publishes. But such a departure, huffs the professor, "would sound the death knell of our discipline." (9)

Here, it seems, Messenger did not recognize a political problem. He dismissed the struggle over a community's effort at self-definition, at place making, and understood the intellectual problem as separated from these community concerns. He represented himself and anthropology as entirely objectivist and did not deign to consider anthropological discourse as articulated to power.

Messenger's contested "ethnographic" portrait constitutes "the Irish" as a particular sort of "other," as a seamless whole marked by negative characteristics. He refused to reflect on his position with this reaction. In fact, he described reflexivity as "the death knell of our discipline" when Viney mentioned the possibility of discussing controversial findings with the people studied. Messenger would accept no type of reflexivity and demonstrated that what the headline to Viney's story calls an ethical problem is also a political and epistemological one.

The islanders Messenger studied were marginalized people living in one of the more remote parts of Ireland. They have had plenty of experience with defining discourses—from the past colonial state, to the present independent one, to the Roman Catholic Church in Ireland. The discourses of these institutions contributed to making the islanders particular kinds of subjects, ones idealized by Irish nationalism but relatively voiceless. Their idealization contributed to the forgetting of their past difficulties, which may be, as are those for the people in Ballybogoin, so alive in the present. Messenger, like many ethnographers in the two decades following World War II, did not seem to think the pursuit of these problem areas important. He presented a body of data and interpreted it, but he never went into detail about how that data was made (through talk and writing) in the field.

Writing Differently, Reorganizing Knowledge

The "writing culture" debate in anthropology deserves consideration when addressing the problems between ethnographers and the people they have studied in Ireland. The criticisms of realist texts do not offer solutions to the conundrums of ethnography, but they do offer suggestions for experimentation. This book has taken up some of these and will try to expand upon them here.

The critics of realist ethnography do not figure language the way classical ethnographic realism does.[3] They privilege meaning, experience, and reflexivity over objectivity. They presume that discourse constitutes "reality," and they hold that people cannot have a "reality" without a sign. They believe not only that language does the work of persuasion but also that it makes subjects and renders the world in which conviction (acts of belief) and production (acts of doing) take place. Those who espouse this view hold that ethnographic texts originate in the language game of the anthropologist author, that of Western academic discourse. They believe "Power and history work through them in ways their authors cannot fully control" (Clifford 1986, 7).

The proponents of this new ethnography see neither the texts ethnographers make nor the ones they collect as perspicuous emanations of experience. To perceive them so would require a perspective they reject, the siting of meaning as a thing in the text ("text" being understood here as whatever is articulated by language), not as something done to a text. For them, meaning resides in relational action, the placing of text in cultural space—in relation to another's action, another text, a new or repeated experience (see Chambers 1979). If ethnographic realism's critics admit of such a thing (truth), Vico's "*Verum ipsum factum*"—the truth is the same as the made—echoes their calling.

By adhering to Vico's battle cry, this perspective on ethnography reduces the space between the anthropologist and the "other." Not absolutely but relatively. It does not claim to replicate the meaning of those others, to reproduce what is in their hearts and minds, but it does believe itself to be engaged in an analogous activity, text building, which is the invention of a way to understand the world, a cultural act. From this point of view, the metaphor of the quest or search is the appropriate one for anthropological knowledge (see Tyler 1986).

Advocates of what has been named "postmodern ethnography" question the hegemonic view in Western thought that it is the accuracy of representations that constitutes knowledge. Instead, they suggest that anthropologists examine taken-for-granted categories and not slot the people studied into the conventional intellectual artifacts that generations of anthropologists have created. This position demands more thorough dialogue between native and anthropologist and requires a more widely contextualized translation when anthropologists move from the cultures they study to their academic ones. These should extend through time and space and should shift back and forth from persons to their contexts (see Becker 1979, 211–43).

In this book I have tried to address some of these concerns, not by rejecting realism but by rearranging its form. I have tried to use a narrative form that puts events into their spatial and temporal relations. The focus on place making in chapter 1 attempts to move away from locating a culture in a specific place the way much realist ethnography does. Instead, the chapter describes the processes by which places are made and the relational aspects of place making. Ballybogoin town, it is implied, can only be understood in terms of its differences within the space of the town, its relations to its variegated hinterland and to the area east of the Bann. It is made into a differentiated space by the bodies that move through it and by the complex meanings those bodies bear.

Chapter 1 implies that categories such as "the Irish" are quite slippery ones. All the people in that chapter except Ian describe themselves without ambivalence as Irish, but they distinguish themselves from each other. Ian commented many times that he is labeled as Irish when in England or Scotland and identifies himself as such. Identity making for all of them is a negotiated process and entails practices of articulation, the joining of differences at several levels, and entanglements with various temporalities.

"Talk" and Talk about It

Henry Glassie (1982), in his ethnography of a remote rural area of Northern Ireland, shows how people construct material worlds through song, story, and work routines. He fills his ethnographic text with the voices of the people he studied and with their views of what makes social actions significant. His ethnography has been a cause for celebration in that area: a folk festival took its title from his book. This difference occurs not only because Glassie did not find the sense of anomie among the bachelor farmers he studied but also because he presents the text-building practices of the people studied as he demonstrates his. An identification between him and them gets produced in the text, not an identity of sameness but one of relationship. Through his discussions and his participation in talk, storytelling, work, and song, he gives ample evidence of those relations, and the ethnographic form Glassie deploys conveys that.

As Hayden White reminds us, there is "content in the form," there is a relation between narrative discourse (form) and representational meanings (historical, ethnographic, psychological contents), one that,

White insists, "entails ontological and epistemic choices with distinct ideological and even specifically political implications" (1987, ix). Glassie's text, often resembling Irish storytelling, produces a different style of thought, a different morality, a different politics than the ethnographic texts on rural Ireland that Viney discusses.[4] He, too, focuses on talk and its importance in how Irish people connect to each other. He does not read talk as a symptom of problems but as an exercise in world making. The world he represents does not demonstrate the qualities of "the Irish" that Messenger invokes as explanation.

The Irish nationalists of Ballybogoin do not fit that description either. Despite that their region suffered some of the highest unemployment rates in Western Europe during the 1980s, they did not suffer the anomie so often described by the ethnographers of the Republic of Ireland's rural west. Much of that can be attributed to the political struggle in which they were engaged and the fact that their identities became solidified in that context. Those identities also depended on everyday social practices, particularly talk.

Irish nationalists in and around Ballybogoin talked about talk in relation to telling. Telling, unlike talk, did not fit into the Ballybogoin Catholic narrative of itself as a "moral community." If we take morality to be, at bottom, a form or system of coherence, a meaning system that appeals to intellectual honesty, as Roman Catholic theologian Herbert McCabe does, then this telling goes against the grain of their text-built morality (McCabe 1987, 200). Ballybogoin Catholics said that to see someone you know and not talk is an insult to that person, which strains or breaks a relationship: it does something to them. "I let myself down," or "we let ourselves down," several Irish nationalist Ballybogoin people told me when they did not adhere to what they called "good form," talking to people and recognizing them.

Ballybogoin Catholic morality adhered to a belief that to make gestures of friendliness in formal settings but not talk to that person when you saw her at a later time was hypocrisy. Relationships need talk to be kept intact, they implied. For instance, at St. Columbanus's Roman Catholic masses, on both Sundays and weekdays, people never exchanged the sign of peace—shaking hands and saying "peace be with you"—that the contemporary Roman Catholic liturgy recommends. Their priests never asked them to perform this ritual gesture. Only once, when a missionary who was in the area for a visit home asked the congregation to do so, did I see it done at mass, and people were quite hesitant. Why perform this act of signification, they wondered, at the ritual of the mass, an act that signals the formation of a relationship, and then relinquish the relationship as soon as the gesture is over? Why go out on the street and not talk to the person with whom you shook hands, not "give them the time," the talk, that a relationship demands? Catholics felt a responsibility to keep their social and symbolic forms full of meanings. Otherwise, why have them? To pretend to the form and not fill it up was hypocrisy in their eyes. Hypocrisy, they believed, should not be performed at the mass. One woman told me on the day that missionary asked them to give the sign of peace that "to shake the hand and say peace be with you at mass, then walk down Irish Street and not give 'em the time o'day would be hurtful, so it would."

Moral content inhered in this form as political content did in the form "telling." The hospitality one is shown, the talk (which can be answered by attentive listening, not only by talking back), the reciprocity entailed in buying rounds of pints at the pub, the desire for all to contribute a song when "everyone at the pub is in great form the night"—these relationships had morality inscribed in them. And this morality was carried by the stories, the narrative forms, that told "what needs doin'" in everyday life, that admitted to the ambiguities in life but reduced them, bit by bit, as those stories were told. Talk and its associated practices gave meaning to everyday life. One Drumcoo glassworker told me as we participated in talk, *craic,* and song one weekend night, "This makes life worth living."

"A mean person" or "an ignorant person" was one who did not follow the practices these forms required: the person who accepted a pint but did not buy one in return; someone who neither listened very well nor responded with a story of her or his own; an individual who showed no hospitality; the rushed man or woman who hurried by when an acquaintance stopped on the pavement and uttered, "nothin' strange?"; a child not yet schooled in the forms that needed filling. "Nothin' strange?"—one of the more common greetings used by Irish nationalist people in Ballybogoin on people with whom they had a relationship—meant "Do you have an interesting story?" or "Is anything happening you can tell us about?"

The greeting "Nothin' strange?" produced and reproduced relationships. It created social situations. "I'm fine, how are you?"—a query concerning the state of an individual's mind and body—was not a proper response, as I found out when I was learning how to be a person in Ballybogoin. "Nothin' strange?" asked for a story—a reflection on the past; a small narrative; a report of an event, perhaps one about the prior evening's conversation; an interpretation, something that might serve as a template for higher-order constructions about the past or the future. It elicited utterances that worked to make relationships. In interactions set up by this greeting, it was not style, a feature that can be recognized by sight, or social position that located self and other; rather, it was talk and listening that people desired. Within the Ballybogoin Irish nationalist community, people made identities through such interaction. Usually, not always, they presented selves as relational, not categorical, when interacting within their communities.

Individual subjects and group identities were formed through such practices, and solidarity across gender, class, and even (though not often) sectarian lines could be formed through mutual engagement in them. The stories elicited by "Nothin' strange?" performed narrative as a "transactional phenomena," as Ross Chambers describes it:

> Transactional in that it mediates exchanges that produce historical change, it is transactional, too, in that this functioning is itself dependent on an initial contract, an understanding between the participants in the exchange as to the purposes served by the narrative function, its "point." Although narrative content is not irrelevant, of course, it is this contractual agreement as to point that assigns meaningfulness to the discourse. (Chambers 1984, 8)

From this perspective, historical worlds are not only built through narrative but also come to us through them. Narrative and world cannot be separated, and the sharing of a narrative—getting its "point" and assigned meaning—can produce both subjective and objective changes.

Every narrative, then, simultaneously makes up and creates a reality. It presents and represents a world. Every story has two contexts, the context of telling the story, the immediate one (the act of presentation), and the context of telling what happened, attempting to make the telling independent of that happening, representing it, objectifying it, while giving it (that past situation or event) voice, a concept whose function it is to tell someone else that something happened and do something with it—to relate it. The significance of stories is determined by the point of their being told, "the relationships made by the act of narration" (Chambers 1984, 3). Stories, narrative acts through which people tell others that something happened, are always available as vehicles "whereby people may 'do things'—that is (and the double meaning is itself significant), *relate*" (Chambers 1984, 4).

In other words, narrative entails both relating a story and relating to another. So, in Ballybogoin, the discourses circulating around "Nothin' strange?" represent as they present: voice is given to those things that make the "strange" (the work of representation), and speaker addresses listener, who, more than likely, becomes speaker in turn (the work of presentation—of self, of other). "Nothin' strange?" provides a space where "experience folds upon itself, refers backwards and forwards to itself through the referents of hope and fear; and by the use of metaphor which is at the origin of language, it is continually comparing like with unlike, what is small with what is large, what is near with what is distant" (Berger 1985, 14–15).

In Ballybogoin, unionists and Irish nationalists adhere to different identifying narratives. They do so because of a shared past that the ancestors of each side experienced differently and that, today, is remembered differently. Each of these communities socially reproduces itself through separate and distinct institutions (schools, churches, community associations, sport and social clubs). The different institutions articulate the past and present in opposition to one another and make relating, sharing, and getting the point of the other side's stories about local spaces and places difficult and unlikely.

Consequently, people avoid the attempt to engage members of "the other side of the house" in storytelling. In my fieldwork, I saw people do this only when they participated in the same institutions. I witnessed such relationships at the Drumcoo Glassworks, although very seldom, and occasionally I saw relationships made through narrative in rugby and soccer matches. Even being next-door neighbors did not produce interactions of this sort between Protestants and Catholics, as the stories of Patrick's family and their Protestant neighbors indicate. The Catholic middle-class people from whom I rented housing did not talk to their Protestant neighbors next door. They interpreted this as their neighbors' refusal to be "neighborly," which they understood to require the sharing of stories and the relation of selves. Those neighbors, however, held to the view that they fulfilled the duties of neighborliness. They maintained their "decency," a quality that Protestants valued in the same way that Catholics valued talk. This structure of feeling indicated that people maintained respect for others by respecting themselves, disciplining themselves, not interfering in the lives of others, and being honest. The signifier "neighborly" possessed different meanings for Protestants and Catholics in this neighborhood situation.

Talk and Telling

This difference in meaning made a difference in Ballybogoin. Irish nationalists in the area differentiated themselves from unionists, "the other side of the house," on the basis of talk. The following joke outlines the practices upon which Ballybogoin's Irish nationalists made this distinction.

> Did you hear about the six men stranded on a deserted island?
> Two Irishmen, two Scotsmen, and two Englishmen.
> The first night, Paddy Irishman and Paddy Irishman stayed up all night talking. They talked about everything, told jokes, and laughed the night through.
> The *craic* was ninety, so it was.
> Paddy Scotsman and Paddy Scotsman talked a bit and went to sleep.
> Paddy Englishman and Paddy Englishman waited to be introduced to one another and had a silent night.

The first time I heard this joke was on a Thursday night, the warm-up to the three or four nights of drinking and dancing that constituted the weekend for the single men (and some married ones) in their twenties and thirties with whom I worked at the Drumcoo Glassworks. They had brought me to this particular pub to introduce me to the quiz matches that were popular there on Thursday nights and that provided an opportunity for them to show what they knew about geography, history, current events, sports, and popular culture.

This joke was told by Brendan, a man around fifty, who had taken over the microphone from the quiz match's master of ceremonies as the pub was about to close. I had seen Brendan often in the streets around the town square as he moved through the town delivering messages for a local bookmaker. That night Brendan's charm, wit, and storytelling skills surprised me. We had been introduced to one another twice before, and he once told me that he had a brother in Philadelphia, a place he desired to visit. He never said more in my presence, although I had seen him on many other occasions. He walked the streets with a cigarette pursed between his lips, the collar of his dark coat up, and his face buried into it. He looked at the ground, not up and around. To get his attention, a person would have to speak very loudly or shout his name. I did not know him well enough to do this, so we had passed each other in silence.

On this particular night, he presented a much different self as he told jokes and stories, broke into song, and cajoled others to come to the microphone and sing. As he brought others out, he specified which of the participants were "real Ballybogoin," people whose families had lived in the town for as long as people could remember, and which were "blow-ins," people whose ancestors had migrated to town in the past two or three generations from as little distance as two miles from the town center. Brendan acknowledged and valued difference that night, and he produced and reproduced local identities.

When I expressed my surprise at Brendan's garrulousness, the workers and the group of their friends who had joined us laughed and told me, "once he has a few drinks in him, he shows what he is really like." In fact, they told me this event would show what they, the nationalists of the town, were really like, and they said that this joke, one often told when "strangers are about," put them into perspective. They were the "Paddy Irishman and Paddy Irishman" of the joke while their Protestant neighbors in Northern Ireland were represented as "Paddy Scotsman and Paddy Scotsman." Their Protestant neighbors, like those present in the pub, were somewhat like them but different. My interlocutors referred to them, as usual, as "the other side of the house" and classified their practices of interaction as less distant than those of the English. Protestant people were represented as able to perform important cultural practices, but only with each other, not with their Roman Catholic neighbors, against whom, as the metaphor of the "other side of the house" suggests, a wall had been built. "You cannot talk to 'em," these workers said.

The English were represented as not able to perform these valued practices at all, and the British security forces, who were omnipresent in the area at that time, most acutely embodied this incapacity. The RUC often garrisoned the security gates that blocked the entry and exit of automobiles to and from Ballybogoin Square, and the army set up random roadblocks throughout the area. The formulaic set of questions they asked were often mimicked by nationalist workers at the factory, who said of "the Brits": "They would not speak to you at all."

This difference between the English and the Irish was remarked upon in a variety of nationalist and Roman Catholic spheres of interaction. It was often used to make points about the perceived changes in the moral order during Sunday sermons at the local Roman Catholic church, where one priest repeatedly preached against the materialist drift of his parishioners and interpreted their removal from social and religious concerns as their becoming like "those English people who would not speak to you and show no neighborliness." At the pub that night, the workers told stories about visiting their relatives in England and about the lack of talk and *craic* "over the water." Several expressed the opinion that their kin in England were hardly Irish anymore, "west Brits" they called them. These kinsfolk, they believed, had lost the ability for talk, for *craic*.

Talk and having *craic*—demonstrating wit in conversation and having a good time (Glassie 1982, 36)—was an important marker of nationalist identity in Ballybogoin, and it received its powerful symbolic valence because of its relationship to silence in the Northern Ireland cultural practice of telling. To elaborate on its previous discussion, "'telling' is the sensory identification of the ethnic Other through the reception of the body as an ideological text," Allen Feldman writes, and it constitutes a complex decoding of the other that encodes the self. When strangers meet on the street, they piece together the "conjuncture of clothing, linguistic dialect, facial appearance, corporal comportment, political religious insignia, generalized spatial movements, and inferred residential linkages" of the person encountered (Feldman 1991, 56–57). From that interpretive act, they discern how to interact. If an individual reads the approaching body as being from "the other side of the house," then silence will characterize the ensuing engagement. If those parties interpret the other to be one of their own, then some sign of communication will likely be emitted—a look in the eye, a nod of the head, a verbal greeting, a comment about the weather.

Telling was a topic brought up by the workers during the second week of my fieldwork on the glassblowing shop floor.[5] During my first week in that shop, I had explained to them what an anthropologist does. On the next Monday, a senior glassblower brought me a cassette tape that he had recorded from a local radio show the previous weekend. It discussed "something about us that an anthropologist might be interested in," he told me, and during the lunch hour he brought Seamus, the shop steward and another senior glassblower, and me out to his car to listen to it. It was an interview with a retired teacher from a Roman Catholic school about life in the nearby countryside. The teacher told about the signs (the clothing, the twitches of the head, the body posture, the look in the eyes) entailed in the telling that he and the generations of students he had taught knew. That teacher said that Roman Catholics performed the practice with almost total accuracy and unconsciously, but he took little pride in this. He felt there was something immoral about telling, that it was wrong to identify others as so different that conversation with them was nearly impossible. The workers agreed with him in the discussion that ensued. They classified telling as "shameful." They told me, "you must think us very strange with all this carry-on, but that is how things are around here." They saw no exit from this existential state.

Acknowledging others through talk constituted a moral responsibility for these workers and for other Irish nationalists around Ballybogoin. What they labeled "strange" in "nothin' strange?" seemed to be the complex dialectic of talk, telling, and silence in which talk as a social practice, through which Catholic nationalists in and around Ballybogoin created the value they believed necessary for the viability of their community and the constitution of self, was bounded by the practice of telling, which produced talk or silence. Silence restricted the space of agency and denied a properly moral selfhood to nationalists while, paradoxically, it increased the value of talk, the practice through which these workers constructed a meaningful sociocultural order and, in the process, constructed themselves in its terms (Munn 1986). The workers said the moral thing to do was to greet people and talk to everybody, so not engaging in talk was "to let your self down."

Acts of telling that produced talk extended connections among people. Talk enabled people of the same neighborhood, village, or town to make relations, to form networks between townspeople and villagers, among people from different villages, and among a wide variety of localities. This capacity rendered talk a value, an implicit, not explicit, one, and, like all values, talk did not come disconnected. Values derive from networks (social organization), while they work to form them (see White 1993), and talk, as a valued practice, produced aspects of subjectivity and extended intersubjective space-time. The telling that produced silence did not lead to anything beyond the immediate present: it read bodies and assumed their substance. The telling that produced talk had the capacity to turn the moment beyond itself: it read bodies, substantiated them through the interactions of selves, and moved beyond the moment by creating material for memory.

The encounters of strangers may move from bodily acknowledgment to talk, to *craic,* an entertainment, and such entertainment functioned like a gift. In parts of rural, western areas of Northern Ireland, "entertainment" is the name given to the gift of food. "Entertainment is also a name for speech—not all speech, but that which does the work of food: gathering personal energy into a gift to others which pleases them in the moment, then carries them on to further life" (Glassie 1982, 36). Like Irish hospitality, talk may connect people in acts of reciprocity that are remembered and returned. Different from many of the practices and techniques that subjected nationalist people in Ballybogoin during the 1980s, especially the surveillance techniques that pervaded the public spaces of everyday life, talk received much signification and was remembered.[6] Ballybogoin nationalist people highly valued the spaces of subjectification where *craic* took place—firesides, dinner tables, pubs, sporting matches, clubs—and differentiated them from the spaces of subjectification enacted by the state—bureaucratic transactions, military and police roadblocks—and the spaces controlled by unionists, especially the neighborhoods defined as loyalist that were believed dangerous and whose boundaries were deemed impervious to nationalist penetration.[7]

That day in the car, the Drumcoo glassmakers called themselves to account for their acts and found themselves wanting. They could not justify telling because it contradicted the value they attributed to talk. If, in their accounting of it, they justified telling and the silence to which it may lead, then they would have challenged the communal value talk had for them in extending networks. It would have signified acceptance of the practices of the police and soldiers who did not talk and represented, for the workers, a disordered state, because Ballybogoin nationalists created order, social and moral, and made sense of the disorder around them through the category and practice of talk. Talk and telling established connections, produced selves, and formed boundaries. They were symbolic forms through which "people actually represent themselves to themselves and to one another" (Geertz 1975, 48).

Talk marked Catholics as different for Ballybogoin's Protestants. To Catholics themselves, it distinguished them. They made identities through it and recognized that fact. Their processes of identification, they understood, were made through the myriad social practices that constituted talk. It entered into how they classified their social world and how they evaluated it. It formed a category that helped them order themselves, others, and social space. It became an important compass for Catholics on the shaky ground upon which they had to travel.

4

Living the Limit

Ballybogoin town's center approximates the hub of a wheel. Streets and alleys radiate from the busy, elongated, rectangular space Ballybogoiners call "the square" and meander by sundry small shops, bakeries, bookies, pubs, and Protestant churches. The southeasterly roads follow past car parks (parking lots), the Masonic Lodge, a cattle market, gospel meeting houses, and the still-occupied mill village with its abandoned factories. The northerly roads pass some small shops, a hardware store, the social security offices, a hospital, a large police barracks, the Roman Catholic "chapel," state schools (Protestant), maintained schools (Catholic), and the local headquarters of the UDR.[1]

Outside the circumference of commercial, governmental buildings, the residential areas begin. Large single-family, red brick and stucco houses built by the rising Protestant bourgeoisie in the late nineteenth and early twentieth centuries sit back from the main roads close to the town. Their emerald green lawns and multicolored rose gardens appeared to enlighten the near permanently gray, north of Ireland sky.

Just beyond these homes the roads, the old roads, diverge. New roads intersect them, wend their way around the government-run housing estates, swing into them, and come "to full stops," dead ends, once you pass through the estates. If driving, you must exit these complexes from where you came. "These new roads, they go nowhere," Ballybogoin's Irish nationalists said, "for security reasons."

The older, primary roads do go somewhere. They roll along the drumlins, through the rural, Gaelic-named townlands. They pass through Ballybogoin's hinterland villages and "go the length of," lead to, the other provincial towns with which Ballybogoin has contact. They go places.

These spots, "townlands way out the back o' beyon'," as mentioned previously, represent Irish nationalist peoples' pasts and help form present identities in both town and country. Their Hiberno-English names roll trippingly from local tongues as they frame family histories and help people tell their stories. In the most distant of these places, Irish nationalists formed a clear majority. There, political sympathies to Sinn Féin were strong. Irish republicans predominated in the poor, sparsely populated hilly lands that are the outermost territories of Ballybogoin's jurisdiction.

From the top of Ballybogoin Square, the hill that rises from it, you can see these western hills. On the northeastern horizon, the depressed lough shore with its barren, boggy surrounds can be viewed. To the south can be seen a series of drumlins that run along the border, a boundary line created in 1921 that divided the island of Ireland into two states—the Republic of Ireland and the United Kingdom of Great Britain and Northern Ireland. From spaces accessible to the public the east cannot be seen from the apex of the town. But the country beyond—the factories, mill villages, and "Protestant housing estates," as the local Catholics called them—was easily imagined in the 1980s. In that direction lay fertile, flat farmland whose vanishing point was as far away as the eye can see. "Aye, ye can see all from up here," a man who introduced me to the hill said. Imaginary landscapes are easily perceived in Ballybogoin as this statement indexes.

At this acme, however, the square, as a hub, was incomplete. The road heading into it from the west extended to the apex, the highest point in the area, but did not go up and over it. "The wee road," as local people called it, stopped at the top, at the steps of the town's Loyal Orange Lodge, one of the many Orange Order meeting places scattered throughout the district. This edifice sat directly adjacent to a British security forces post, whose structures were the only ones that rose above the building that housed the meetings of Ballybogoin's Loyal Orange Order.

The Loyal Orange Order, a worldwide organization, is dedicated to the defense of the Protestant religion, Orangemen argue. They claim the organization preserves political and religious liberties. Orangemen trace their ideological roots "back to the beginning of the rise of the Dutch Republic against the tyranny of the Spanish Sovereigns"(Dewar, Brown, and Long 1967, 9). They look upon their victories over the native Irish as one of the crowning glories of that tradition, a terribly misunderstood one in their view. In his foreword to the Order's official history written in 1967, Captain L. P. S. Orr, M.P., Imperial Grand Master of the Imperial Grand Orange Council of the World, writes, "it is to this movement that the world owes the establishment of the concept of Civil and Religious Liberty" (Dewar, Brown, and Long 1967, 9), and he outlines his organization's tale.

Through this famous story runs the continuous thread of the leadership of the House of Orange from William the Silent to our own King William III. The principles of this movement (which we call Orangeism because of this leadership) were constant throughout the struggle. They were to establish and protect the Protestant Religion (by which general term was understood not any particular sect, but the general concept of freedom of conscience in religion) and to establish Civil and Religious Liberty.

The destruction of the doctrine of the Divine Right of Kings and the establishment in England of Constitutional Monarchy, while its roots in English history may in fact go very deep, was nonetheless accomplished by Orangeism; and the tradition of opposition to European dictatorship can fairly be claimed to have started with the same movement.

When, therefore, the Protestant citizens of Ireland saw themselves and their freedom threatened in later times, it was natural that the great Institution formed for their protection should carry the Orange name. The Orange institution is, in fact, the direct descendant of that Orange movement which established amongst mankind the idea of liberty under law in both religion and politics. When this historic fact is understood and when it is realised how small a proportion of mankind enjoys the liberties enshrined in Orange principles, and how these ideas of liberty are on the retreat throughout the world before the time of collectivism, dictatorship and resurgent tribalism, the relevance of the modern Orange Institution can clearly be seen.

Although this new history of the Order naturally dwells upon the part it has played in Ulster, it should be remembered that the Order has a worldwide membership and that wherever its Lodges exist, whether they be in Nigeria or Australia, Canada or Ghana, Ulster or Tasmania, there is to be found a brotherhood of men pledged to uphold the ancient, but more than ever valid, concept of the Protestant faith and liberty under the law. They are neither bigots nor extremists. They are pledged not to "injure or upbraid any man because of his religious beliefs." They stand for tolerance and compassion towards all men, but they stand also for that underlying principle of the Christian faith, the dignity and rights of the individual against the tyranny of a soulless state or an authoritarian Church. (Dewar, Brown, and Long 1967, 9–10)

As Captain Orr tells it, the Orange Order views itself as the institutionalization of a spirit of freedom, "Orangeism," and, as the authors of the account Mr. Orr introduces inform us, the order will exist until "Religion, laws and liberties are so far secured by us in a Free Parliament that they shall no more be in danger of falling into Popery and Slavery" (Dewar, Brown, and Long 1967, 40).

That day has not arrived in Northern Ireland. The institution must still perform its work. The rallying slogans of Ulster loyalism and the need to repeat them—"No Pope Here," "No Surrender," "Ulster Will Fight and Ulster Will Be Right," and "Not an Inch"—have not died in the region because victory has not been won. In the Ballybogoin area, this repetition has been deemed necessary since the seventeenth century. The 1980s IRA strategy of local assassination reinforced the notion, as does the memory of the Ballybogoin area's past that this official Orange Order history produces.

This "Native Irish" victory on the River Blackwater took back from the Planters much of the "Old Irish" territory in Tyrone and Armagh, as well as the military strongholds of Charlemont and Mountjoy. It was regarded as a great victory for the Roman Catholic faith. The "Ulster Scots" had lost 4,000 men, the "Native Irish" only 300, and the captured Covenanter Colours were sent to the Papal Nuncio to Rome itself. So a dark night descended on the unconquerable colony, and the infant settlements seemed likely to be strangled at birth. But the Northern iron is incredibly tough, and in the eighty years between the Plantation and the Williamite Wars, it was forged till it had the consistency of steel. Steel may be bent but it cannot be broken. Rather it rebounds on those who seek to bend or break it, as thousands have discovered since the days of Jeremiah the Prophet, who asked: "shall iron break the northern iron and the steel?" To this rhetorical question, from the deep heartland of Ulster, from the Plantation garrisons of Derry and Enniskillen there came the firm and uncompromising negative which generations of Ulster's enemies have learned to know, to understand, and to respect. (Dewar, Brown, and Long 1967, 52)

And, to underscore the northern Protestant's will, the same author adds, citing another text, "When the Southern Irishman [i.e., Catholics] says, 'not an inch' he means not more than three or four inches, anyway, or not for a moment at least; when an Ulsterman says 'not an inch', he means just that, 'not an inch ever'" (Dewar, Brown, and Long 1967, 191–92).

The majority of Northern Ireland Protestants have exhibited this constancy, in word and deed, through recent history. In the late 1960s, when local Catholics took to the streets to protest discrimination against them, "the Ulstermen," with the police usually in support, "beat them off," according to Catholic memory.[2] In 1974, when Irish nationalists and some renegade unionists, at the behest of the London and Dublin governments, signed a power-sharing agreement that had nationalist participation, unionist and loyalist leaders called a general strike that was supported by trade union leaders and the leaders of the several Protestant paramilitary organizations. These organizations effectively closed down the state. Protestant workers who dominated employment in the manufacturing industry, utilities, the civil service, and the security forces shut off power and stopped production. Security was lax, if existent at all, during this crisis. British state leaders squashed the already compromised arrangement and returned to the status quo.[3]

Throughout the 1980s, Orangemen, in general, and the vast majority of Ballybogoin unionists felt under constant threat. The IRA had waged a war against the state since the early 1970s. But that insecurity, "the siege mentality," existed long before the current wave of violence.

Surrounded by the indigenous people, overturned by native uprisings, the settler colony, according to this Orange Order account, became haunted by the specter of revolt, and this fear has remained a constant since the early years of the seventeenth century.

I got a sense of this the very first time I climbed up "the hill atop the square" when I visited the town to find out if the place I had chosen seemed as interesting a site for possible fieldwork as it had appeared on paper. Naively, I walked up that hill with a camera armed with a tele-photo lens. A man leaving the Orange Order hall greeted me with a friendly warning: "Don't aim that camera over there, they'll come out and take it from ye." He nodded toward the security base across the lane. Then he proceeded to show me the surrounding country. To the west, the areas of which we had a full and panoramic view, was what he called "bandit country"; then he indicated the large lake to the north. The people living on its shore, he said, were "half primitive like." He turned me to the south and southwest and commented on the rich farmland in that direction. We could not see the east. The high security fences of the military outpost blocked our vision. That structure was the reason the square only approximated the hub of a wheel. No road went up and over that hill. Police cars could get in from either side, from both the westerly and easterly directions, but even they could not drive over the hill without passing through the security gates of this fortification and entering it.

If you could have crossed over the hill you would have arrived at a row of older, well-designed terraced houses. Across the street stood the entrance to an old and prestigious state grammar school. Inside that entrance, visible from the street, stood an imposing statue of a military man with his saber unsheathed. A monument to colonial service and its value, it represented Major General John Nicholson, an alumnus of the school. He led the British military action against the Indian Mutiny of 1857. The statue, originally located in India, was scheduled for destruc-tion as India prepared for independence, so alumni of "the Protestant grammar," as Ballybogoin's Catholics called it, organized to bring it to Ballybogoin. It functioned as a monument to the many alumni of the school who served the empire.

From the purview of the Ballybogoin Orange Order hall, at the very top of this hill overlooking the square, only the gaze east provided any security for unionists. Protestants occupied the housing estates and private houses on that side of the town and predominated in the flatter, more fertile farmland beyond. Their story, the Protestant Ulster epic, not demography and geography (although they provided the spaces where this story takes on its specific meanings), helped them decipher the world around them. The narrative (objectified in the Orange Order text excerpted here), its rhetoric, and its emplotment of events constituted omnipresent danger as social fact. The "darkest hour" to which the Reverend Dewar refers in the official Order history, for example, occurred near Ballybogoin. Protestants there remembered it through the commemorations they performed on Ballybogoin's town square and the annual reenactments around the province, the Battle of the Boyne particularly, that the Orange Order performed to remember victory over the natives.

"The Battle of the Diamond," for example, a story often remembered in Orange Order ritual, tells the tale of the Orange Order's founding in 1795. This founding moment occurred in one of the townlands beyond the square's eastern horizon. One Orangeman author, the Reverend John Brown, contextualizes it by noting the influence of the American and French Revolutions on some Irish Protestants who called for " 'an abolition of the Popery laws, and an extension of privileges to Roman Catholics' " (to extend them the right to vote, to own property, to own a horse, and to carry firearms, among others). The Reverend Brown writes this about the natives, whom he calls "the rather oddly named Defenders":

> By 1795 trouble was appearing again in County Armagh. The Defenders were aggressive—more so than in the earlier period of their activity, and the Peep o' Day Boys were not slow to oppose them and to take the offensive on occasion. It was the old story—raids and counter-raids for arms, attacks on individuals and groups at markets and fairs, destruction of property, challenges between one party and another. But now things were coming to a crisis. It was no longer to be just a matter of personal grudges, or competition for farms and employment, or a continuing and obstinate social, religious and racial dislike. All these things were there, but it was now believed that local outbreaks of Defenderism were only part of a widespread conspiracy, and evidence of a dangerous plot against the government, and more especially against the Protestants of the County of Armagh. It was obvious that the Defenders had an effective organisation. They could

gather men not only from the mountains of South Armagh, but from Monaghan, from the hills of Tyrone, and from beyond the bounds of Ulster itself. Many of them were comparatively well-armed. (Dewar, Brown, and Long 1967, 92–93).

This history, whose version of events Orangemen and their sympathizers celebrated in ritual and song, presented the forward-looking Protestants of the eighteenth century, the pro-"rights-of-man" bourgeoisie, those Protestants who often led the republican-minded groups on both sides, as decidedly mistaken. Colonial institutions had softened under their liberality, and loyal Protestants had to take action, this history of the Orange Order suggests. Papists had plotted all along. If the state (recruiting Roman Catholics to the southern militia) or loyal Protestants (some of the rising Presbyterian bourgeoisie were sympathetic to the writings of Thomas Paine) gave an inch, this text implies, then disaster would result. The Reverend Brown describes and inscribes:

> What was widely believed to be a fierce and inveterate hatred of Defenders for Protestants, their treachery in breaking up the treaty at the Diamond, what seemed to be a deep conspiracy, all caused a natural reaction. There was what a correspondent of Lord Charlemont calls "a deadly and irreconcilable rancour in the minds of the lower people." The obvious thing to do was to disarm the Defenders, and if troops were not able to do it, others were quite prepared for the task. (Dewar, Brown, and Long 1967, 102)

Catholics did not remember "the Battle of the Diamond" the way this Loyal Orange Lodge writer did either in content or in form. Catholics could not recall any completed narratives retelling these events. They have simply recorded the event with a sentence or two within their own very different stories. One "mountainy man" who said his family originated from one of the very places that the Orange Order story says it cast out the plotters in 1795 told me, "Aye, we were pushed here by those'ons after that. We don't belong up here. . . . My name's on the land down there in County Armagh." This man held to a narrative that opposed the Orange Order's. He believed "the Battle of the Diamond" was an act of colonial appropriation. He represented his attachment to that land almost as a natural relationship. His name was on it.

These Orange Order stories, remembered through ritual marches and public ceremony, reconfigured social space. They fostered the social imaginary that transformed the higher hills to the west and the low country to the northwest of Ballybogoin Square into dangerous spaces. The other resided there, and the Orange Order commemorations recalled the perfidy of those who lived there in times past. Catholic Ballybogoiners did not have such publicly elaborated narratives in Ballybogoin itself. Their political rituals were performed far less frequently, if at all. They had no officially recognized public ritual spaces. Irish republicans, supporters of Sinn Féin and the IRA, commemorated the Easter Rising in one of the western mountain villages every Easter Sunday, a place inhabited by "mountainy men," from the Ballybogoin point of view.

Only one Protestant family lived in that village, local people told me, and they left the area for this Irish nationalist commemoration, which Catholics and Protestants alike figured as an act of insurgency. It consisted of a relatively short march from the village center to the local Roman Catholic Celtic cross near the village's edge, where speeches were given every year by a prominent Sinn Féin leader. When I went to the march, Martin McGuiness spoke. Rumored to have been the chief of staff of the IRA in the late 1970s and early 1980s, he was well liked by the republican audience. He read a speech. The British army helicopters flying low overhead, "taking pictures of all of us," one of the men who brought me there told me, drowned out every word he said.

During the march prior to the speech, to the accompaniment of a loud roar, an IRA color party of masked men entered into the midst of the straggling marchers. When they did, their supporters locked arms and surrounded them, a sign of protection from the police and army who were massed on the surrounding hills and whose vehicles, at a distance, blocked off the side roads that ran perpendicular to the main thoroughfare along which the people, almost entirely men, marched.

The IRA color party fired shots over the graves at the cemetery to honor their republican dead. Afterward, the members of this IRA color guard ran off into the crowd and disappeared into one of the buildings along the route. Before the march, one of the parade officials warned me not to take photographs, but after a few conversations the glass-workers who had accompanied me arranged for me to do so. They "worked moves" on an occasion that was largely one of "workin' work." Most Ballybogoin Irish nationalists had no desire to attend this political rite in the mountains.

Orange Order marches had a much different relation to geography and the security forces than those of the Irish republicans. Orange Order marchers were orderly, and they made public space their own. Dressed in black suits, bowler hats, and sometimes white gloves, these walkers cut a much different image than did the Easter Sunday marchers who wore jeans or casual pants and cool weather jackets. In the summer after that Easter march, the summer of 1985, one Protestant woman said to me, "We'll walk where we say we'll walk, when."

Usually this woman and her people have the will and the power to make her statement true. The RUC often walked in front, behind, and alongside "traditional" marchers, allowing them to walk where they pleased. They seemed a constituent element of these parades, not a guardian and surely not an enemy of them. But the day this loyalist women uttered this statement about walking, things were different. The British government had promised to put an end to the symbolic, yet no less real, intimidation of Catholics in Portadown, County Armagh, during the summer of 1985. The government had banned a "traditional" Orange Order march, and she was protesting this government act. She had much company.

About a week beforehand, in a drinking session I attended, a policeman joked with his Protestant mates (the only type present) about his upcoming duty at this march. "I'm gonna head-butt the first brick that comes my way. I'm not gonna want to be there," this constable said. To Catholics the police appeared to be in step with the Orange Order marchers. Catholics say that "Protestants have the state."

Ballybogoin People

Ballybogoin people bisect the past and experience history in the present, bifurcating their everyday lives as well. Ballybogoiners live at least two histories, a Protestant/planter version and a Catholic/native one. Each side vitalizes those experiences of the past through participating in and constructing separate social institutions, differing modes of daily interaction, and varying stories, rituals, icons, images, and songs. These representations not only were surrounded by history but also were in it. They were in history as instruments of efficacy, symbols of power, producers of situations, and forces of society. History was in them "as enabling condition, shaping force, forger of meaning, censor, community of patronage and reception" (Greenblatt 1988, viii). Representing the past in the present, these historical creations were not the inert artifacts of experiences long past but were integrated into the lives of the Ballybogoin people who make and remake the present through their daily practices. In polarized Ballybogoin, one community's view of historical and political reality refuted the other community's.

For the townspeople the term "Ballybogoin people" had two meanings. It referred to the community of the person speaking, either Protestant or Catholic, and excluded the other group with whom that speaker's "people" lived. Ballybogoiners used the terms "Protestant people" or "Catholic people" when they were making a specific comparison between the two groups. They seldom employed the terms otherwise. "Ballybogoin people" signified one or the other side, with no middle ground. "Ballybogoin people" was "we Protestants" or "we Catholics," depending on the speaker. People most often used the term "Ballybogoin people" to describe their side only.

Those distinctions made in the category "Ballybogoin people" were impossible to dissipate in the 1980s. Lived history served to strengthen them. The IRA bombing campaign throughout the 1970s that disfigured Ballybogoin's architecture and rearranged how people moved through space had slackened but not stopped in the 1980s. The town's courthouse and two hotels as well as some army vehicles in the area had been exploded. Despite these blasts, the most feared activity during that time was the IRA assassination campaign. Guerrillas of the Provisional IRA assassinated members of the security forces and others. These people were usually, but not always, highly regarded people within the Protestant community.

The IRA also murdered noncombatants, people who were not members of the security forces. It claimed the majority of these civilian murders were unintentional, cases of mistaken identity (there were several of these cases in the Ballybogoin region during my fieldwork). The intentional killings of noncombatants, they asserted, were punishments inflicted, after several warnings, for conducting business with the state's armed forces or for "antisocial activities." But, contrary to the media image—an image reinforced, if not created, by the state—it was not only Protestants whom the IRA killed. They killed several Roman

Catholic members of the security forces in the Ballybogoin region during my stay there, and they murdered two contractors from the Catholic side whose firms were carrying out work for the state, servicing the RUC, or building security facilities.

The state also carried out an assassination campaign in the area during those years, and their work made those bifurcated distinctions within the category "Ballybogoin people" crack with clarity. State agents, the police and army, did not name their strategy, and they denied it. Critics called it "shoot to kill," a policy of combating terrorism through killing rather than arrest, and it became an item of controversy through the 1980s and still is.

Amnesty International addressed the question of this policy in their 1983 report.

> Towards the end of the year there were a series of incidents in which police and army personnel shot and killed unarmed suspects in Northern Ireland. Among victims were members of the Provisional I.R.A, and the Irish National Liberation Army. There were allegations that the police had undertaken a "shoot-to-kill" policy to eliminate supporters of the group by killing them rather than by arrest. The killings took place in a context of repeated shootings and attacks on the police and army by supporters of these groups, and it was therefore difficult to assess these allegations. (Amnesty International 1983, 290)

Such security force killings of alleged IRA men were contested events in and around Ballybogoin in the mid-1980s. These victims of the state had received multiple bullet wounds. Several were unarmed. Some of the armed showed no evidence of having fired a shot. And several of those killed had no connection with the IRA whatsoever.

One story that received no public attention in the United Kingdom or in the Republic of Ireland when these debates raged was that of a Protestant man killed just outside Ballybogoin, in a rural area just north of the town. The news stories in Northern Ireland reported that the victim had been caught in the crossfire between the IRA and the British army. One of the major daily newspapers in Belfast even published a photograph of the man's car, riddled with bullets, to illustrate this tragic incident. Witnesses at this man's place of work and the information his family found out through hiring a private investigator corroborated a different story. This man left his place of work driving fast, as usual. When he got to the end of the driveway of the factory, he slammed on his brakes. When he did, a member of the British army's special forces, the SAS, jumped up from the ditch beside the road, pistol in hand. The soldier reached through the side window and shot the Protestant businessman in the back of the head. He died shortly thereafter.

This event took place nearly a mile away from the place where the British army and the IRA exchanged fire that fateful morning. No evidence of shooting existed besides the pistol shots that killed this man. The private investigations initiated by the family of the dead man yielded this revised story, but the family did not pursue it publicly or seek justice. The victim's brother, a Protestant and a unionist, initiated the private investigation because he was afraid his two nephews, the sons of the deceased man, "would join the IRA, they're so angry." He spoke to a reporter for the *New York Times,* and after that story appeared this gentleman and his family got hassled.[4] The British army visited his shop in another town and knocked things about. He got frightened and stopped seeking the truth behind his brother's death.

As it turned out, the photograph of the automobile shown in the newspaper had not belonged to the victim at all. It was an SAS car that had lain in ambush for the IRA a mile away. The dead man was nowhere near the gunfire, so the unmarked SAS car that had been damaged in the shoot-out with the IRA was presented as evidence for the state's story of the Protestant businessman's murder. The SAS vehicle was represented as the dead man's car. No British or Irish news reporter bothered to follow up this fact. No correction ever appeared in the Northern Ireland daily that ran the photograph.[5] The British government, it was said, lobbied the *New York Times* to remove the reporter who investigated these "shoot to kill" incidents (Thomas 1988). No critical narrative of the state, one that perhaps both local Catholics and Protestants could take up, was voiced in the media that Ballybogoin people consumed.

Like this killing, the majority of the "shoot to kill" incidents in the area in the 1980s involved controversial deaths. Several of the dead were not members of any political group. Differing positions on the "shoot to kill" policy existed on "both sides of the house." Catholics remembered well two remarks made by prominent unionist politicians in response to what they felt were unnecessary "murders" committed by the security forces: "Two swallows do not a summer make" (presented in a different context in chapter 1), after the deaths of two IRA men who did not fire a shot in return, and "Christmas has come early this year," after several more IRA men were gunned down without clear evidence that they had fired.

Northern Ireland civil society has not yet addressed these particular events in a public forum in which members of the three sides have been represented. By early 2001, no body sanctioned by the state had convened to question the official versions of these events, although some families of victims had mobilized for such civil society action. No local public space had opened up to ask the questions, Who shot whom? Why was this unarmed Protestant unionist man not given the choice to put up his hands and surrender? What were the rules of engagement at this moment and why? Who manipulated the information involved in the telling of this killing? How and why? Protestants, by and large, believed the official stories and still do. Catholics, by and large, did not and still do not. The state abets the division that was and is "the Ballybogoin people."

For Catholics, these events evidenced more of "the same old story": "the Brits" and "the prods," in the guise of the British army and the RUC, doing them in.[6] "They don't want us," was the common Ballybogoin Catholic refrain when asked to interpret these events and put them in context. "It's always been this way, and it'll never change, the police are just like the rest o' them." And when pressed, when asked to account for a Protestant who had a bit of *craic;* who could snap dialogue forward with wit and be entertaining; who talked, laughed, and joked with "the Catholic side of the house" in the small minority of the town's pubs and few social spaces where mixing took place, they said, as one white-collar employee of the glassworks, an Irish nationalist but not a republican, told me:

> Sure, he's a green Protestant, a decent fella, but when ye scratch 'em, they're all the same. . . . They're always goin' on about how the Catholics, the Catholic religion is not democratic; but we're the democratic ones. They're the ones that are always stickin' together. Like now, they're not goin' to our shops, not even to Devlin's which

is cheaper. . . . Ye couldn't get the Catholics to do that. We do what
we want when we want. We're the democratic ones.

Yes, there were decent Protestants, there were differences among
them, Ballybogoin's Irish nationalists believed, but that did not change
the interrelations between the two groups or Irish nationalist perceptions of unionists. The associations and disassociations that characterized their "house" as "a place apart" were difficult to deconstruct by
friendly social interaction alone. The state and the fact that its terms of
identity saturated society had to be addressed for such deconstructions
to occur.

The Catholic white-collar worker who spoke of the relative commitments of Catholics and Protestants to democracy was talking to me
about Devlin's grocery store, one based on the American model. It had
opened on the outskirts of the town less than a year before to service the
town and its hinterland. It was hugely popular with Irish nationalists,
and unionists patronized the place in substantial numbers at first. But,
after the signing of the Anglo-Irish Agreement, which gave the Republic of Ireland's government a consultative role in the administration of
the north (but with no real power), some unionist political leaders organized a boycott of Irish-made products.

In Ballybogoin, Protestants circulated a rumor, totally unfounded,
that Devlin's, which was Catholic owned, had placed Gerry Adams, the
president of Sinn Féin, on its board of directors. Some of the unionists
who worked there resigned, and almost all unionists stopped shopping
there, at least for a time. A local Protestant paramilitary organization
phoned in several bomb threats that closed the store down on a number
of occasions during this period. After the everyday uproar over the signing of the agreement subsided, Protestant shoppers trickled back. To
Catholics, this was not surprising. They expected the Protestants to
stick together. Such adhesions, they believed, overrode economic concerns. Still, they constantly reminded me, "the Protestant people think a
lot of a pound, so they'll go back." This thrift, Catholics believed, could
alter Protestant programs of protest but would never undermine their
solidarity. Catholics respected this solidarity and commended Protestants for it. "We need to stick together like that, fair play til 'em,"
Catholics often told me.

Crossing the Divide

Some Ballybogoin Catholic businessmen described themselves as "great with" Protestant customers and businessmen from that community and said, "if you need a turn done, ask a Protestant, not one of your own." However, the majority of Ballybogoin Catholics said these people, almost always men, maintained these relationships for business purposes and opined that these "friendships" were not very meaningful: they became strained and dissipated in times of political strife. I saw this happen a number of times during my stay in the town.

This waxing and waning of "across the divide" friendships not only followed the state's political developments but also fluctuated with the Protestant political ritual cycle. During the "marching season," which focused every year around the Twelfth of July celebration of William of Orange's 1690 victory over the forces of King James II ("James the Shit" is how he is remembered in the Irish language), Catholics said those Protestants who may have spoken to them often stopped talking during these commemorations of state victories. Silence reigned on the streets, at work, or in business. "They are so bitter, they work themselves up to hate," one Catholic worker whose family had a history of working in a "Protestant firm" told me. He said his family has had to endure these midsummer silences for three generations.

Yet, not all "mixed friendships" were put on hold during these "public holidays." There were some individuals who could balance communal identity and solid camaraderie across division. A number of Protestants simply went on vacation to the Mediterranean or to "the mainland," and a few went to the Irish Republic. The majority of these seemed to be young people who did not belong to any unionist community associations and professional people who may or may not have served "both sides of the house" in their official capacities. The shopkeepers, farmers, factory workers, and unemployed did not get away so easily. These people were deeply tied to the established associations and the networks, both formal and informal, of their local communities through band memberships, sports organizations, and other activities. Not only their livelihoods but also their senses of self depended upon these social connections. Few had stable friendships with Catholics, and they were not aware of what these practices signified to Irish nationalists.

One subgroup that did manage "mixed friendships" was "the doggie men," whose hobby was training and racing greyhounds on both sides of the border. Members of this group joked, "We don't have two groups about Ballybogoin. We have three—Catholics, Protestants, and doggie men." Male and largely Roman Catholic, this group included a substantial Protestant minority. They spent many evening and weekend hours together running their dogs through the fields and along the roads around the area, giving the dogs time trials, racing them in official events, breeding them, capturing hares so their dogs could course them, and traveling both the Irish and British countryside bartering with breeders for the best of their litters. "Doggie men" spent much time together, developed friendships through the sport, and delicately balanced their identities when those relationships crossed social boundaries. However, people did not forfeit their friends and did not give up their invented or imagined "traditions" so easily in Ballybogoin, so the cross-community friendships of "doggie men" were tested every Twelfth of July.

One middle-aged Catholic, middle-class man told me when I headed off to my first Twelfth of July parade:

As a wee lad I used to go to my aunt's house; she lived on one of their routes. I would lift up the corner of her front room curtain and watch them march by. I was a wee-bit scared, so I was, but I had to admire those farmers—all dressed up in their bowler hats, white gloves, and best suits that they take out only once or twice a year. And so determined. I wish I could go there now, with you, and see 'em, but I'd be afraid they'd recognize me and do something to me. You'll be okay though. They won't recognize you as anything. It's best for us to stay away.

He then drove me along some back roads into the mountains where that year's Orange Order march was to take place, in a town with a population that was at least 85 percent Roman Catholic, strongly Irish nationalist, and sympathetic to the IRA. He stopped about a half mile from the route and said he did not want to get any closer, wishing again he could have gone but deeming it too risky. He was a moderate nationalist who tried to understand unionist positions, but he knew he would be recognized as a Catholic and a person out of place.

A few evenings after my second Twelfth of July, when the regional march took place in Ballybogoin, Garrett, a Catholic "doggie man" I knew well, asked me whom I had seen at the march and what I thought of it. He had fled the town with his family on the morning of the Protestant's "big day" to take a week's automobile tour of the Republic of Ireland. With his wife and his children, he promised to "explain" these marches to me. "We'll learn ye about the Twelfth," he said. "You have til live here til know what it's like, but." Although he and his family had never been to a march, they heard about them from Protestant "doggie men" friends, whom he named and asked if I had seen.

I said that I had run into only one of the people mentioned. Then Garrett told me, "no, those'ons wouldn't march or cheer the speeches, but they would have to show their faces so their side wouldn't talk." His teenage children and young adult children, though, smarted when I answered their queries about the people they knew who marched. One of them felt slighted that a workmate of his, who had been treated well by "the Catholic firm" where they worked, had paraded with Ballybogoin's Orange Lodge. He could not imagine that such "a decent fellow" with whom he had such good *craic* at the factory and at work-related social activities would engage in such sectarian practices. But his mother, Bridie, interpreted. She said she knew that lad's father and grandfather. "They were Orangemen, so of course he would march," she said. Marching does not mean he is a "black protestant," a bigoted one, she added. Another son, Sean, commented, "You have to remember they grow up with this, and they don't know anything else. Some don't know what it means to us, but." Garrett, their father, then told us about his two Protestant "doggie man mates."

Godfrey, whom I had met in one of the local pubs after the marchers had paraded through the town, neither marched nor went to the field where Orange leaders gave their speeches. He had stayed in the pub all day, buying pints for his Protestant mates and saving face among them in that way. Godfrey told Garrett that this was the extent of his participation, being part of the celebration but not affronting his Irish nationalist "doggie man" friends by marching or cheering. Graham, Garrett's other Protestant "doggie man" friend, also told Garrett that he had not engaged in the sectarian aspects of the celebration. Graham did not drink, so he could not negotiate his dilemma as Godfrey had. Instead, he went down to the field where the speeches were made and, he told Garrett, talked to as many people as he could without paying strict attention to the rhetoric coming from the speakers' platform. "The prods" would remember his being there when they recalled "their day," and Garrett added, "They won't be able to talk about him too much."

Sean, the one family member who had to work and could not leave town on the day, then told the story of his observances of "the Twelfth." He was drinking in one of the more militantly nationalist pubs on Irish Street (no Protestant drank there even though "that side of the house" occupied most of the town's pubs on the Twelfth of July) when a fellow Catholic came in and said the last band was marching by the corner. The bands and the Orangemen marchers turned to leave the town at the foot of Irish Street. "They wouldn't dare march up and down there," Sean said. So Sean and his mates went out to have a look. A group of stragglers, having spent a long morning in the pubs, followed the last marchers on their way to the field where the speeches were to take place, and one tossed a bottle that splattered on the wall just above their heads. "A couple of RUC men standing at the corner saw it but did nothin'," Sean said. "That's right," Bridie added, "they never would," and she ended "the chat" by angrily recalling the headline story of one of the two local weekly newspapers, the one read by nationalists: "And did'ya read about them [the police] attacking the Killybackey Road ones when they tossed a few stones at the Orangemen to keep them away? At the end of the day they're all the same, so they are. It'll never change." The family nodded in agreement.

After Garrett's family's attempt to differentiate Protestants, to understand them as something other than members of "the other side of the house," the actions of the police entered their recounting of "the Twelfth's" drama. The Protestants became undifferentiated when the state entered. The storytelling that recognized differences among the Protestants halted.

Catholics often opined that they could not talk to Protestants about politics because of the unionists' strong political will, a strength of character that united them and solidified their support for the armed forces of the state. Catholics respected them for it. One Irish nationalist shopkeeper in the town told me:

> Fair play til 'em, they stick together. We just fall out. Bobby Sands won the election here because there was only the one party runnin'. It's a shame Sinn Féin and the SDLP don't work together. We can't

get together on anythin'. It's the same in business. Kevin McSorley opened up a gift and record shop to compete with Patterson's, and our side wouldn't support him. He had to close up shop. The other side sticks together and supports their own. We don't, and we lose out.

Catholics credited the secular political qualities of their neighbors on the other side of the divide and implicated themselves when, as several Ballybogoiners said to me, "Ye can't talk politics with them because they're so bitter." "Bitter about what?" I asked. "Bitter about some o' the terrible things we've done til 'em."

Protestants, in return, did not regard Catholic political qualities highly, and I was able to get very few reflections about any "terrible things" their side might have done to Catholics. Catholics have partici-pated very seldom in the Northern Ireland state's political institutions since it began, under their protest, in 1921. Protestants say this absten-tion was the Catholics' fault. "They could have done something when they had the chance," one young man told me. But they did not, and some Protestants interpreted that as just another example of their priest-ridden behavior. "Their church kept them out cause their hands weren't in it," several Ballybogoin Protestants repeated.

In one late-night, after-hours ending to a marathon, all-day drinking session that "crawled" through several of the local pubs, the nailer O'Quinn, a Catholic working-class man, and the three Protestant lads—"Wee Sammy," Trevor, and Ian—to whom the nailer had gone out of his way to introduce me, got drunk and indirectly addressed the topics of religion and politics. It came up in the context of a discussion on South Africa in a Catholic-owned pub with a mixed clientele that, with lights dimmed, stayed open after legal closing hours. It was the first time the subject of politics had come up all day.

With the pub's lights diminished and the security shutters bolted, Bop, the Catholic barman, "a mate" to all of the men, kept our talk intact by listening for the footsteps of army and, especially, police patrols. He signaled us to quiet down whenever the sound of a jeep or several pairs of feet could be heard on the pavement. When a knock came and an arm, an off-duty policeman's, was inserted through the heavy mahogany door he had unlocked and partially opened, Bop delivered a previously prepared parcel of "drink" and surreptitiously secured the entry. We returned to our talk.

"Wee Sammy," Trevor, and Ian, one of several Ballybogoin Protestants I knew who had lived and worked as a technical professional in South Africa for several years, were arguing that the media had exaggerated the apartheid problem and that, like Northern Ireland, journalists were a large part, if not the cause, of the political violence they all had experienced. They commented that if the media stopped butting their noses in, the problem would probably go away. At the same time they agreed with Ian's stories, based on his experiences with South African blacks, that you could not have democracy, one man–one vote, in South Africa because the blacks did not have the "know-how" to run the country. "They only listen to the old people, don't want to learn and are stupid. But I don't think the Afrikaners are right either," Ian told us. He related a story that I heard on several other occasions to prove his point.

When Ian lived in "Jo'burg" in a rented house with several of his workmates, all white-collar professional people, they had a black servant who spent most of his time in a shed at the back of the house and did odd jobs for them. One night when they were watching television, the group ordered the servant to go down to the shops and buy them some food and drink. They waited and waited, thought something had happened to him, until finally, after about two hours, he returned to the back door telling them he could not find the shops and did not get the items they wanted. Ian said, "Can you believe how stupid? He'd been by there dozens of times. Unless you give them directions step by step they can't do anything. The only ones they listen to are their grandfathers, the old people." The nailer, having listened intently, said, "That story don't prove nothin'. Catch yerself on! He caught you out, so he did!" And the nailer continued to patiently argue with "Wee Sammy" (a salesman), Trevor (a bricklayer), and Ian while I listened.

The three Protestant men disregarded the nailer's insistence that South African blacks would get the "know-how" if they had the chance. Finally, frustrated, the nailer blurted out, "The trouble's not the media at all. It's just like Northern Ireland. The problem is whenever they go out into the street to get somethin', ye just shoot 'em." I intervened at this point. Feeling the anger boiling in the nailer and the shock from his three "Protestant mates" that the nailer would believe in such "bigotry," I tried to defuse any drunken escalations of ire. Speaking as the expert I was often taken to be in such matters, I addressed the nailer: "You can't equate the two places. In South Africa the blacks can't vote. They can't live where they work. They have no rights. At least here you've got democracy, you can vote. They haven't got any." Silence ensued. I had intended to defuse anger with this utterance. I desired to keep the *craic* going, but I did not succeed.

After a minute or two dragged by, Bop, the barman, asked what we thought of Liverpool's chances, the nailer's favorite English soccer team. "Would they take the cup?" No one returned his service. Instead, "Wee Sammy" remarked, "Ach, we must go. The nailer has to get up for chapel the mornin'."

To which the nailer volleyed, "You know I don't believe, Sammy."

"Well neither do I, but ye know the difference between yous and us when ye don't believe."

"No, Sammy, what?"

"You all go to the chapel no matter if you believe or not," Sammy said. "We don't."

The nailer said, "I don't go, Sammy."

Bop again broke the silence: "That's right, the nailer's wife has to go to mass twice every Sunday. Once for herself, once for him. Okay, drink up, boys."

None of us ever mentioned that conversation again, although we often recalled the *craic* of the all-day drinking bout. The four of us departed amicably despite the hot-tempered ending to our "day-out." Ian and Trevor went off singing in one direction, and the nailer, "Wee Sammy," and I went off in the other, Sammy tutoring us in a "Protestant drinking song"—a bit pornographic—that neither the nailer nor I knew but that echoed the tune of Ian and Trevor.

The abrupt ending to our discussion surprised me, because of all the Ballybogoin Catholics I knew the nailer most staunchly defended the Protestant point of view. He by no means adhered to their opinions, but he would listen to them and tolerated their political positions, an attitude he did not maintain for the ideas and political program of Sinn Féin. "I'd vote for the unionists before I'd vote for them boys," he often told me, but the stories told and discussed with his "Protestant mates" suffered more constraints than those I witnessed between him and "them boys," the known supporters of Sinn Féin with whom we had occasions to drink.

The Politics of Identity

The nailer's seemingly contradictory relationships with his Catholic and Protestant friends demonstrate that cultural politics interpellated everyday lives. Cultural classifications and categories set the field of politics and they were part of political and personal struggles. In Ballybogoin the political field extended to people's constructions of subjectivity and social identity. The nailer negotiated his identity continually, and it came out differently in different contexts. He had to balance a multiplicity of personally and politically charged situational definitions, read the flow of interaction, and take his chances. Language had to be constantly examined to maintain relationships across the unionist/Irish nationalist divide. Poetics, in the sense of paying close attention to the figures of everyday language, marked these encounters. It was not easy to speak if you wanted to keep a relationship going. "Speaking your mind" was a practice idealized by Ballybogoin Protestant people, and they identified with the practices entailed by this phrase. Catholics found this very difficult in their everyday encounters. To them "speaking your mind" was "workin' work," and they believed they had to "work moves" to make it through nearly every day.

The nailer's identity depended on relationships in particular times and places. When he talked politics with his Protestant friends and engaged them outside the topics of sex, sports, and popular music, he took what they labeled a typical nationalist position, so he did not address political subjects with them. Yet, with his Catholic, nationalist friends, the nailer almost never talked politics either. His Catholic mates often said to me, "the nailer, he's as deep as a well," implying that it was difficult to know what he thought on a lot of issues, especially political ones.

The nailer certainly had some *craic* in him and loved to talk about music, sports, and popular culture generally, but on politics he was mum. A skilled worker in a local factory, he did not extend a uniform self out into Ballybogoin's social world. His nationalist self came to the fore with his Protestant mates that night in the pub. It seldom, if ever, did with his Catholic fellow workers and friends. This suggests ambivalence and a context-dependent cultural identity. The nailer's actions show that identities, even in this environment of supposedly permanently solidified ones, get decentered in specific contexts. This is not a question of self against society but of social discourses, social context, entering and passing through selves, making the self what Renato Rosaldo (1989) calls a "busy intersection."[7]

The nailer tried to refuse those discourses of Irish nationalism that objectified people like his Protestant mates. But he employed that discourse when he argued with those friends. He demonstrated a complex subjectivity that was politically produced and has theoretical importance. Feminist theory has proffered the notion that the personal is political; that power is at play in domestic as well as public spaces; that lived experience is political, is negotiated in everyday life, and is an object of struggle constituted by different discourses enmeshed in relations of power.[8] It points to the importance of meaning and the intersubjective relations it makes possible. When those meanings, made in a chain of signifiers, get rearranged, they can transform political subjectivity and produce new meanings (Aretxaga 1997, 20).

The nailer's case evidenced such transformation, but his was a transformed subjectivity that always required negotiation. Specific political discourses fixed him. The state did a lot of the work of fixation in 1980s Ballybogoin, as this story implies. In this case, the location practices of the nailer's mates positioned the nailer's knowledge of the South African servant as illegitimate. After his remarks, his friends typified him as Catholic, a follower of superstition, a character in Roman Catholic "group think." When his friends did not acknowledge his perceptions, he, too, was marginalized and became subaltern: his knowledge became illegitimate. The comments made about his need to attend Sunday mass represented him as an unquestioning follower.

This episode demonstrates how difficult identifying with "the other side of the house" was in Ballybogoin during the 1980s. Neither the unionist exclusionary narrative nor the nationalist one of usurpation had total meaning for the nailer.[9] He skirted them both, a difficult thing to do in Ballybogoin, but, from his Protestant mates' point of view, he placed himself on the nationalist side. He did not fully identify with one or the other position, but others put him in one or the other. There was little room for maneuver in Ballybogoin, Northern Ireland. It was, as the Scotsman Sir Walter Scott said in 1825, "narrow ground":

> I never saw a richer country, or, to speak my mind, a finer people; the worst of them is the bitter and envenomed dislike which they have to each other. Their factions have been so long envenomed, and they have such narrow ground to do their battle in, that they are like people fighting with daggers in a hogshead. (quoted in Stewart 1977)

Ballybogoin's social space was "narrow ground" indeed. There was little room to maneuver in the mid-1980s, and people were positioned and repositioned in an everyday life saturated by politics.

Landscapes of History and Memory

"Words are never transparent," the writer John Berger notes, "They create their own space, the space of experience, not that of existence" (1988, 3). The words of both Ballybogoin people and ethnography make places. That the language of the Ballybogoiners does so is obvious. That ethnography does so is less evident, but I have tried to write ethnography in this chapter that attends to this, to present experience lived, not essence experienced. In attempting to do so, I hope I have demonstrated the impossibility of fully relating experience.[10] Rather than envelop lived events in social scientific categories, often ones that the state in Northern Ireland deploys to organize society—ones like class, ethnicity, religion, national identity (ones that claim that what is true for the whole of society is also true for its parts)—the attempt here has been to present social practices in the terms the people living them used and to represent the effects of those practices. Experience comes here not from direct association and perception but from depictions of the often contradictory discourses that make events (see Scott 1992).

The ethnographic descriptions written in this chapter present themes that cannot be separated from one another—land as a cultural construction; community division and conflict; religious rhetoric and social exclusion; the presence of the past in the present; the intrusion of the state, both as physical force and discursive power, in everyday Ballybogoin interrelations; the assessment of political positions in relation to global politics; and the legacy of colonialism. They ran into and entered one another in daily life. To separate them, to close each off into the elaborated categories of class, state, history (colonial and contemporary), and ecology, imposes arbitrary boundaries not recognized by Ballybogoiners. Our analytic languages do not present "reality" or "experience" transparently.

Following Susan Buck-Morss, I hope the themes presented here produce coherence "due to an objective affinity within the material itself" (1987, 200). One experience led to another, left a little less ambiguity in its wake and created new uncertainties. Using the material in this chapter, I will try to illustrate how these themes and these events attracted one another.

The Irish language names on the hills and low country remind "one side of the house," the Catholic side, of loss and evoke dispossession and displacement. Many of the inhabitants, referring to the time when the Irish names for these places were conceived, a period long before the Elizabethan Conquest, used the first person plural, "we," as they took me around these places and told their story. Carboniferous limestone, upper basalt, and metamorphic rock did not explain very well the "ground" we stood on. In and around Ballybogoin, signifying practices created their own space both literally and figuratively.

"The top of the castle hill, up above the square" was at least two spaces. The members of the Loyal Orange Lodge saw it as a place of triumph, a sign of firm resolve: they firmly believed this edifice and the practices it embodied were a sign of the preservation of freedom and democracy. This belief represents a partial truth. For Catholics, however, this truth was imperceptible. Catholics metaphrased the top of the hill: it was "nowhere" for them. The road that led there did not go anywhere. It did not lead to a space with affective meaning. For Catholic nationalists, both the army lookout and the Orange Order hall were best avoided. Catholics warned me, "Don't go up there." For Protestants, "the top of the hill," and "the square" were and still are places where only they should assemble. Their record of preventing Catholics, often by violent means, from gathering there goes back to at least 1871, when a group of "home rulers," people organizing for Irish people to govern Ireland in a parliament of their own, tried to assemble in the square but were forced back to the Catholic shopping street, Irish

Street, by the army. Memories of such events invade friendships. Catholics perceived the state, the historical agent of such events, as the source of division.

With Garrett's family, talking stopped when actions of the state— the seeming complicity of the police in a Protestant attack (the throwing of the beer bottle) and the actual actions of the RUC against Catholics for a similar Catholic act (the throwing of the stones)—were brought up in the conversation. From the Catholic point of view, the security force observation post at "the hill atop the square" reinforced the exclusionary practices of the Orange Order.

The nailer, considered by Catholic Ballybogoiners to be an apolitical person, if that is possible in a place where people constantly remind each other that "everything about here is political," immediately identified with South African blacks although he did not articulate it directly. He did not simply say, "When they try to get somethin'." He said, "It's just like Northern Ireland, when they go out into the street to get somethin' [when they go out into public space, in the land of the pass laws, the tribal homelands, the exclusionary state, and the siege mentality], ye just shoot 'em." By saying "ye," not "they," the nailer put his "Protestant mates" on the side of apartheid's forces and brought the exclusionary state back home. His utterance jolted the gathering, but we all understood it. Its change from "they" to "ye" changed the subject of our talk, and the transformation came from prior texts, from past meanings that "the two sides of the house," the two interpretive communities in Ballybogoin, knew but valued differently.

The nailer's "Ballybogoin people," the Irish nationalists (among them supporters of Sinn Féin, with whom he vehemently disagreed), gave him stories on the topics of space, social power, and social force. They belonged to all of them, and relevant to this discussion on South Africa are the stories of Ballybogoin's 1960s campaigns for social justice and civil rights that the nailer told me the first time I interviewed him, narratives often told and retold by Catholics in Ballybogoin.

A little too young to march in the NICRA demonstrations of the 1960s, the nailer remembered the tumult they caused around the town and his experience of them. At that time, he lived in a slightly "mixed area," far more Protestant than Catholic, at the edge of the urban district. He had lots of Protestant friends, he told me, but his friends from the neighborhood, eleven- to thirteen-year-olds, stopped talking to him at the time of the marches. "And some don't to this day," he told me. "They're afraid I'm gonna take away what they got. It's daft."

Daft or not, the nailer's negative remembrances have been reinforced by the stories he knows from older Catholics about those events. The stories, which I heard but never tape-recorded, tell how the police (an almost entirely Protestant force back then as now) stopped the civil rights marchers at the Ballybogoin roundabout (the traffic circle), at the edge of the urban district, and did not let them march to and assemble at the square. I heard differing versions of these tales, each constituting an argument for or against the police. Some Catholics said the police saved them from death. They believed that loyalist paramilitaries hid in the buildings just on the other side of the roundabout, guns at the ready, aimed to fire. A former editor of one of the local "Catholic newspapers" legitimated this version because he said he got his information from a "Protestant reporter" for an out-of-town "Protestant newspaper" who saw the armed contingent when he innocently went into one of the buildings, a government one, to use the bathroom. His story was never printed, but many people believed it.

Some Catholic townspeople saw the event differently. They said of the police, "no, not at'all, they were only doin' their job, sure," and they do not believe that anyone waited in those buildings. The RUC, in these people's view, feared trouble and stopped the marchers to preserve public order. Others disagreed. They believed that the gunmen were ready to fire and asked why the policemen did not go in, disarm, and arrest them. Their story only proves what they see as the RUC's murderous bias against nationalists. Either way, by police force or by death, Catholics believe that Irish nationalists were not going to assemble on the square, were not going to be allowed to exercise their rights.

The nailer knew all these versions. They resonated with the news stories from South Africa that prompted our late-night discussion. The square belonged to the Protestants. They would not allow its appropriation, symbolic or otherwise, for an Irish nationalist demonstration. Echoes of the over one-hundred-year-old history of these spatial struggles reverberated when the nailer made his response. "It's just like Northern Ireland, when they go out into the street to get somethin', ye just shoot 'em." For a moment, talk stopped. But the nailer, as Northern Irish people say, "soon got put back in his place."

"Wee Sammy" called to mind the nailer's Roman Catholic roots. "The nailer has to get up for chapel the mornin'," and he stated that the nailer, like his fellow Catholics, went even though he did not believe. Sentiment, not rationality, motivated the nailer in "Wee Sammy's" representation. The nailer did not question his priests. He did not question the media image of South Africa. Like the blacks who blindly followed the desires of the old people, the nailer's people obeyed their priests. "Wee Sammy's" discursive practices defined the nailer. The forces of state and the legacies of empire invaded the friendships of people who struggled to live at the limit, to face "both sides of the house." The security state and the legacies of the colonial one saturated social space despite the many decolonizing struggles that permeated Ballybogoin life. The nailer and the "doggie men" were invested in such decolonization struggles in ways that differentiated them from the majority of their sides' citizens.

5

Organizing
against History

Sir Walter Scott's description of early-nineteenth-century Ireland as a "narrow ground" remains an apt depiction of Ballybogoin in the new century. Events of centuries past have been objectified in state institutions, in associations such as the Orange Order, and in everyday lives as people move through social and physical space. Although repetition marked these sites, difference was produced. Homogeneity did not mark either side of the Ulster unionist and Irish nationalist division, although each side reached some form of cultural coherence. The simple binary of colonizer and colonized cannot be sustained from an examination of these social spaces, as the previous chapter shows.

At each of the sites discussed in this book, difference was negotiated in complicated ways. The past entered the present, primarily through Irish nationalists, who, as subalterns, were often considered to be a time lag (see Bhabha 1994, 192–93). But Irish nationalists have challenged the typifications of them as living in the past, as having arrived late to modernity. Through their everyday acts of memory, they questioned the locally hegemonic notion of progress that positioned them as other in the 1980s. In a variety of social spaces, they took up the discourses of modernity and became its agents. They "worked work" and "worked moves."

In the 1960s, Catholics in Ballybogoin founded movements for civil rights and local development that, until political violence erupted, gave them hope for the future. They organized around issues concerning the region west of the Bann and created institutions that remain important for Ballybogoin's political economy. This chapter briefly discusses the political and cultural economies of the region during this time in order to provide the context for the following two chapters, ones that describe the place making, social positioning, and shop floor struggles of workers who found employment in a firm these 1960s social movements fostered.

These Ballybogoin organizations were motivated by the economic policies of the Northern Ireland state and Catholic perceptions of it as discriminatory. The northeast corner of Ireland that became Northern Ireland in 1921 was the fastest-growing industrial area of the island in the nineteenth century. Protestants had accumulated the vast majority of its wealth, and this industrial development was coded as a Protestant phenomenon.[1] During nineteenth-century industrialization, Protestant political allegiances became solidly associated with Britain, and unionist citizens identified with urban and industrial developments in Belfast that were associated much more with those in Manchester, Liverpool, and Glasgow than with economic activity in Dublin, the other major Irish city.[2]

The island of Ireland's economic differentiation produced an excess of meaning in the nineteenth century. Through the signs of capital accumulation, Protestants identified themselves as disciplined and hard working, unlike their largely peasant compatriots in the south of Ireland and in the hill country in the western parts of Ulster, the region west of the Bann.[3] Descendants of the seventeenth-century planters were more apt to join the British armed forces, its imperial armies, and the Irish police during this period, although Catholics joined them as well. The social disciplines, the experiences of industrial work, and military service correlated well with the Sabbatarian and total abstinence practices advocated by the dissenting Protestant denominations. It is not surprising that the northeast corner of Ireland demonstrated little support for the nationalist and proindependence movements that waxed and waned throughout the rest of Ireland during the nineteenth century.[4]

The republican and pro-rights-of-man Protestants, largely the urban bourgeoisie and skilled tradesmen, who actively campaigned for an independent Ireland at the end of the eighteenth century drastically decreased in numbers throughout the nineteenth century. Loyalty, self-discipline, integrity, and speaking one's mind became the publicly exalted forms of Protestant-identifying practice, and the republican values that some Protestants held dearly in the eighteenth century came to be associated with peasant struggles for rights to the land. Republican values dissipated drastically within this remade Protestant identity, and its consequences for the development of a class politics similar to England's were pernicious. Organizing along class lines proved very difficult when nation and state were the central terms of political affiliation (see Rowthorn and Wayne 1988).

These cultural codes inscribed the map of Northern Ireland after its formation in 1921 and, Catholics argued, informed the decisions state bureaucrats made about locating and funding industry. In Ballybogoin, Catholics believed they were discriminated against and began to organize against this discrimination in the early 1960s.

The Ballybogoin Social Justice Movement

Prior to the founding in 1968 of NICRA, the Ballybogoin area had its own local human rights organization, the Ballybogoin Social Justice Group. Middle-class Catholics led it, and the organization sought housing and social services for Catholic families, mostly working-class ones. The Social Justice Group looked to the civil rights movement in the United States for inspiration.

Although Ballybogoin was a majority Catholic area, it had been gerrymandered to give Ulster unionists a two-to-one majority on the Ballybogoin Council, which Catholics believed discriminated against them. The local council was responsible for allocating housing in the region, and they did as they pleased, without the constraints of fairness required in England and Wales. Northern Ireland's devolved government put its own laws in place and used considerable discretionary power in providing social services.[5]

In the early 1960s, houses were being built, but they were not going to Catholics in Ballybogoin. Married Catholics with several children remembered living with their parents in small two-room flats that had, as an older Catholic middle-class woman described to me, "so many beds ye couldn't see the floor." Conditions were overcrowded and unsafe, and a group of women, mostly young mothers, started to publicize the fact that houses were not distributed justly. "People in the most need did not get them. People in the know did," one woman who protested said.

To protest what people remembered as the discrimination of "the Protestant state," some young Catholic women in the town formed a group to make this situation public and called themselves the Homeless Families Group. They had little formal organization and no leadership experience when they started. A group of neighborhood women who got this idea from talking among themselves started to collect stories and information about the housing needs of families and the social and psychic displacement that unfit and overcrowded housing caused. These women, working class and not well tied to Catholic status networks, went to a local priest for help. They scheduled a meeting at the parish hall, and that priest was supposed to chair it. He never showed up, and the female organizers were frightened that their efforts would come to nothing.

A middle-class woman, whom I shall call Brigid, volunteered to be the group's secretary. Brigid had never been active politically, but she got up to speak and chair the meeting because she felt so angry that these earnest young women had been abandoned by their priest. She, along with her husband, took on the leadership of the group.[6]

After this meeting, the women organized marches and started to keep a record of discrimination by noting which people were getting houses. They evaluated this distribution by comparing the family situations of those who got houses and those who did not. Their understanding of the developing welfare state was that families with children and without housing should be given priority. They found that the local housing authority did not operate accordingly. Protestant women were promised housing when they announced their engagements, while married Catholic women were often waiting for a house twelve years after their marriages. The league publicized their own members' needs and let people in the area judge whether discrimination was a social fact. Catholics believed there was discrimination. Protestants did not.

Brigid and her husband organized the publication of the data that the young working-class women gathered and brought it to the local council, where they got nowhere. The women organized protest marches, but they were never allowed to assemble on the square. One of the women remembered their very first march. She said they got dressed up in "pressed clothes," cleaned up their babies, and put them in prams for their march around the town. But "Orangemen off work for their dinner" stood around at the corner leading to the square, spit at them, and told them to go away. Stone throwing was added to these insults, several women remembered, after the second or third such march.

Finally, fed up with their lack of progress, these women, without middle-class Brigid's approval, decided to squat in some temporary houses that were scheduled to be torn down. Protestants had lived in them while they awaited permanent, newly built council housing. At this time, in 1963, the league's published literature claimed that no new housing had been built in the town's Catholic ward in the post–World War II era. It also reported that no Catholic had been allocated a permanent house for thirty-four years.

The squatting by the families who needed housing took place after Brigid and her husband, along with some educated, Catholic middle-class men whom Brigid had recruited to help represent the women of the Homeless Families Group, had gone to the local council and Northern Ireland's devolved parliament, Stormont, with their information. They got no action from those government bodies. And, although they received an interested hearing in the British Parliament at Westminster, especially from Labour party members, no results were forthcoming from that body either. After these failures, the working-class women of the Homeless Families Group decided to take action to protest not scarcity but discrimination. By making this move, these young women acted on their own agenda and did not follow the advice of the middle-class leaders who had filled the vacuum in that first meeting.

Group members' patience ran out as the government of the United Kingdom built new houses in great numbers during the postwar period. Ballybogoin was no exception to this, but it differed. The Homeless Families Group repeated their findings that "young Protestant women were being allocated houses and picking their homes in the new estates before they were married," while area Catholic women "were waiting up to twelve years for a house." When the council announced that the sixty-seven prefabricated houses (they had been put in the district immediately after the war for Protestant married couples waiting for permanent housing) were not to be distributed to Catholic couples who had been on the waiting list for any available housing, the activist women of the Homeless Families Group were irate.

Those temporary domiciles had housed Protestants, except for a very few exceptions, over the years, and they were being removed because their occupants' new, permanent government housing was completed. The Catholic women, tired of being on a waiting list they never thought they would get off, thought this "a terrible waste" that prevented them from starting a proper family life. They protested.

The young women moved their families into these houses in the middle of the night and received some press coverage for it. Ballybogoin Catholics remembered that these squatters impressed people when they showed "the nice, decent young people they were" and proved to the press the good condition of the houses that were to be pulled down. The council had promised to sell them to local farmers, mostly Protestant, to house poultry and other farm animals. When the women were able to show the press how local landlords, both Catholic and Protestant, gouged them, they engendered political sympathy in the Republic of Ireland and in mainland Britain.

After these successes, members of the Homeless Families Group expanded their concerns under the auspices of an umbrella organization that Brigid and her husband had instituted. They collected data on factories, especially newly built ones, and, by their count, there were 114 factories east of the Bann and 14 west of the Bann. Jobs as well as housing became their basis for organizing and petitioning the government. The leaders made clear they were not nationalists stirring trouble, and that became the narrative line of the Ballybogoin social justice groups as a whole. They asserted that they were fighting for the rights of people in need, whatever creed or nationality. They never joined forces with the Nationalist party or the Irish republican groups of the time. They made their object of complaint neither the border, as the nationalists did, nor class, as the transforming 1960s Marxist-oriented republican groups attempted to do.

"We were pure civil rights," some leaders remembered. The women in the Homeless Families Group presented themselves as upright citizens. They paid their rates to an escrow account rather than boycott the payment of taxes. "They tried very hard to make a good appearance," on the advice of their leaders, who believed it most important that these homeless women showed they had the discipline of the middle class and the "decency" toward officialdom that the Protestants had. They tried to present themselves as establishment people who supported the social forms of the status quo.

The leaders of the Homeless Families Group recognized the union with Great Britain and at all times made that quite clear. That stance, however, did not carry much weight with Protestants. Protestant paramilitaries threatened them. By the late 1960s, NICRA had been created, and counteractions from the loyalist "side of the house," often violent ones, had accelerated.

Violence in the Ballybogoin area increased significantly during and after 1969. In 1971, when internment without trial was introduced, all but 2 of the 342 internees in the initial morning's swoop were Catholic. The two Protestants were known to have Irish nationalist, republican sympathies. Many young men in the Ballybogoin area, descended from republican activists of campaigns long past, were picked up even though they had no political involvement ever. The RUC and British army forced young civil rights activists out of their homes at dawn. The RUC provided the intelligence, and the British army carried out the door-to-door operation. This turned many Catholics adamantly against the soldiers (Rowthorn and Wayne 1988, 39–50, 176–83). The political space in which the Homeless Families Group operated was lost as violent politics took over.

Up to that point, the British army was thought by many Catholics to be their community's protectors. In 1969 when the army entered Northern Ireland, they prevented attacks on Catholics by organized loyalist groups, and they intervened when police confronted Catholics: there were several cases of constabulary attacks on peaceful civil rights demonstrations (see Farrell 1976). Catholics had welcomed the British troops. Almost all Ballybogoin Catholics remembered that members of their side in Belfast served the soldiers tea and biscuits when they arrived. This was a trope that Catholics remembered, and the news media often reproduced it. The event, televised and retelevised in the many documentaries and docudramas dealing with Northern Ireland that appeared on British television, was well known to Northern Irish citizens of all ages and all denominations.

In 1971 there had been thirty deaths (the majority of these were civilians killed by loyalist paramilitaries, but there were several IRA members and British security force personnel killed as well) for the year until

August, when internment without trial was introduced. By the end of the year there were 143 more deaths and 700 people held without charge (Rowthorn and Wayne 1988, 42). In the latter part of that year, the IRA, practically defunct militarily for over fifteen years, was reorganized. It split into two groups, the Official IRA and the Provisional IRA. The Officials were those who had been running the organization since the IRA's border campaign of the late 1950s. Because of the failure of their military strategy, these IRA leaders had chosen party politics over armed struggle and were trying to form an organization based around social class. They adopted a Marxist analysis of Ireland, and this never went over very well with their more nationalist, Catholic members, who formed their own organization, what became the Provisional IRA, as the violence around civil rights demonstrations accelerated. The Provisional IRA carried out many political murders of security force members and engaged in fighting with the Protestant paramilitary groups that had been organized and well armed from the late 1960s. The Provisional IRA bombed many business enterprises to economically hinder the British social order.[7]

Ballybogoin suffered substantially from this bombing campaign. The square, as discussed previously, was bombed over twenty-five times through the mid-1970s and received the largest bomb of the first fifteen years of the troubles, local people said. Homes and housing estates were not bombed, although several small rental houses received damage. In the Ballybogoin region, the IRA murdered members of the security forces, both Protestant and Catholic, by planting car bombs, and they carried out numerous assassinations. Ballybogoin Catholics claim that none of the IRA's "economic" bombs ever killed anybody. People said they always gave a warning when these bombs were planted. Protestant paramilitaries did not follow the same procedures, in the Catholic worldview. They planted several no-warning bombs in Ballybogoin's Catholic pubs, killed several people, and wounded dozens. IRA bombs wounded many as well. The area was in desperate political and economic crisis in the 1970s and 1980s.

Ballybogoin's Political Economy

On the periphery of the area that harbored the nineteenth century's linen boom, Ballybogoin was one of the towns in the north of Ireland's "linen triangle." Since World War II, it gradually lost its position relative to other areas that produced linen, all of which were in decline. During the 1960s, the largest linen firms in the area were either closed down by their local family owners or sold to multinational corporations. A South African multinational bought the largest linen factory in town and moved most of its production to a site east of the River Bann. Some Protestant workers moved there, but no Catholic workers did as far as people could remember. Catholics had been concentrated at the bottom of the firm's skill hierarchy and stayed in Ballybogoin to look for alternative work.

A similar process took place in the largest, nontextile-producing employer in the area. Owned by an English multinational, this firm made fiberglass products. The factory in Ballybogoin carried out the primary, most dangerous part of the process, the making of the glass fibers. These were transported to factories on the British mainland, where finished products were made. This firm shut down its Ballybogoin operations in 1970. The most dangerous and unhealthy part of this process was moved to South Africa. Some of the Protestant white-collar workers moved to England and South Africa when these firms relocated. A few of the most skilled blue-collar workers moved to South Africa as well, where South African blacks, so the Catholic story goes, did the "dirty work" that Catholics did in Ballybogoin. All those who moved were Protestant in the accountings that Ballybogoin Catholic employees of this firm gave of this economic history.

Some scholars contend that violent paramilitary acts, especially the "economic" bombing campaign of the IRA, caused Northern Ireland's economic decline (Kennedy 1986). Others hold that violence resulted from general economic decline and the practice of discrimination (Rowthorn and Wayne 1988).[8] In fact, the effect of violence on the overall economy is hard to gauge. It created jobs as it destroyed them. Employment in the security forces and in the building trades increased during the IRA's military campaign. The industrial decline and faltering manufacturing investment in Northern Ireland correlated with the industrial and investment patterns of other marginal areas of the United Kingdom and may have been only peripherally related to Northern Ireland's political troubles. Bob Rowthorn, an economist who has studied the effects of the violence and correlated them with regional economic trends, estimated that the effect of "the troubles" on the economy was plus or minus 4 percent in the 1980s (Rowthorn 1981, 16–18). The serious decline in industrial output and the acute rise in unemployment arose from secular trends in the economy more than they did from Northern Ireland's political problems.

It has been argued that the island of Ireland has been treated as an internal colony by Britain. Michael Hechter holds that a cultural division of labor characterized the British economy throughout its modern period. In Northern Ireland, he notes, that division is complicated by the complexly "British" identities of the Protestants. Hechter, however, does not read the dynamics of class and secular trends in the economy into his understanding of these complicatedly situated people (Hechter 1975). Rather than understand Protestants as subjects formed in power, he blames them unduly for situations of culture and economy that are, in many cases, beyond their control. Nevertheless, he provides a historical context for understanding the contemporary political economy of Northern Ireland as powerfully influenced by cultural contexts and the classificatory powers of the state.

Combined with Rowthorn's economic analyses, Hechter's sociocultural interpretation offers insights into contemporary Northern Ireland. Neither he nor Rowthorn provides understanding of the regional variation within the Northern Ireland economy, however. The geography of uneven development cited earlier is needed to supplement their work. Doreen Massey and Richard Meegan's "geography of employment," especially, seems to offer some helpful concepts. Massey and Meegan move away from conceptualizing regional differences by associating the map of employment decline with the characteristics of the physical geography of an area and the cultural traits of its people. They find these approaches analytically deficient because the form of production through which jobs are lost or relocated is as important as the local physical and cultural features. Furthermore, they find these perspectives politically wanting because they tend to blame the people in these areas for job loss: motivational and physical factors are given precedence over structural ones (Massey and Meegan 1982, 121–26).

Massey and Meegan develop a three-part schema to decipher transformations in production—intensification, rationalization, and technical change—that are based on their own empirical studies on the British mainland and that may be used to analyze the structural features of decline. Each production change influences regional development differently. By looking at these production level changes, a more incisive depiction of uneven development in the Ballybogoin area can be constructed.

Intensification, "the reduction of aggregate labor costs per unit output by cuts in the number of workers employed," does not generate mobile employment, jobs that can be moved (Massey and Meegan 1982, 124). Changes that occur through this mode of raising productivity create layoffs without relocating industries. It is a common way of changing labor practices in the small firms around Ballybogoin.

Rationalization differs from intensification in Massey and Meegan's formulation. It may foster changes in the geography of employment. It does not involve investment in new productive capacity, and "all changes in employment levels take place within the existing geographical distribution of employment" (Massey and Meegan 1982, 125). Firms that cannot intensify any more in a particular region, that cannot change production relations to get any more production per unit, may move that area's productive capacity to another site that does allow for more profit and more disciplined organization.

The activity of the South African multinational in moving part of its Ballybogoin operation to a site east of the Bann is an example of this, as is the glass fiber operation that moved to South Africa. A Catholic firm, started up and helped by government grants even though it was making a healthy profit, adopted a similar rationalization procedure in the late 1970s. That firm moved part of its operation across the border to the Republic of Ireland to take advantage of Irish government subsidies offered to firms investing in undeveloped areas.

Qualitatively different than rationalization and intensification, technical change involves the introduction of new productive capacity. New capacity always has the potential to be mobile, so locational decisions may be based on factors such as the political violence in Northern Ireland.

Using these categories of organization as a guide, the political economy of Ballybogoin and Northern Ireland becomes more complex. The differing cultural constructs the two groups have about economic relationships can be put in better perspective. In Ballybogoin, Catholic workers are not a mobile labor force as Massey and Meegan conceive it. They are a part of the labor force subject more to intensification than to mobility. Also subject to intensification procedures, Protestant workers relocate, but at a cost. During the 1960s and 1970s their moves, spurred by changes in the larger economy, forced new identities upon them. The old family firms for which generations of linen workers labored either went out of business or were sold. The Protestant working-class neighborhoods near these old factories, the "wee houses" these paternalistic linen mill owners built, became dilapidated and, as one older man in desperation put it, "started to look like Catholic houses," unkempt and in disrepair.[9]

In the 1960s, when the Homeless Families Group started, everyday unionist classification and categorical systems, such as the classification and imagination of certain house forms as Protestant, were undergoing reconfiguration as a result of economic transformation. For the first time in the postwar period, that community's members were experiencing unemployment, and their definitions of themselves and others' definitions of them began to change. Protestant neighborhood and workplace identities were being rearranged as they, too, suffered from an economy in decline. Like Catholics, they emigrated from local communities, but, unlike Catholics, they emigrated to jobs and often stayed within Northern Ireland. The Ballybogoin social justice activists claimed that Catholics were discriminated against and were forced to emigrate outside of Northern Ireland so that the Protestants could preserve their majority. Ballybogoin Protestants did not accept this and responded that they were forced to move, too.

Regional variation and economic inequality have characterized the Northern Ireland state through the 1990s, although the last decade has brought increased economic activity to both Catholics and Protestants. Many poorer people in Ballybogoin's Catholic community say things have not changed. Many middle-class Catholics say, however, that they have altered significantly, and they point to the many new middle-class, private homes that Catholics have built in the 1990s. The Catholic middle class notes that they have invested in education to a greater extent than have the local Protestants, who used to have apprenticeships they could enter on leaving school. Now, these Catholics say, their focus on education is paying off with the transformation of work in the information economy.

In Ballybogoin during 1981, the last census taken before the shop floor study discussed in the next chapter took place, Catholic male unemployment for the year was 36.7 percent and Catholic female unemployment was 24.1 percent. Non-Catholic male unemployment was 12.7 percent, and non-Catholic female unemployment was 11.6 percent. In the jurisdiction adjacent to Ballybogoin, Catholic male unemployment was 43.3 percent and non-Catholic male unemployment was 14.4 percent. The region as a whole had one of the highest unemployment rates in the European Economic Community during the mid-1980s.

Northern Ireland Catholic males and females had the highest unemployment overall in the United Kingdom of Great Britain and Northern Ireland, the highest of all the ethnic groups tabulated in the census. For males, the unemployment rate was 30.2 percent overall in 1981; for females, it was 17.1 percent. For Northern Ireland's non-Catholics, the respective unemployment rates were 12.4 percent for males and 9.6 percent for females, not far above the United Kingdom's average of 11.3 percent for males and 7.4 percent for females. In 1983–84, the Northern Irish Catholic unemployment rate was 35 percent for males and 17 percent for females. The category "West Indian" or "Guyanese" followed them on the United Kingdom's ethnic unemployment list with a male unemployment rate of 27.6 percent and a female one of 18.0 percent. Obviously, a large percentage of Catholics still remained near the bottom of the class hierarchy in the United Kingdom of Great Britain and Northern Ireland when I studied workers. Catholics, especially those west of the Bann, who have made it into middle-class income levels have done so by entering the service professions—teacher, doctor, solicitor, social worker, and nurse—where they often serve "their own side of the house." In the 1990s, however, there has been much more entrepreneurial action by Catholics around Ballybogoin.[10]

In Northern Ireland the changes in the economy since World War II have recast Protestant-made identities, especially those of the working class. Communities centered around shipbuilding, heavy engineering, and linen manufacturing had to redefine themselves. One definition remained constant in this transforming situation, however—the position of Protestants compared with Catholics—but that, too, began to be reconfigured in the mid-1980s. Catholics, too, have remade their identities during the last thirty years of upheaval, and that remaking has affected "both sides of the house." Around Ballybogoin, Protestants say, "There's more Catholics driving Mercedes around here than anyone else." Catholics have created many of the small service-oriented enterprises that provide new economic development in this economically marginal area. Ballybogoin Catholics now say, "We're the only ones who know how to start a business around here."

6

Working Memories

In May and June 1985, a five-week strike took place at the Drumcoo Glassworks, one of the Catholic, nationalist enterprises inspired by the movements for social justice in and around Ballybogoin in the 1960s. Prior to the strike, a long one by local standards, the workers had reestablished relations with their national trade union, the Amalgamated Transport and General Workers Union (ATGWU), for the first time in more than four years. The ATGWU, a British union, promised to back the workers but chose to remain neutral on management's final offer, which was draconian. If the workers did not return to the factory and the status quo, management said, the glassworks' furnaces would be extinguished. Once the fires were out, the factory would take one to three months to reopen. Management hinted darkly that the glassworks might close permanently.

Of the sixty workers who cast ballots on that final offer, only four voted to continue the struggle. Two of these were the only Protestant unionist workers to attend the final meeting.[1] But the failure of the strike was only the first casualty. The second was the embryonic sense of class solidarity the workers had felt with the union and with each other. Back at work, not a single skilled worker would take a shop steward position. No one wanted to negotiate with management. No one wanted to organize fellow workers to fight another day.

Although it was not apparent, the workers' inability to sustain momentum was more than a failure of will. It had much to do with other struggles under way in Northern Ireland. The workers' attitudes toward class issues were profoundly affected by the culture and politics they brought through the door. Political and class identities were negotiated simultaneously, and none was determining. Instead, they were articulated to each other through cultural and linguistic practices, especially the practice of talk, as Catholics in and around Ballybogoin perceived it.

The practices of Catholics were particularly influential in this Ballybogoin factory because Catholics made up more than 85 percent of the workforce.[2] A Roman Catholic priest, Father Finbarr, who was concerned about discrimination against Catholics in employment had founded the firm. Since the 1960s, the factory had been classified as an Irish nationalist firm, linked, on the level of local politics, to the fight against discrimination in employment and housing and, on the national level, to the Irish nationalist desire to unite the six counties of Northern Ireland to the twenty-six counties of the Republic of Ireland.

The cultural practices exhibited at the Drumcoo Glassworks and their effects on the strike should be examined in the context of current debates about working-class formation and the concept of class because the profound economic, political, and intellectual transformations marking the past quarter-century, in all areas of the globe, have put the concept of class under scrutiny (Joyce 1995, 3–16; Hall and Jacques 1990). Global markets have transformed labor relations, patterns of investment, and the articulation of capitalist institutions to nation-states (Appadurai 1996). Many manual sectors of employment have moved to the industrializing states, leaving a less organized working class in Europe, the United States, and Japan. New forms of industrial management, the expansion of service work, the widening of the female labor market in the United States and Europe (much of it part-time), and the feminization of industrial work through free-trade zones and subcontracting firms in Latin America and Asia and in sweatshops scattered throughout the globe have challenged established models of economic development, class formation, and collective identification (Ong 1991; Rouse 1991).

These economic transformations have profoundly affected the organized working class. In places where women and men have organized politically around the category "worker," the shift in investment and employment from manufacturing to consumption has weakened working-class institutions. In this situation, collective and personal identities cannot be assumed to derive from positions in the social division of labor. Consumption, too, can be a source of identity (see Berdahl 1999, 104–39).

Along with these economic, political, and social transformations, structuralist, poststructuralist, and feminist theorists have challenged the assumption of rationalizing actions that both liberal and Marxist social theories have propounded (see Bourdieu 1987, 1991, 1993; Eley 1996; Joyce 1987 for this important discussion). These theorists conceive language not as a reflection of reality but as a conventional and arbitrary structure of relations and differences that constitute social worlds. They hold that identities such as gender and class do not derive from an external referent that confers meaning on them. Instead, such identities are understood as discursively produced, as the product of histories and cultures, as constructed in social action.

As Joan Wallach Scott writes,

> Class consciousness and class are the same thing—they are political articulations that provide an analysis of, a coherent pattern to impose upon, the events and activities of daily life. Although the rhetoric of class appeals to the objective "experience" of workers, in fact such experience only exists through its conceptual organization; what counts as experience cannot be established by collecting empirical data but by analyzing the terms of definition offered in political discourse. (Scott 1988, 56)

From this perspective, the study of discourses, understood as the material existence of linguistic and cultural practices and recognized for the effects they produce beyond and including the making of meaning, is necessary to discern the processes of working-class formation. As Scott implies, calculating a fall in real wages and demonstrating that worker productivity has simultaneously increased may reveal the dynamics of the structural position that the affected workers occupy, but those facts alone do not explain the motivations and justifications for an ensuing job action, a strike, or an organizing drive.

The analyst cannot assume that these conditions of exploitation and the acts that workers organize to protest them index the Marxist move from a class in itself to a class for itself, where the first term, "class in itself," represents the set of objective class conditions while the second term, "class for itself," represents the range of subjective factors that mark workers as conscious of that objective position and willing to struggle against it.[3] Instead, experience itself is conceptualized as constituted by discourses that render it complex and multiple (Scott 1992). A strike cannot be assumed to be a class experience only or even primarily. Discursive analyses, ones that emphasize discourses' effects on the formation of political subjectivity and its work in forming groups, may provide a more apt starting point for a strike situation and its articulation to working-class organization than the usually conceived sources of social structure and economics (see Eley 1996, 216–23).

Histories of nineteenth- and twentieth-century working-class formation have demonstrated the salience of this position (Joyce 1995; Scott 1988; Stedman Jones 1983). They have shown that working-class organizations from trade unions to political parties were made through a series of discursive oppositions through which people related to or excluded others. These inclusions and exclusions often relied on discourses of gender, race, ethnicity, nationality, and democracy to construct their boundaries (see Ignatiev 1995; Jones 1998; Roediger 1991). As Geoff Eley writes, it "was at this discursive level that the operational collectivity of class—who got to be included, who set the tone, and who received the recognized voice—was defined" in the nineteenth century (1996, 218). Consequently, ethnic, class, gendered, and national groupings were constructed alongside working-class ones. None was necessarily prior, although theories and historical works privileging the determining power of economic structures label such events "class struggle" (Thompson 1978).

Other struggles were engaged simultaneously. Working-class men opposed the bourgeoisie when they fixed social identities around class, but they often defined themselves against women and culturally different others (Baron 1991; Scott 1988). They used gendered, racist, and ethnic discourses to bolster their sense of collectivity and distanced people who were different. In the process, they contributed to positioning women, racialized groups, and differing national groups as lower in a hierarchical social order that their practices contributed to making.

Contemporary ethnographers have observed similar contests over positions and positionings while studying contemporary workplaces and class formations (Fernandez-Kelly 1983; Lugo 1990, 1999; Ong 1987,

1991; Yelvington 1995). These ethnographers demonstrate that the developing regimes of flexible accumulation depend on the control of social spaces beyond industrial sites. Often issues of gender control, their relationship to kinship institutions, and the representations of racialized groups enter into labor struggles.

Neighborhoods and domestic spaces are disciplined in these locations, and an effect of such practices is the production of docile workers. The context of industrial work enters the workplace not as background but as a social force (see Ong 1987). Aihwa Ong (1991) suggests substituting a concept of "cultural struggle" for class struggle to address this changing milieu of production, one that foregrounds the fact that daily workplace practices address cultural meanings, values, and goals along with the exigencies of production.

Arguing for the embeddedness of "race" and "class," Daniel Segal makes the related point that racism, a set of linguistic and cultural practices that makes "races," structures positions in the social division of labor. He writes, "We would find a significantly different constellation of class relations (in the United States and throughout the world) were laboring and underemployed persons not divided and disadvantaged by invented racial distinctions" (Segal 1998, 56). He argues that analyses of race and class that do not relate one to the other as mutually structuring abstract race from its social context and naturalize it, contributing to the construction of "races." Again, invented divisions such as "races" do not merely form a contextual background. They structure class relations and enter into workplace and other labor struggles. People such as African Americans in the United States or Irish Catholics in Victorian England, who were marked as other and made into devalued groups in nineteenth-century formations of the working class, often took up jobs that descended in the social order because those occupations were identified with them (Jones 1998; Lees 1979; Stallybrass and White 1986). Masculinist ideologies, racism, and the devaluation of positions and people in the social division of labor had a structuring effect on class relations and still do.

Shop Floor Struggle

Ballybogoin's dramatic economic and political situation provides the context for this chapter's discussion of shop floor struggles and the strike at the Drumcoo Glassworks, but, unlike accounts that treat such backgrounds as independent of the practices being studied, the ethnography that follows does not separate the events focused upon from the background. Like the historical studies of nineteenth-century working-class formation, the shop floor ethnographies in regimes of flexible accumulation, and the reconsiderations of the relationship of race and class cited previously, the shop floor ethnography presented here moves away from notions of determination that assume that objective social spaces, such as positions in the division of labor, are accompanied by social and cultural groupings that correspond to those positions in direct mechanical relations.[4]

Rather than work with specific cause-and-effect relations, a concept of articulation is used here that denotes the practices of linking together elements that have no necessary relation to one another (Hall 1986; Grossberg 1992, 37–67). For example, religious identity and class have no necessary relation, but social actors link them when the dominant religious group excludes and devalues a subordinate one or when it positions members of the less valued religious group as incapable of taking up certain jobs or professions. Such exclusionary practices pervade colonial situations and the histories of women in labor markets.

Social actors engage in articulation when they construct one set of relations out of another—race relations out of workplace relations, for example. Social analysts form articulations when they analyze an event by depicting the network of relationships to which it is connected and, by so doing, account for structures, the relations among the effects of social practices (Grossberg 1992, 54–57). Articulations, then, work to build structures, but, as social actors construct one set of relations out of another, they transform those structures. In keeping with theories of practice, this Gramscian interpretation of articulation and its place in the structuring of the social world understands structures as entities that have real effects, although it does not conceive structures as having the power to determine the articulations made by agents within social worlds.[5]

Tracking and analyzing the linkages social actors make among differing sets of relations require not only the usual anthropological commitment to ethnography but also a commitment to theory. In this case that commitment constitutes awareness that categories such as "the working class," "the people," and "the community" are neither primordial nor unitary political objects but are constructed in discourses (e.g., Marxism, trade unionism, Irish nationalism, Ulster unionism) that are in tension with one another and have different objectives (Bhabha 1995, 11–12).[6] From this perspective, I read the shop floor of the Drumcoo Glassworks, the ethnographic site here, as "the point of intersection and of negotiation of radically different kinds of determination" (Frow and Morris 1993, xviii). Rather than represent struggles at the factory as an expression of "class" in late-twentieth-century Northern Ireland, I offer a reading of the glassworks as organized by a range of diverse and overlapping systems (local, religious, demographic, economic, regulatory, and political) and the object of very different discourses.

The starting point of this analysis of the Drumcoo Glassworks is neither class structure nor class struggle. It is cultural struggle, but questions of class and class identity permeate this treatment of the factory. I understand class neither as a composition of individuals nor as an aggregation of individuals. What is important about classes is that they, as David Stark writes, "exist in an antagonistic and dependent relation to each other" (1980, 97). They are constituted by mutual antagonisms and produced not by individuals but by organizations. Those organizations can be informal—kinship networks, workplace interaction groups, neighborhood groupings—or formal—trade unions, political parties, government bureaucracies (Stark 1981, 98). The approach I deploy focuses on the tensions between and among these organizations.

Following from this approach, the ethnography here does not attempt to explain the strike, a single event, by placing it in a specified category, class struggle, and relating it to the overarching class structure, a practice that abstracts from social action and moves social actors out of time and space. Instead, it develops an identity approach to social action, one that foregrounds discourse, specifically narrative. It assumes that the relationships in which people are embedded ground their actions, not the interests that theories of class impute to them (Block and Somers 1984; Polanyi 1944, 1957; Somers 1997). It adheres to a concept of narrative, one mentioned previously, that understands it to have a dual role (Hart 1992). People use narratives not only to represent lives, history, and the surrounding world as historians, storytellers, and novelists do but also to emplot their lives and develop themselves as subjects by thinking themselves as protagonists in stories (Sewell 1992, 483). Research in a wide variety of disciplines has shown that narratives possess organizational power in everyday life, and this chapter proceeds from a position that holds that social identities are constituted through narratives from gendered ones to class, ethnic, and sexual ones; that social action is guided by narratives; and that social interactions as well as institutional and organizational processes are mediated by narratives (Somers 1997, 87; Steinberg 1996; Steinmetz 1992).[7]

This chapter affirms that narratives are constellations of relationships that are embedded in time and space and that narrativity, unlike taxonomic relations of structure and event, demands that "we discern the meaning of any single event only in temporal and spatial relationship to other events" (Somers 1997, 82). This connectivity turns events into episodes that must be related to other episodes. The shop floor struggles and the strike presented here cannot be understood alone in relation to the class structure: they must be related to the episodes that preceded and followed them, and they must be contextualized in terms of the cultural practices and the social, economic, and political processes in which they are embedded.

Telling, Talk, and Their Articulation to Struggle

The social terrain on which the shop floor struggles and the strike at the Drumcoo Glassworks took place was one in which the discourse of everyday life, specifically the narratives that allowed people to situate themselves in their social world, played an ordering role. As noted throughout this book, Irish nationalist Catholics in and around Ballybogoin understood themselves as a devalued population, and they struggled to transform those positionings through a variety of social movements, from the violent to the nonviolent, and the creation of social spaces like the glassworks.

In the 1980s, several of Ballybogoin's Irish nationalist housing estates had unemployment rates hovering near 60 percent and more, the local Roman Catholic parish priest claimed.[8] Catholics interpreted their neighborhoods, segregated from and generally poorer than those of their Ulster unionist fellow townspeople, as signs of their devaluation in the society at large. They maintained that their housing estates had less state capital invested in them from the start, and they understood the relative deprivation of their housing as the result of that discrimination.

Ballybogoin's Irish nationalists, as mentioned throughout this book, countered these practices of devaluation, ones linked to their past and present colonial situations, less through organized political action in the 1980s than through daily interaction. They did this through "talk," a practice that they often talked about. In analogous fashion, the glass-workers, believing that management devalued them and their labor during a series of events preceding their strike, put talk to work to address their situation of class struggle.

To set the context for the shop floor struggle, the strike, and talk's relation to them requires a return to the story interpreted by the Drum-coo glassworkers in chapter 3. There I retold the joke about talk that the workers used to distinguish themselves from their Protestant neighbors and the English. These workers valued talk in relation to the practice of telling, which they told me in the car that day was an immoral pastime. Talk was interpreted as an important index of Irish nationalist identity in Ballybogoin. The workers acknowledged others through talk and by practicing it constituted a moral relationship with them.

Telling produced silence in the workers' views, while talk produced relationships. Talk extended a person's spatiotemporal relations, enabled memories, and fostered the creation of networks, relationships of import. Talk was necessary for the viability of their community and the constitution of self, while the silence that telling produced restricted the space of agenthood and denied selfhood to them while, paradoxically, it increased the value of talk. Talk was the practice through which these workers constructed a meaningful sociocultural order and, in the process, constructed themselves in its terms (Munn 1986).

Talk made for an ethical sense of self among Ballybogoin's Catholics. That day in the car, the Drumcoo glassworkers accounted for their acts and found themselves wanting. They could not justify telling because it contradicted the value they attributed to talk. If, in their accounting of it, they justified telling and the silence to which it may lead, then they would have challenged the communal value talk had for them in extending networks.

Talk, Social Order, and Social Worth

Talk, a polysemous category, is not only a value but also a means of measuring it. Borrowing from David Stark's contribution toward a sociology of worth, I adopt the view that notes that a social order assigns relative standing based on a standard of evaluation (see Stark 1994). In Ballybogoin's nationalist social order, talk functions as such a standard. Valuable because it makes ties, talk also accounts for those ties. Social order—conceptualized as "the intersection of ties and accounts, of networks and social forms," where accounts are understood in their "etymologically rich sense" as both bookkeeping and narration (Stark 1994, 29–31)—is orchestrated through talk by Ballybogoin nationalists.[9]

Ties, whether they are kinship ones, concretely established social networks, or those binding imagined communities such as nations, mobilize accounts. They transport narratives across settings through networks of affiliation. Accounts, whether they are narratives, bookkeeping formulae, or legal procedures, mobilize ties. They "link social beings in orders of worthiness with measuring instruments that inscribe value" (Stark 1994, 31), and talk as an accounting measure signifies worth among Ballybogoin's Irish nationalists. It figures into the narratives that mobilize ties and the ties that transport accounts across social space. It articulated to the workers' struggles to make groups during the strike in complicated and complicating ways.

People invest in social forms, and Ballybogoin's nationalist Catholics invest in talk (see Thevenot 1985). Talk abets social reproduction by promulgating particular views of the world through which groups generate hypotheses about possible strategies of action. Ballybogoin's Irish nationalist people avail of talk not only to justify past actions but also to perform future ones, as that reflexive moment when the workers discussed telling in the car that day indicated. Structures of justification enter into acts. They do not merely explain them retrospectively. They justify acts that will be taken in the future (see Stark 1994). The Drumcoo glassworkers used talk to make sense of their conflicts with managers and to justify their actions toward them during the 1985 strike.

Unlike the soldiers and militia-like police who represented the dominance and disarray of the state, no group readily represented the disordering power enacted on the shop floor for these workers, the vast majority of whom were the first full-time, long-term industrial laborers in their families.[10] These Drumcoo glassworkers found it difficult to classify local society into bounded groups other than residential ones, collectivities based on the unionist Protestant and nationalist Catholic social divide. Presenting rank orderings of socioeconomic groups posed problems for them. When asked to do so, they constantly qualified the class schema presented to them with remarks like "this one'd talk to ye but that one wouldn't."

Instead of objectifying social groups in their "community," these workers located the town's social structure in talk, as the product of social action. They knew the class vocabularies of social scientific and British political discourses. They tried to translate Ballybogoin in those terms, but their attempts never fully satisfied them. Borrowed terms—working class, middle class, upper class, aristocracy, capitalists, proletariat—seldom, if ever, served as fixed representations.

"Shrewd Paddy," a once poor Catholic who made it, may have been a millionaire, he may have driven a Mercedes, and "he'd surely stick the arm into ye." But "he'd talk to ye," so he was a difficult man to classify. Workers did not classify him unqualifiedly as a member of the upper or middle class, despite that the spaces he occupied were filled with the signs of wealth: the big house, the new Mercedes every year, the BMW for his wife, and the private boarding schools for his children. Ballybogoin Catholics laughed when they told me that he bought the same green-colored Mercedes every year so that people would not notice and talk so much. They said, "He is not full of himself," "He is still one of us, he talks to us," and "He remembers where he is from."

Mairead Maguire worked as a packer at the poultry factory, found a Protestant boyfriend, a salesman there, and joined the golf club. People said, "She talks posh now, if she talks at all," and it is her talk, not her boyfriend ("he has some *craic* in him," people said), that separated her from the women and men living in her nationalist, Catholic housing estate. The nationalist people there made exceptions for a Protestant unionist like Mairead's boyfriend if he talked to them. He was considered an exception that proved the rule, but the workers did not fit Mairead easily into one of the class categories this ethnographer persuaded them to use because, they said, "she forgets where she's from." Either her talk removed her (talking posh), or she did not talk. Categorically she occupied an ambivalent position, and concepts of class seemed to provide people little help in ordering her.

Within Ballybogoin's Catholic nationalist neighborhoods, what you saw was not what you got, as it was in their interpretation of Protestant bodies through telling. It was not what you did for a job necessarily but what you did in everyday life, especially one's practices of sociability, that was important. Nonetheless, Catholics marked some bodies within their "own side of the house" as other and reduced the space of agent-hood in which those people operated. Brendan, the teller of the joke about Irish *craic* and English stolidity, moved through Ballybogoin's streets in silence. He resided in the town's poorest housing estate, which was entirely Catholic, dilapidated, and associated with the IRA and which bore the highest male unemployment rate in the region, one hovering near 80 percent, in the mid-1980s.

Both Catholic and Protestant townspeople identified this neighborhood as violent and dangerous. Both groups used a name for it that brought to mind the Wild West of American motion pictures, "the OK Corral."[11] This naming practice rendered this space beyond the pale, and such accountings not only were inscribed on the bodies of the people who lived there but also were made sense of in terms of talk. The following dialogue was an exchange between a Catholic man who had a business in Ballybogoin and a local, middle-class woman who, unlike him, was born and brought up there.

> Them ones in the "OK Corral" won't talk to ye unless they're full [i.e., drunk].
> Ach, don't talk about those'uns like that. They don't like it when ye call their place that. They've been done to, so they have. They're real Ballybogoin.

Class ideologies did not figure in these nationalist, Catholic accountings of their social order, but cross-class networks made through talk did. Class ideologies did not propel the glassworkers' strategies during the strike at the glassworks either. To do so would have required that they re-cognize relations in their nationalist factory. It would have necessitated the making of new associations, both the rearrangement of social ties among persons and things and a new set of principles for justifying those rearrangements (on such rearrangements, see Stark 1994). Instead, they sized up their situation of exploitation within the accounts of social order that marked their classification of people in Ballybogoin and its surrounding area. They organized their action from their knowledge of talk's function, its work in making groups.

This understanding did not abet their making themselves into a class grouping, a unified historical agent, even though they were embroiled in a situation of acute exploitation, one they well understood and represented cogently. Much like Karl Marx's analysis of the organization of factory time, they argued against the lengthening of their workday without receiving proper compensation for their extra production, but this consciousness of workplace injustice did not easily translate into class identification (see Marx 1967a, 524–63).

Shop Floor Conflict and the Strike

The troubles at the glassworks started with a dispute in the glassblowing shop. The workers at that site had complained that they were owed back wages. They had not had a raise in four years and had walked off the job in protest because they reckoned they were not getting paid for part of their workday. Some qualified glassblowers figured they were producing more than the 100 percent basic wages and the 20 percent bonus for which they were paid, so they calculated the number of weeks they had been producing more than bonus and multiplied that by what they measured to be the average percentage extra. Once they got the numbers, they presented management a bill for back wages, claiming that it was their "inventions," their reorganization of the glassblowing teams, and their knowledge that produced the extra glass, items that the firm sold and for which the workers did not get paid.

These glassblowers demanded to be paid for this production, but management rejected this bookkeeping move. The production manager declared that the timings under which the workers labored were too loose, that the time allotted to make almost every piece of glassware was far too high, and that the glassblowers were overpaid for the work that they did. The glassblowers walked out over this insinuation for one day, and the Northern Ireland Labor Relations Agency (NILRA) and representatives of the national trade union, the ATGWU, were called to examine the issues in dispute. Together with management these institutional bodies arranged to have time management consultants evaluate the timings, a procedure the production manager told me he wanted performed when I interviewed him two months before. He had told me that he wished to institute a piece rate system that would increase pro-

duction without increasing wages. The one-day strike and its consequences fulfilled a management desire. Many of the workers were skeptical of the forthcoming timings. One glassblower said of the union, the
ATGWU, "Now that they've their feet under the table for the first time
in four years, they'll not do anything for us."

Dolan, the managing director of the glassworks, stopped making his
morning rounds at the glassblowing factory after the walkout, ceased
talking to the workers, and stayed in the nearly panoptic observation
window well above the shop floor when he made his daily visit to the
blowing shop. Dolan's silence outraged the workers. When I moved
from daily work at the glass-cutting shop to the glassblowing factory a
month after the walkout (three months before the time-study experts
arrived), the chief complaint among the blowers was that Dolan would
not talk to them. "He does not want to learn about the job, and he's not
like Father Finbarr," they told me. Still, they made some *craic* out of the
situation. Unlike the pure panopticon, Dolan's perch above the shop
floor accorded the workers a view of him (Foucault 1977, 195–228).
They could see him, and they worked very hard to set a stage where
they could watch him surveying them. The four most skilled glassblowing teams out of a total of six teams worked at a feverish pace throughout the day in the hope that they would finish work before Dolan's
arrival, which usually took place about one to two hours before closing
time. These teams knew precisely when they had reached the 120 percent mark. When they did, they stopped work and sat around, talking,
while they waited to punch out.

When Dolan came, they became more animated. The workers convened in larger groups, played "kick the can" or some other game that
allowed them to talk from their bodies, to represent themselves as a collective, as a class (Farnell 1996, 322–23).[12] Such action signs usually got
Dolan's attention, and he reacted by railing at the blowing shop manager. He pointed fingers in the direction of the shop floor and jabbed
them at the manager. This set the workers into flurries of mimicry. They
jabbed fingers at each other, grunted, and jumped up and down miming
simian banter. "Great *craic*," they called it, and they added, "we get our
own back almost every day."

This *craic* did not get the workers further along in their struggle.
Their paychecks remained identical to those they earned when they

worked the full day, but their relations with Dolan deteriorated. As they did, the workers made sense of Dolan and their struggles with management through recollections of Father Finbarr. They kept repeating that they wanted Dolan to come down on the shop floor and talk to them man-to-man like Father Finbarr did.[13] They wanted him to learn what they had invented and to understand the nature of their accomplishments, the investments they made in the streamlining of the production process that they called their "inventions." They imagined that Father Finbarr would have learned these and praised them for their self-organized innovations. Memories of Father Finbarr figured into the shop floor strug   he strike.

Father   ic priest who raised the capital for and establ   orks, constructed a foundational narrative fc   ups such as those affiliated with the local soc   e Ballybogoin Homeless Families Group, he a   rse in the 1960s that explained Northern Irel   leprived social position in terms of their long su   al policy and the discrimination meted against t   the Northern Ireland state's formation.

He wrote open letters to development bureaucrats about unemployment among and discrimination against Roman Catholics. He founded a local development association that was the umbrella organization for the glassworks, and, when he appealed to the Ballybogoin community to start these development projects, he connected the need for local employment to demography and the political processes of dislocation. In one local publication he outlined the goals and reasons for the local development association he was attempting to establish. He wrote that one of its aims was "to provide opportunities for employment by the setting up of small local industries in which the emphasis would be on the personal skill of the worker."

Father Finbarr opined that "drastic action" was required "from a consideration of the following statistical economic facts of life in this area, which are directly attributable to the policies of the unionist government at central and, more particularly, at local government levels." He included among those facts an emigration rate for Catholic school leavers in the nationalist areas of the county that ranged "from 35% to 43% in the age group of 15–25 years" and an average Catholic male unemployment rate in the nationalist areas of the county that ranged from 20 to 26 percent "in spite of the huge emigration rate," while the unemployment rate for the six counties of the Northern Ireland state as a whole totaled only 7 percent.[14]

Father Finbarr elaborated upon these contested demographic figures from his pulpit on Sunday mornings, in the local newspapers, and in his lobbying of Northern Ireland development bureaucrats in the early to mid-1960s. He constructed a narrative that tied the desire for local development to the need for skills among the nationalist male work-force. He addressed the lacks and absences commonly perceived in Ballybogoin's Roman Catholic males by countering the dominant nar-rative about the high levels of nationalist unemployment, the story that held that these men "have no work in them," that they are bound by "tradition" and resentful, that they are "the lazy natives."[15] Instead, he represented the unemployment situation as resulting from a historical relationship, from the Catholics' history as an oppressed people. He emphasized over and over again that young Catholic men were capable of becoming skilled workers, ones who, because of their skills, would not be made redundant. In his story, Catholics had skilled work in them, but they never had a chance to learn and perform it.

Father Finbarr inscribed Northern Irish society this way in the mid-1960s. His local campaign, like the groups started by Catholic women in the town, was a precursor to NICRA. Shortly before the years of nearly continuous political violence began in 1969, Father Finbarr and the Ballybogoin Catholics who established his local development associa-tion built houses for homeless families, established a cooperative for small farmers, and founded the Drumcoo Glassworks, a firm dedicated to producing skills for local men that would not be displaced by tech-nological developments. They did this through an ideology based on Catholic Action, a conservative Roman Catholic movement that emphasized self-help, but their efforts were articulated to Irish nation-alism because Father Finbarr contextualized his group's actions within the demographic crises of Catholic nationalists and the local critiques that held the British state responsible for those population problems.

The glassworks was the late Father Finbarr's largest and most favored project. His name is associated with it by all groups in Ballybo-goin, but particular groups remember him differently. Some Catholics remember Father Finbarr as a saint, while others recall his dictatorial demeanor. For most townspeople, Father Finbarr was related metonymically to the glassworks: he functioned as a sign in place of the whole. He spoke for it and, in a sense, became it. For those Catholics ready to canonize him, by and large the middle-class people who worked with him to establish the local development association and the working-class people who benefited from it, Father Finbarr was a source of power.[16] To those who supported him, it was his representation, his talk, that got the money for the factories. Many among them said, "He was a powerful prayer."

For some middle-class Catholics, the people from whom he got a good portion of the start-up capital and the land for the factory, he was remembered as "a dictator." They recall that Father Finbarr coaxed and cajoled them into giving him money. Some of them said that "he only had time for" them, only talked to them, when he wanted money. They said, "He would have been a success at whatever he chose to do with his life," but to them he only appeared as the source of the power he exerted. They (by and large the shopkeepers, small contractors, successful small farmers, and solicitors) realized they were his real source. They figured they had given enough when they had contributed to the initial capital drive, while the poorer people in the Catholic housing estates, especially the older ones, gave their life savings, never very much, over to Father Finbarr (for the local development association) to, as one old woman told me, "create jobs for the lads."

The most experienced workers, then, those who started at or near the factory's founding, felt a deep kinship with the firm and with Father Finbarr, its first managing director. As sons and grandsons of the many women who gave the father their savings, these lads wanted to make the factory work successfully. They enthusiastically threw themselves into their apprenticeships, as some workers remembered:

> *Brendan:* As Francie was just sayin' there earlier on, even, ye know, ah, it just showed ye how keen we were at that particular time, ye know. We worked nights, maybe two, and three nights a week and Saturday mornin' for nothin'. Isn't that right, Paddy?
> *Paddy:* That's right.
> *Brendan:* We, ye know, just to gain experience. And we done it, ye know, ye know. Fair enough, it was Paddy's first job. I already had been workin'. Francie, I think. It wasn't your first job was it?
> *Francie:* No.

Brendan: No, you had been workin' too and to think, I actually left a job where I was gettin' more money to work for less money.

These men worked late into the night and on weekends, and they warmly remembered Father Finbarr's encouragement while he attempted to learn the crafts of both glassblowing and glass cutting from them. Unlike the company executives who followed him, Francie told me, "He appreciated the craft. He gave us time, not like those'ons running the place now." By "givin' time," talking, Father Finbarr helped to constitute a group of workers in solidarity with the firm. That original group of twelve glassworkers with whom Francie, Brendan, and Paddy identified named themselves "the twelve apostles."

In 1985 the struggling workers at the Drumcoo Glassworks differentiated Father Finbarr from the management with whom they were in conflict by remembering that he talked to them, gave them time, and inquired into their skills and knowledge. They punctuated that memory with accounts of Dolan's history at the glassworks. After taking a leave from pastoral duties to manage the glassworks, Father Finbarr left the glassworks in 1974 to take an assignment in a parish across the border. The local people who succeeded him did not have the knowledge to run the firm and "made a balls of it," the workers remembered.

The firm went into a tailspin, but the British Labour government, for whom the glassworks served an ideological function in that it was used to demonstrate the Labour government's concern for nationalist working people, took it away from the local development association in 1977. The government put the Northern Ireland Development Association (NIDA), a state bureaucracy, in charge. Several London-based consulting firms were hired to study the labor process, and, as a result, production was rationalized. The glassworks continued to lose money, but the Labour government put money back in as fast as the firm lost it.

This failed rationalization period coincided with the election of Margaret Thatcher as British prime minister in 1979. Mrs. Thatcher changed the state's economic role from one of welfare state management to that of entrepreneur. Her government sold many state assets and led investment away from the peripheral regions, where unemployment rose dramatically.[17] To conform to Thatcher's policies, NIDA wanted to rid itself of the glassworks and put it up for sale. Catholics in the town believed the government never wanted the firm to continue but were "caught out" by the wit of Dolan, who in 1981 engineered the purchase of the firm in the name of the local farmers' co-op, the one begun by Father Finbarr, which Dolan then ran.

Dolan had been negotiating in good faith with the government to buy the glassworks. He had the Ballybogoin area nationalists as well as the Protestant small farmers who belonged to the co-op behind him. The government was a reluctant seller, and the negotiations went nowhere. Finally, Dolan, known locally as "a dealing man," got tired of the bureaucracy's prevarication and called the major radio and television stations in Belfast to tell them the government did not want to sell the glassworks to the Ballybogoin Co-op despite that, as Dolan told me, "the co-op wanted to keep jobs in the area and to put the place on the right footing."

The story went out on the 10:00 A.M. news bulletins, and before the 11:00 A.M. broadcast, officials from NIDA had called both Dolan and the media to inform them they would deal. The co-op finalized the sale that very afternoon, and the workers were overjoyed. They remembered the event with the words "one of our own got the factory back." The workers read Dolan's maneuver as a sign of resistance, and this act—combined with the fact that Dolan's move coincided with the IRA hunger strike in the Maze prison, a protest led by Bobby Sands, the IRA commanding officer who had been elected the MP at Westminster for Ballybogoin and its region—made it appear that the nationalist cause in the area was gaining ground. Some workers, not all, remembered that time as one in which they felt empowered.

Many recalled the day that Bobby Sands died because, spontaneously, no workers showed up at the factory, even though it was a workday. Seamus, the glassblowers' shop steward, believed this was a sign that local nationalists were finally united. He joined Sinn Féin, the political party allied to the IRA, during the hunger strike protests, and he, along with other workers, read the co-op's purchase of the glassworks as further proof of nationalist momentum.

Father Finbarr, who had moved back to Northern Ireland to take a position as parish priest in a nearby town, preached against Thatcher's policy on Irish political prisoners and the hunger strikers from his pulpit and published open letters in Ballybogoin's press summarizing one of his sermons. Although he expressed his opposition to the IRA and criticized its practices continuously in his sermons, the workers, the majority of whom supported Sinn Féin in local, regional, and national elections in the 1980s, selectively remembered Father Finbarr's statements and positioned him as solidly with them during this crisis because of his open criticisms of Prime Minister Thatcher.

Although Dolan's position against Irish republican nationalism was well known, he was linked to Father Finbarr's foundational narrative, which articulated the story of the glassworks to the deficiencies of the state, the need for the nationalist community to have its own sources of capital, and the desire to create a space where underemployed Catholic male workers could learn skills. Like Father Finbarr, and unlike the state managers who had run the factory in the intervening period, Dolan, the workers believed, was a man to whom they could talk, one who identified with them when he assumed the role as the glassworks' managing director.

Shortly after taking charge of the firm, Dolan reduced the shop floor workers from 135 to 65 and the management team from 30 to 10. After several months under the new regime, overall production was 80 percent of the previous highs and costs were down nearly 55 percent. Quality improved dramatically. In the period leading up to the strike, there were 105 employees, about 25 of them in a training program subsidized by the state, and production had gone from £25,000 sterling per week before the co-op's takeover to £47,000 sterling per week after the takeover. Dolan explained to me that he completed this turnaround because he fired the workers from the town, especially those from the "OK Corral," whom he said "had no work in them." At the time of the one-day strike Dolan told me, "I only hire those country boys. They have work in them."

The glassmakers accepted the increasing exploitation and the numerous redundancies (layoffs) made by Dolan and his management team not only because the labor market was weak in the area but also because the nationalist narrative was at play on the shop floor from 1981 to 1984. Those workers who supported Sinn Féin understood that party's success in local elections as indexing a transformation of people's attitudes. Dolan's retrieving the glassworks from the government and the increasing success in selling the glassworks' product in England, Ireland, and the United States added to that sense of burgeoning community value. Local shareholders in the glassworks and the co-op that bought it got their first ever dividends in those years, and the success of the firm and Dolan's saving of it became frequent topics in the pubs.

The town and its surrounding villages valued the glassworks and themselves through it. The firm and its employees received recognition as community assets.

The workers' articulation of these events to the firm's foundational story enabled relatively harmonious relations despite the redundancies that contradicted the discourses stating that economically marginalized nationalists would become productive workers if given the chance at a skilled job. The workers described those laid off as "wasters," "slackers," and people who "work moves rather than work work." Many of those laid off were from "the OK corral" and, although Irish nationalists, were known for not talking and remembered for their dishonesty. Dolan, because he talked and was figured as a savior of jobs in the town, someone who proved the Catholics' worth, was identified with the nationalist narrative up until the 1985 strike. Those workers made redundant were not.

In late 1984 when the workers billed management for back wages, they articulated this local narrative to shop floor relations differently. The company was doing well, and the workers wanted a return. They had not had a raise in four years, and when Dolan stopped talking to them after the one-day walkout, the force of the local nationalist narrative began to dissipate.

Father Finbarr's foundational narrative of the firm mediated not only the nationalist narrative but also the labor exchanges that took place on the shop floor. Narrative is transactional, as Ross Chambers writes, because "it mediates exchanges that produce historical change, it is transactional, too, in that this functioning is itself dependent on an initial contract, an understanding between the participants in the exchange as to the purposes served by the narrative function, its 'point'" (1984, 8). In the glassworks, talk, as a valued practice and as an instrument of evaluation, served as the contractual agreement upon which the meaningfulness of the nationalist discourse was built. As long as talk took place, the basis for the nationalist narrative as transactional, for producing historical change, indeed, for producing production, was kept intact. Without talk between management and workers, the nationalist narrative lost its performative, exchange-mediating force on the shop floor, and the space for outright class struggle opened.[18] The events surrounding management's reorganizing efforts at the glassworks demonstrate these changing social and cultural relations.

Time Management and Worker Resistance

The time management team brought in by the NILRA, with the agreement of the national trade union, arrived in March, when management and labor were not talking. The workers' strategy was to slow down, talk to the time management consultants, and convince them of the difficulty of their highly skilled job and the adequacy of the timings they had labored under for the previous three years.

Working in slow motion, the workers hoped to confuse the "time-study men" and tried to engage them in *craic*. These tactics failed. Two of the six teams did not participate in the slowdown, and no *craic* came from the time-study men. The glassblowers believed that the first time expert who arrived, a Catholic, could be persuaded of the legitimacy of their positions. The workers took him out to some local pubs after work on the Thursday of the first week he observed them. He got "footless drunk," one worker remarked when he arrived to his glassblowing job the next day; the time-study man missed a day's work and lost all credibility with the workers.

The other two time-study men never established a relationship with the glassmakers. The workers named the junior one "Peter Robinson, Peter Robinson," after the dour deputy leader of the most anti-Irish nationalist political party in Northern Ireland, the Reverend Ian Paisley's Democratic Unionist Party (DUP). They named the leader of the time management team "Ian himself," a representation indicating that this was a man with whom *craic* could not be had. No solidarity seemed possible with these men, and the workers believed they could not persuade them to the justice of their position. When I remarked to "Ian himself" that "they are doing great things around here," he said, "not at all." He told me that the firm in which he had worked on his previous assignment in Larne (which for Ballybogoin Catholics was a notoriously exclusivist, unionist, Protestant town east of the River Bann) was truly doing great things. They were modernizing their factory, computerizing it, and had no time for arcane operations like those in the glassworks. These remarks showed that the workers were likely right in their telling. This man would not have taken up the narrative of the firm that emphasized the workers' "traditional" skills and the need to maintain them to prevent redundancies in an era and area of such high unemployment.

As the workers in the glassblowing shop were being observed by the time-study men, the glass cutters, who had been timed and analyzed before the time management consultants arrived at the blowing shop, tried out their new timings and realized they would lose pay. They voted to strike after several informal appeals to management for a reconsideration of the new prices, and they walked out to picket the factory gates. The cutting shop's ancillary workers joined them the next day, and the blowing shop workers joined the strike five days later.

No group of workers consulted with the regional representatives of their trade union before making this move, but they tried to contact them immediately afterward. They received no response for three weeks. When the trade union representatives did come, there was a marathon meeting in which little connection was made between the two bureaucrats, both unionist and identified by the nationalist workers as Protestant, and the Catholic nationalist workers.

These union men invoked stories of the shipyard workers, a notoriously sectarian workforce, to narrate the importance of perseverance. They spoke of the struggles of workers who were soldiers in both World War I and World War II to invoke the overcoming of hardship, because by the fourth week of the strike some workers were in financial trouble. Several had just bought houses, and more than half of the skilled workers were making payments on new cars. The nationalist workers did not identify with these stories of soldiers and perseverance, while the only two Protestant workers at this meeting did.[19]

At the end of the second meeting between the workers and these union representatives, Seamus, the glassblowers' shop steward, approached one of the union representatives to apologize for missing some days at the picket line. He told this union man that his wife was running for a local council seat and that he was helping her to campaign and take care of their children. The union representative asked him which party his wife was in, and when Seamus told him "Sinn Féin" the union representative's response was, "Well, I guess you don't have much choice. Them SDLP are all middle class, teachers and university professors. You wouldn't want to join them." Narratives that linked members of the working class across their Irish nationalist and Ulster unionist divisions were difficult to produce in these trade union meetings. No political party that explicitly took up the cause of workers existed in the area. Discourses of class did not have the power to link differences of national identity in this context, even though they were active at this moment in the strike's history.

Within days of the meeting, management issued their ultimatum. They wrote letters telling each worker that, if they did not go back to work within the week, management would shut the glassmaking furnaces down. They warned that the cost of doing so would be enormous and that the furnaces might never be reignited. Over sixty workers turned out to a quickly organized meeting, and all but those two Protestant unionist workers and two angry Irish nationalist ones voted to end the strike and go back to work on management's terms. The two unionist men who wanted to continue had won the respect of their nationalist workmates during the strike. They appeared faithfully at the picket line every day and, for the first time, had associated with their fellow workers outside the factory.

These Protestant workers began to be discussed as having some *craic* in them by the nationalist workers with whom they had seldom socialized. Prior to the strike these men were marked as docile and loyal workers. After the strike management and workers understood them differently. On the weekend following their return to the shop floor, a member of the management team, one born and raised in Ballybogoin, called me aside in a pub and wanted to demonstrate the knowledge he had gleaned about the strikers. He knew that four of them had voted to stay on strike. As I remained silent, he named the two Protestant workers and said, "Ach, you can't trust them ones who'll never talk to you."

On returning to work, "talk" and "giving time" ceased between workers and management and among some workers themselves. A new piece rate system was institutionalized, and production had to be considerably increased to make the wages that workers earned before the strike. The features of everyday life, "talk" and "giving time," which made a group among Irish nationalists around Ballybogoin, were debilitated at the glassworks. In the period after the strike, the glassworks became "modernized." An internal labor market—a set of internal bureaucratic rules whose governing principle is not membership in an interacting group but membership in a category of persons—was instituted and was adhered to (Stark 1986).

Talk does not function as a means of contract in this type of organization. A worker is assigned a category from management after having met bureaucratically defined criteria, and the struggle is over categories delineated from above. Management instituted a new set of skill categories. They differentiated skills and offered workers incentives to upgrade their craftsmanship status.

Many workers focused on these newly named skills, and the glass-blowers moved their attention away from the inventions they created as blowing team members with different skills to meeting the requirements for attaining hierarchically organized titles. These classifications were not made through the talk of relational selves but enacted by bureaucratic authority. Opportunities for the joint creativity that had led to what the glassblowing teams called "our inventions" were sharply curtailed in this new organization and so were the spaces for talk and labor solidarity.

Talk as a social practice, at least as Irish nationalists in and around Ballybogoin understood it, assumed that people used it to forge groups, to organize selves and others at particular sites, to make the future.[20] This did not happen for the glassworkers in this struggle because talk, as a cultural form, articulated to class relations, transforming social structures and local power differences in complex ways. Seamus, the shop steward in the glassblowing shop who was a key negotiator for the workers in the period before the strike, alluded to these contingencies when I asked him about the divisions that disjoined workers after their defeat. He responded:

> Well, there's a relationship where ye go. Ah. Ye have carriers, and ye have to shout, and ye have to use language that ye wouldn't normally use, ye know. And I hate that. I hate to do that there, but I can't get anything done if I don't do that cause that's accepted terminology. It's accepted to shout at people, and it's accepted to use slang, and it's accepted to tell dirty jokes, and it's accepted to, ah, accepted to be, be just crude at times. And if ye don't do that, ye won't, ye won't progress, ye know. Ye won't get your thing organized. Ye won't get your ship on the water, ye know. Ye have to do these things to go on. It's hateful. It goes against my character completely. When I walk out that door, I'm a different guy, a totally different person. . . . It's an industrial culture, ye know where people, where people, where they do things out of their character. What I would consider normally to be crude and obscene behavior, ye have to do that. And there's a greed, there's a greed in there something terra'.

After a pause, I asked Seamus what he meant, and he told me.

> Like behind all the niceties and the people saying about the job, it's a
> lovely job and it's a skilled job and this here, a lot of them guys in
> there don't give a shit about that. Let's face it, all they want is money.
> That's all. Like you know Malachy, Malachy's worked with me four-
> teen years, Bill, and Malachy's building a house, and he's never men-
> tioned to me yet that he's building a house. I mean that's the type of
> thing, ye know, and I find that terrible so I do.

What Seamus found terrible was the lack of talk between him and
Malachy, the deformed interaction that he believed predominated on
the factory shop floor, and the consequent inability of the workers to
build sustained relationships, to make themselves into a group. Seamus,
one of the firm's most skilled glassblowers, had been known for his consideration of the less experienced workers on his glassblowing team and
had been elected shop steward, an apprentice glassblower told me,
because he was "the best fella in the factory," the experienced master
craftsman who had the most time for the younger apprentices trying to
learn the craft, the man with the most *craic* in him, the man who talked
to everybody and could hold his own talking to management. Seamus
valued wit in interaction, as did his fellow workers, but the contrast
between the modes of command required at the workplace and the
everyday relational modes used by nationalists to forge group identities
proved profoundly disappointing for him.

Seamus did not continue as shop steward after the strike. When the
strike ended, he attributed the workers' loss to their inability to perform
as a group, a deficit he now believed preceded the strike. He thought
that those negative interactions that characterized everyday shop floor
life rendered him and his workmates unable to unite. He summed it up
by saying, "we let each other down, we let the side down," a statement
that referred to the workers' lack of talk, as Catholic nationalists in and
around Ballybogoin understood it.

The three other shop stewards did not want to retain their union
positions either for complicated reasons explored in the next chapter.
Even the four glassmakers who wanted to continue the strike, workers
who seemingly identified with the trade union, would not take a shop
steward position. No other skilled worker would either. Each of the

two groups of skilled workers had a trade union representative, as did the semiskilled and unskilled workers whom management classified as "the ancillary workers." Two unskilled workers assumed the glass cutters' and glassblowers' shop steward positions, and the skilled glassmakers felt humiliated by this action. They believed their identities as men who had built the firm had not been recognized by management. They stated that the trade union and the ancillary workers had conspired in this lack.[21]

Indifference, that social production that denies identity and selfhood and may lead people to acquiesce in the humiliation of others, had infiltrated the glassworks' social relations of production and existed not only between workers and management but also among workers themselves.[22] Paradoxically, after a bitter and highly emotional cultural struggle at the glassworks, the skilled workers did not care to participate in their trade union organization and to sustain their performance as a class.

Making Sense of the Strike

The reasons for this indifference and for management's stunning victory are complex. The Drumcoo glassmakers did not fix their identities around the category "worker" because the trade union did not engender commitments from them to its project. Understanding agency and agenthood in their neo-Gramscian senses—where agency refers to the long-term or "tendential" social forces, such as capitalism, socialism, nationalism, and colonialism/postcolonialism, that struggle to determine the future and to shape the course of history, while agenthood indicates the individual actors, institutions, and organizations that struggle to make history in the terms of particular agencies—the union failed to make the vast majority of workers its agents (Gramsci 1971, 175–85; Hall 1986; Grossberg 1992, 113–27). The workers, instead, articulated the class relations at work that trade unionism addressed to other sets of relations, particularly political relations, those that related the force of colonialism (colonizing/decolonizing processes) to the British state and to talk and the relations of value that talk produced.

The political relations that entered the glassworks articulated to Thatcherism, the economic, social, and ideological policies of Margaret Thatcher's government, which at that point in the United Kingdom's history embodied capitalism and was a transformative social force (Hall 1988).[23] Thatcher's policies rearranged, adapted, and reconfigured existing organizational forms, particularly the institutions of the welfare state. More than a background for the struggles at the glassworks, Thatcherism entered them when NIDA tried to sell the glassworks, a state asset, in 1981.

At that time Thatcher served as the prime figure of political opposition for Ballybogoin's Irish nationalists. Her government's law-and-order policy did not recognize the political status of IRA prisoners on the H-Blocks, and this led to the hunger strike of 1981 (see Beresford 1987). As the ten hunger strikers died, there were mass protests by Irish nationalists, to which Ballybogoin Catholics of all political beliefs went, those who supported the military campaign of the IRA and those who condemned it. These demonstrations and the election of Bobby Sands gave the majority of workers who supported Sinn Féin a sense that their political views had value despite the condemnations of IRA atrocities both within and without the nationalist community, including criticisms from their fellow nationalist glassworkers.

Thatcher became a figure that most Ballybogoin Irish nationalists opposed despite these divisions over the politics of violence. Her government's economic policies led to a decline in the economic position of Catholics, so while many of the workers revalued their political positions, the dramatically high levels of unemployment devalued the nationalist community. Politically, Ballybogoin nationalists struggled against Thatcher. Economically the glassworkers had very little ground for a challenge until Dolan outmaneuvered NIDA and, as one of their own, got the glassworks back for the workers and those community members who had invested in it. He provided a local economic ground for resisting Thatcher, not through any direct ideological challenge but through a response to the political and economic devaluation that the region's Catholic nationalists experienced.

The workers read Dolan's maneuver as an act of usurpation, and they identified with it.[24] When Dolan took over the firm he, along with the workers, began to transform it into a valued community asset. Assets, according to David Stark, embody economic value, and, like social and cultural values, they are only mobilized in and through networks of social relations. They cannot be reduced to social networks, Stark notes, because to circulate through "the ties that bind (and thus contribute to that binding) an asset must be bound in a network of measuring instruments, tests and proofs of worth" (1994, 30). In this case, the network of measurements operated at the levels of politics (state/community interrelationships), profit, and everyday interaction. On the political level, the making of the glassworks into a valued community asset, one that did not depend on the British state, signified for the workers the possibility of local autonomy and proved Irish nationalist worth in relation to the state.

The production of economic value, profit, was required for this revaluation. As profits began to be made the firm became accredited in the eyes of Ballybogoin's nationalists and the nationalist and unionist communities throughout Northern Ireland. Community investors started to earn dividends from their long-dormant stock. The glassworks, through regional and local advertising, became a source of pride, and this, from the workers' perspectives, depended on talk, both the instrumental talk that took place among glassblowing team members to create the inventions that increased productivity and the everyday talk that was valued as a sign of communal viability.

At the same time as the glassworks countered the political and economic effects of Thatcherism, it articulated to its economic ideology. Transforming the glassworks into a community asset required a reorganization of the firm that emplaced a boundary within the nationalist community when Dolan fired over half the workers. Both management and workers classified those Irish nationalists made redundant by Dolan as "slackers" and "wasters" who "had no work in them." Largely from the poorest Catholic housing estates in Ballybogoin, such as "the OK Corral," they were sometimes classified as people who would not talk. In these representations, they were subjects who "worked moves" only. Both management and workers marginalized them. Essentialized as unable to contribute to community building, their social worth was questioned, as was the larger Catholic community's by Thatcher's policies.

When Dolan and the rest of the management team stopped talking to workers, the workers who "worked work" were placed in a marginal position in the firm. When they shortened their workday after Dolan stopped talking to them, the workers protested not only the fact that part of their day went uncompensated but also the lack of recognition they received from Dolan in making the glassworks a prized community asset. As one worker said, "Everyone worked hard for him because we thought he was more or less like us. Now, he gets all the credit. We never get any, and we created the profit." Dolan became distanced from the workers, but they still did not represent him as the embodiment of a middle class that opposed them, the working class. They posed the problem in terms of lack, the lack of recognizing them as productive persons by a valued community member.

As the strike proceeded into its third and fourth weeks, the workers' standing in the community slipped. "Ballybogoin people" they encountered told them that "the factory belongs to the community" and they should "get back to work." Many townspeople cited Dolan, not them, as the reason for the firm's success, and the workers said the people came to this conclusion because Dolan had "the media locked up." Only his side of the story was reported in the local press. This was one of the last two issues addressed before the workers voted to accept management's ultimatum at that last trade union meeting. The workers acceded to this draconian move not only because they needed the income from their jobs but also because their value as persons and the value of the glassworks were intertwined.

The glassworkers remade themselves as they transformed the glassworks, making it a valued community asset. They fought for the recognition of themselves as persons, as productive community members, throughout their struggle. Their struggles at work articulated to their struggles to be recognized as valued community members and to the making of social transactions through the nationalist narrative. This complexity did not easily render a space for a focus upon the formation of class identities. The workers' articulation of the Ballybogoin nationalist narrative to the relations entailed in the strike made it difficult for them to negotiate a space where they could differentiate themselves as a distinct working class within the nationalist community.

At that particular historical conjuncture, trade unionism and the discourse of class that accompanied it were difficult to take up for the Irish nationalist workers. For them, the firm was a vehicle for their personal and their community's value formation, and when management threatened to shut the glassworks down, they ended their strike. The unionist, Protestant workers did not articulate the firm to themselves and their political community in the same fashion. They, too, talked about talk and noted its effects, but they did not associate their value as persons with the firm as a community asset. The category "worker," in and for itself, was salient for them, and they wanted to continue the fight against management. The narrative of soldiering on that the ATGWU representatives used to represent the importance of struggle persuaded them to carry on. The nationalist workers did not identity with this rhetoric, one linked to the British military.

After their return to work, the majority of the skilled workers made deals with management on an individual basis. They correlated their individual skill levels to productivity goals to increase their wages. Seamus, who was an advocate of ending the strike when community members disparaged the workers' walkout, would not do this, and neither would those two Protestant workers who opposed him on the strike issue. Seamus, as his comment cited earlier concerning Malachy indicated, interpreted the continuation of the strike as antagonistic to the nationalist narrative as enacted at the glassworks. He used Malachy, with whom he had worked and had traveled to work for fourteen years, as an example of the deformed interaction that had infiltrated the workplace. He understood Malachy's silence on the house he was building as a negation of the values associated with talk, and he refused that individualism when he declined to negotiate within the internal labor market until long after the strike ended.

James and Ken, the two Protestant unionist workers, did not participate in the new labor organization because they desired to act collectively and retain the effectivity of the trade union. They, too, declined the shop steward jobs. These workers took the same position as Seamus, but it was an ambivalently constructed one. They arrived there through different articulations than Seamus did. Their indifference to the internal labor market was linked to their dismay at the individualization it effected and the passivity among workers that it fermented. Seamus's indifference connected more powerfully to the long-term struggle of nationalists to be recognized as valued persons and to the factory as a valued community asset.

The individuated workers who made deals with management represented Seamus and the other workers who did not negotiate for themselves as "ignorant men from the country" who, once they got on the motorway that ended at a roundabout just east of their small towns and villages, lost their way. "They're lost once they've passed the Ballyish roundabout," one worker commented to laughs from others. They represented these workers as the yet to be modernized working class from the backward, western, rural areas, just as management did, even though a significant number of these so-called men from the country lived in the urban district. The understanding that these "modern" workers and management shared seemed to be that these "rural people" might have work in them but they were ignorant of the ways of the present, ones that, although they did not represent them as such, articulated to Thatcherism and a politics of consumption. The increasing privatization of life and the need to pay for goods had become their priority and signified their modernity.

Malachy had bought the house he had rented for years from the housing authority, a change in the organization of housing that the Thatcher government instituted, and he was selling it at a profit to build a new one. Several other workers were involved in similar negotiations. In my first interview with Dolan, ten months before the end of the strike, he told me that he could keep the union at bay because the workers were beginning to get mortgages. He implied that their financial obligations would keep them under control. This replicated the discourse of Prime Minister Thatcher, who disparaged the use of class as a concept, fought trade unions, and privileged the freely choosing consumer in her political discourse (Cannadine 1999, 1–24, 176–84; Hall 1988). "There is no such thing as society," she said. "There are individual men and women and there are families" (quoted in Strathern 1996, 64). In buying up council houses, the workers became agents of Thatcherism, albeit unwitting ones, and this United Kingdom level of politics entered the struggles at the glassworks.

The indifference toward the trade union and the feelings of humiliation that were engendered in the aftermath of this strike were produced by factors that included but went beyond the exigencies of the national and local political economies, the bookkeeping mechanisms deployed by the firm, the new piece rate system, and the introduction of internal labor markets. Rationalizing instruments like the internal labor markets imposed at the glassworks do not affect every workplace situation in the same way. Their effects depend upon developed narrative identities, notions of self, the existing social relations of production, the discourses that shape the workplace, the practices of subjectification in the social spaces outside it, and the cultural constructions of group identity that people involved in such reorganizations have worked out. The strike at the glassworks demonstrated this.

The workers who submitted to the internal labor market and reaped benefits from it also formed a cultural intimacy with management (Herzfeld 1997). The recalcitrant workers suffered misrecognition on two levels: their trade union was not recognized and they, as persons, were not. This has had negative consequences for all workers. In keeping with the Thatcherite project, the glassworks was selected to be a tourist site by the Northern Ireland Tourist Board and NIDA. These two organizations provided the major investment to build a new factory that arranged work spaces so that tourists can observe the labor process. Discipline on the shop floor has increased since the new factory opened in 1992. As workers perform for the visitors and conform to the practices narrated by the tour guides, there is little space for their inventions (the changing techniques that they created in the early 1980s and for which they desired recognition), their talk, and their *craic.*

Workers' issues were not part of the negotiations entailed in the construction of this new factory. The trade union was not consulted, and the workers had no alternative representation. In the years since the 1985 strike, the trade union has not been active. Hegemony has been established, although it remains a contested process. All the actors have not taken on the same identity. Difference has not disappeared. A collective will has been constructed through the articulation of differences, but these differences remain. The Irish nationalist glassworkers have not been incorporated into the British state, but they are actors, different ones, in its 1990s projects, such as the glassworks tourist site (see Hall 1991, 58).

This chapter has shown that social and cultural differences get rearticulated as people negotiate them through time and space. It has examined these workers not from a theoretical perspective that represents their acts as deviant, not class conscious, but from a position that highlights their complex sociality, the relational matrix that constitutes their lives as persons. At base, this chapter concerns the classical anthropological and sociological problem of the formation of collective identity and concludes that, at the Drumcoo Glassworks, this is a continuous negotiating process inextricably connected to state power and its organizational and cultural forms. Class and ethnicity do not battle one another as formed entities. Relations of class work in terms of relations of ethnicity or race, and in a place like Northern Ireland, where so much trouble arises because, among other reasons, the typifications associated with the terms "Protestant" and "Catholic" rule, it is crucial to demonstrate this.

7

Struggling
Masculinities

When sturdy John Bull (England) forcibly married dreamy Hibernia (Ireland) with her artistic temperament, it was a marriage doomed to failure. Even their children have deserted her, as thousands of their sons have left her shores. Much as we abhor divorce, Hibernia ought to get a decree against John, on a plea of incompatibility.

St. Marys Star, St. Marys, Kansas, 1916

A variety of feminist scholars has cleared a path toward more fully relational studies of class, race, ethnicity, and gender through their critiques of notions proposing an ontological specificity to women as childbearers, as social mothers, or as essentially relational. Such identity categories not only describe but also normalize women and, therefore, exclude the complex differences that characterize them. To contest such marginalization, poststructuralist feminism has elaborated the position that the category "woman" cannot be totalized and ought to signify "an undesignatable field of differences," as should the category "man" (see Butler 1992, 16).

This position holds that both women and men are constituted in relations, as are the adjectives "masculine" and "feminine" that attach to them. "Feminine" and "masculine" designate symbolic references, not the physical bodies of female and male. In the Enlightenment tradition, one that applies to Northern Ireland, "masculine" and "feminine" define abstract qualities through opposition: masculine as strong, rational, and public and feminine as weak, irrational, and private provide a partial listing of these abstractions.[1]

Joan Wallach Scott has connected this critique of identity categories to the category "class." She holds that gender, understood as social understandings of sexual difference, constitutes class relations. Gender marks class relations and class struggle because it provides a convenient and available resource to register difference. It refers to nature, to physical bodies, so gender appears natural and immutable, even though it varies across space and time (see Scott 1988, 1–11). Gender categories often work to naturalize social hierarchies and render their production as a specific organization of relations difficult to perceive.

From this perspective, gender is apprehended not as a thing added to social relations but as social knowledge that may exert force in those relations, may transform them, and gets made and remade in various locations. It has material effects. "As a social process, we need to think of *gender* not only as a noun but also as a verb," Ava Baron writes, and the study of gendering, in this sense, "is concerned with how understandings of sexual difference shape institutions, practices and relationships" (1991, 36; emphasis in original).

This chapter examines the making of masculinity among the skilled glassworkers and the effect of this construction on shop floor relations. Masculinity, particularly that of Irish Catholic men, entered the history of the firm, was attached to its geographical location, and was expressed in the struggles that occurred there at the end of 1984 and in the strike that ensued in the spring of 1985.

Masculine identities profoundly shaped the institutions, relationships, and practices of the glassworks as well as the subjectivity and actions of those who worked there. It figured into the events described in the previous chapter and articulated to political and ethnic identities in complex ways. This chapter will track this identification process and will attempt to understand masculinity's effect on social action, drawing on the identity theory of action developed by Margaret R. Somers and Gloria D. Gibson, who combine the insights of feminist theory with the recent research on narrative that emphasizes its ontological and epistemological dimensions (see Somers and Gibson 1994, 40). From this position, no ontological specificity is accorded to any category whether it is men, women, or workers. Instead, narratives, as discussed in the last chapter, are understood to provide the means through which social actors come to know their world. Actors become who they are by locating themselves in stories that are negotiated in time and space.

Somers and Gibson have proposed four dimensions of narrativity—ontological, public, conceptual, and metanarrativity. Ontological narratives are the stories actors deploy to make sense of their worlds and to act in them. These are discourses that are about the self and that define persons. A person, then, is a narration made intelligible through ongoing relationships in time and space. Actors understand themselves and others by placing their actions in the context of preceding and subsequent events, and the ontological narratives they construct are integrally related to public narratives.[2] Public narratives are the products of the interpersonal webs of relationality that transform ontological narratives over time. They include narratives of family, nation, church, and workplace, among many others, and persons configure their ontological accounts and changing relationships in close relation to these public narratives.

Emplotment gives significance to events. Social actors get confused when they are not able to integrate an event into a plot they can understand. In emplotting events, social actors measure some types of worth and not others. In doing so, they endorse some narratives and disclaim others. Power works upon those emplotments.[3] Through narratives, social order is linked to evaluations of social worth and to moral positions.

Social actors make their social orders and, in turn, are made in relation with them. Somers and Gibson's third dimension, conceptual narratives, addresses this process. They acknowledge that ontological narratives and public narratives alone do not produce social action and that analyses of social action must include such social forces as market patterns, institutional practices, and organizational constraints. The challenge for conceptual narratives is "to devise a conceptual vocabulary that we can use to reconstruct and plot over time and space the ontological narratives and relationships of historical actors, the public and cultural narratives that inform their lives, and the crucial intersection of these narratives with other social forces" (Somers and Gibson 1994, 62). Social scientists, among others, perform conceptual narratives when they lace their stories with theoretical constructs and material histories.

Metanarratives may require consideration in the conceptual narratives of the social researcher. They may come into the researcher's story because they enter the discourses and practices of the actors being studied. Metanarratives include, among others, those epic dramas of modernity associated with the cold war, colonialism versus anticolonialism, communism versus capitalism, the individual versus society, and the West versus the rest. Metanarratives enter lives when the discourses of historical agencies (nationalism, capitalism, socialism) are taken up by actors who become agents of those discourses. This chapter is a conceptual narrative of the glassworks and the struggles that occurred there, especially gendered ones.

Men and Masculinity at the Glassworks

"He's a bull of a worker," Dolan, the managing director, told me as we watched Liam, a highly skilled glasscutter, approach his cutting wheel. Liam, who overheard, gave Dolan a broad smile and pulled four crates of heavy glassware to his cutting machine from the marking area, the one place in the main shop floor space of the glass-cutting factory where a woman worked. Most other workers pulled one crate at a time or possibly two.

Liam was one of the most skilled glass cutters. With the highest production and the best weekly pay, management considered him their model worker. They pointed to him and his work habits when other workers complained of poor pay. They used him, as Dolan did at this moment, to produce public relations. When the few 1980s tourists and government officials visited the factory, Dolan explained the glass-cutting process by highlighting Liam. On this day, Dolan told Liam that I was an anthropologist who had come from the United States to study the factory. Dolan said, "Usually we visit the Yanks to learn about business, not the other way around." The three of us had a short conversation during which Dolan identified with Liam. Dolan uttered, "We are doing great things around here," as we departed Liam's work site.

This statement of identification between Dolan and Liam, the "we" that Dolan invoked, was part of a complex social positioning that the events of the next ten months would show, but, at that time and place, Liam identified with the subject position in which Dolan's discourse placed him. Dolan's speech action was determinate: it was taken up by Liam because it followed the story line of Liam's ontological narrative, his worker autobiography, one closely articulated to the public narrative of the firm.[4]

At that time, Liam's fellow workers considered him to be management's man. In his mid-thirties, he was one of the three remaining employees from the glassworks' original blue-collar workforce, "the twelve apostles," and his job had enabled him to fulfill his responsibilities and desires. With pride, he showed me the house he was having built for his family, his wife and two sons, at the end of 1984. Satisfied with his situation and his choices, Liam identified with the subject position that Dolan rendered to him.

Dolan articulated his identity to Liam's because he connected to Liam's productivity and masculinity. Dolan's utterance positioned Liam as hypermasculine and positively productive, "a bull," and the first-person pronoun, "we," enabled Dolan to take responsibility for the "great things" the firm was doing and the fact that its success story attracted foreigners. Dolan assigned joint responsibility for that success to Liam and his bullish practices. Liam accepted that partnership in productive prowess, so Dolan's utterance became a speech act: Liam and I took it up and made that utterance part of our reality. The pronoun "we," as used in that situation, is best understood as fulfilling the function of an indexical, not as a substitute for proper nouns. An indexical carries information about the speaker's identity, and it is creative when it sets up new relations or makes them explicit.[5]

The "we" here indexed Dolan and Liam as occupying the same spatial location and the same position in the local moral order's categories of person types (see Harré 1995). This was a positively valued position. It depended on the speaker's moral standing in relation to the counterspeakers and others in the moral community, and, at the time Dolan produced this speech act, he was a revered figure in Ballybogoin.

As discussed in the previous chapter, Dolan had rescued the glassworks and had won the respect of both Protestant and Catholic members of this bitterly divided town. His takeover of the firm enabled it to survive at a difficult historical moment, and Dolan's appropriation of the firm worked to sustain the ontological and public narratives with which Liam identified. Dolan's speech act indexed these narratives, and they abet understanding as to why masculine person types were valued by Liam, Dolan, and the townspeople more generally.

Liam's ontological narrative makes that interpretive process possible.

Liam had left school in his mid-teens and had been working as a laborer for two years in the mid-1960s when Father Finbarr raised enough money to start training workers. Apprenticing at the glassworks paid very little, even less than Liam's laboring job at a building site, and offered little status. Nonetheless, Liam joined the twelve young men who constituted the original group of trainees, several of whom had given up better paying jobs for the chance to become a skilled worker. They collected jam jars from parishioners of the local Roman Catholic parish, cut them, and sold them cheaply at local demonstrations. Liam told me he joined the glassworks because he wanted to settle in the area and have a family, and the cutting job offered the possibility of stability.

Meanwhile, as the previous chapter details, Father Finbarr was institutionalizing a foundational narrative for the firm, a public narrative he used to raise money from his parishioners, other townspeople, and the state development authority. Father Finbarr chose to address the crisis of social reproduction in the Ballybogoin area's Roman Catholic population by attending to the family. His first project was a cooperative housing development for families who were living doubled or tripled up in the homes of parents or siblings. His second community undertaking focused on employment and the discrimination against Catholic men. He did propose a series of home-based paid employment schemes for women that began but never materialized into any long-term work for them. The major aim of the local development association, then, was to provide skilled work for unemployed Catholic men.

Father Finbarr persuaded the young Catholic, underemployed workers that, as Liam told me, "we had something better in us." He enabled them to deploy a narrative that held they could support a family in Ballybogoin without having to emigrate. Father Finbarr enabled choice. He provided an agentive discourse, speech acts oriented to "the taking and assigning, accepting and repudiating of responsibility for actions" (Harré 1995, 123) to Liam and his workmates.

Father Finbarr's narrative thematized the glassworks as a firm that required skilled craftspeople who, once trained, would not be "made redundant." The founders of the firm believed that Catholics, if given a chance and a stable work environment, would become reliable workers and produce a quality product. The founding narrative also contested the dominant discourse about culture and economy in the area, that which held that Catholics operated from personal and cultural deficits that disabled their economic agency. One economist who became a key advisor to Northern Ireland's unionist government in the 1960s stated this position in 1955: "For generations they were the underdogs, the despised 'croppies', the adherents of a persecuted religion, who were kept out of public affairs by their Protestant conquerors. They were made to feel inferior, and to make matters worse they often were inferior, if only in those personal qualities that make for success in competitive economic life" (Wilson 1955, 208–9).

Several workers and many Ballybogoin nationalist townspeople remembered feeling inferior during the time that Father Finbarr was building his local development association and remembered that he countered that feeling. Liam remembered those days and identified the struggles of many people he knew who did not have proper houses as his motivation for deciding to become a glass cutter.

Asking, as Joan Wallach Scott does, "how implicit understandings of gender are being invoked and reinscribed" (1988, 49) in general social processes allows these narratives of the 1960s to be connected to the strike events of 1984 and 1985. Liam's ontological narrative deploys an agentive discourse, one that recounts the choices he made for his working life. He related his work autobiography to the desire to support a family, to work hard, and to be a man, an opportunity that the public narrative of the firm holds was denied to him by the local labor market. He realized his family obligations and his masculinity working at the glassworks, and they formed important values for him. The glassworks, in this reading, has afforded Liam's self-realization as a local masculine subject while meeting the instrumental values attached to providing for his family. Both ideal and instrumental practices constituted the glassworks.

Dolan narrated stories that reproduced this masculine ideology when I asked him about his history at the firm. He also performed it in his everyday managerial practices, such as his daily visits to the two shops, the glassblowing shop and the glass-cutting shop, which were housed in two buildings over one mile apart. At both these sites, Dolan produced speech acts like his description of Liam as a bull, and those acts articulated to a variety of stories of masculinity analogous to but different than Liam's.

Dolan, a Roman Catholic whose religious identity was revealed by both his Christian name and his surname in the Northern Ireland process of telling, was born and raised in an eastern region of Northern Ireland, a majority Protestant one. This marked him as different for local Catholics. They believed he did not interact artfully the way Ballybogoin people did. Many local Catholics considered him bullish and brutish.

For his part, Dolan desired his difference from the Ballybogoin nationalist community to be recognized. During my first interview with him, he told me how he transformed sales by going personally to a variety of clubs and ladies' societies, the vast majority of which were politically unionist and religiously Protestant. He told me that he hated the immediate interpreting of him as Catholic in those spaces, and he tried to make his political position clear. Dolan said that he did not want to be identified with nationalist politics, especially the republican nationalism of Sinn Féin, an identity that most unionists assigned to Catholics from this western region of Northern Ireland.

Dolan was known around Ballybogoin as "a dealing man," one who "could buy and sell you." Roman Catholic nationalists represented him as blunt and to the point and used metaphors like "bull" to describe him, figures they also used to name their Protestant fellow townsmen. He was "a dealing man" because he would become bullish and ignorant, meaning he would not listen, if his desires were not met. He "worked work" constantly. Although he was both respected and reviled for this trait, the quality of being like a bull was one he valued and identified with, as his comments about Liam show.

Dolan identified with Liam's bodily acts, his strenuous physical exertion and his speed at work. These bodily practices represented qualisigns of value for him: they signified value iconically. They exhibited value in themselves, and as signs they were part of a more comprehensive whole.[6] For Dolan and Liam such signs and their associated values constituted that whole, their intersubjective relations.[7] Dolan attempted to institute those practices and values through his favoritism of Liam. He desired to create networks that fostered the masculine values for which Liam's work practices served as signs.

The stories Dolan recounted about his strategies in reorganizing the glassworks when he took over in 1981 served to justify the reorganization he imposed on the workforce and his departure from the firm's foundational narrative. Dolan offered a different accounting of the workplace than did the workers and local people. In interviews, Dolan referred to Liam as "a man with work in him," and he opposed Liam, a man from the rural areas outside the town, to men from the working-class housing estates in the town who, Dolan said, "had no work in them."

Dolan identified himself as "a man from the country" as well, but he differentiated himself politically from "the men from the country" around Ballybogoin. He told me that "men from the country around here are daft" as he recounted to me the fact that the majority of Catholic nationalists from those areas voted for Bobby Sands as their MP at Westminster. Bobby Sands and his fellow hunger strikers were "bullish," too, but Dolan did not recognize their bodily acts as qual-isigns of value, whereas many of his workforce, who were supporters of Sinn Féin, did. Dolan believed that the men from the town with "no work in them" were solid supporters of Bobby Sands and the IRA. He fired most of those workers when he became managing director of the glassworks. Most men from the country kept their jobs even though many of them, Dolan believed, had questionable political ideas, but they were quiet about it. Liam was a quiet supporter of Sinn Féin, so, for Dolan, even he was marked with ambivalence.

Still, Dolan regarded Liam's acts as valued ones because they had the capacity to produce value in its economic, objective, and sociological, subjective senses. His acts produced more glassware and, therefore, profit for the firm. They fitted the accountants' story line that Dolan highly valued and extended the social relationship between Dolan and Liam, manager and worker. Linguistic practices, like the masculine banter that took place when Dolan visited the shop floor every day, signified the subjective links between this manager and his workers. Dolan's connections were made through commonalities of masculinity, the bullish practices that made profit, and the cultural practices that signified the manly mode, not the foundational narrative of community.

When I asked Dolan how he viewed Father Finbarr's dreams for the firm and his narrative about it, he scoffed. He said he admired and respected Father Finbarr but believed his idealism was wrongheaded. The business was about sales, Dolan insisted, not about community. Dolan understood Liam's acts as profitable, manly, and valuable because they opposed the discourse that Catholics had no work in them, but he did not see the glassworks as an employment scheme for Catholics. He told me that the workers he kept on were interested in building houses for their wives and children, as Liam and several other of the better paid workers had started to do. Dolan saw Liam's upward mobility as insurance for his firm.

As mentioned previously, during my first interview with Dolan, he told me he could keep the trade union at a distance if the workers were building houses and had mortgages, as Liam had. Such practices served as a hedge against the firm's uncertain future, and Dolan invested much in that narrative of masculinity and family responsibility that articulated to the firm's foundational narrative. Dolan did not take up the community discourse, although he was read by the workers as doing so.

Identities: Narrating Struggle, Emplotting Masculinity

Dolan's and Liam's ontological narratives articulated differently to both the firm's public narratives and the local nationalist ones. These differences indexed the nonfixity of their identities. They registered the evanescence of the unity that Dolan's speech act had achieved when he introduced me to Liam. The relationship between Dolan and Liam was an unstable ordering of multiple possibilities, as was that between management and workers generally and among the workers themselves. The social order at the factories constituted incompletely managed factors of difference from 1981, when Dolan took over, until late September 1984. During that period, there were no strikes and no extended conflicts, although Dolan fired more than one-third of the total workforce. That uneasy stability began to transform in September 1984, as the previous chapter notes, when labor unrest at the glassblowing factory became public.

The glassblowers' one-day strike led to the NILRA's (or LRA) proposing a fact-finding study of the entire glass-making process. That study resulted in a set of eleven recommendations. These included adding an additional shop steward for the glass cutters, who had no skilled worker to represent them, and the retiming of jobs in the company by outside time-study experts who would reassign value to the items workers produced. The glass cutters elected Liam as their shop steward and anticipated the 1985 retimings with trepidation.

The workers, both cutters and blowers, feared time studies because when they first underwent them in 1977, they transformed them into masculine contests, racing each other to see which man was the strongest and fastest. They had no knowledge of workplace struggle at the time, and those races, they later realized, led to more stringent timings and lost wages. They had no desire to repeat that history, so in the 1985 conflict they exchanged stories that hypothesized possible strategies of struggle. The rank-and-file workers worried about Liam, whom they admired as a worker but mistrusted as a shop steward. They identified him as "a company man" and believed management got the shop steward they desired. They believed Dolan's "we" had effects.

Glass Cutter Struggles

In early 1985, the production manager, Sean Murphy, lowered the prices the glass cutters would get on 1984 glassware items, and the edge cutters struggled to make the wages to which they were accustomed. At the end of March these cutters protested, met with management, and agreed to prepare lists of unsatisfactory edge-cutting piece rates. Two days later the edge cutters banned overtime, pending a determination of those piece rates they found unsatisfactory.

Liam, a flat cutter who was not directly affected by the new prices, prepared the edge cutter list in consultation with that group of workers and discussed the issues several times with management. But management remained adamant that the new prices were just, so the edge cutters, in protest, walked out of the factory after a May 6 meeting. That evening Liam told me, "The strike is the fault of one man, Sean Murphy." Liam believed that Murphy had arbitrarily assigned new prices to old items and that someone from outside the factory should have retimed them.

Still, Liam felt management's timings offered possibilities. He thought the edge cutters could try them for two months and then discuss the wages by looking at the average earnings over the period. "Some of the edge cutters are being stubborn," he said, adding, "the LRA report was a useless whitewash and I don't know why they bothered." The next morning the flat cutters and the ancillary workers in the cutting factory voted to strike and joined the edge cutters' picket line. Six days after the edge cutters walked out, both the skilled glassblowers and the blowing factory's ancillary workers voted, with some reluctance, to strike in support of the cutting factory strikers.

The picket line was manned for twenty-four hours a day, but it was not well organized. Ten to fifteen men participated regularly while the rest showed up sporadically. Divisions between men and women, who worked in different spaces in the factory, were evident from the beginning. All the nationalist, Catholic women workers and two of the four unionist, Protestant women workers came to the factory gates the first two days, but they did not walk the picket line. They stayed in their cars and watched. Most of them polished or packed finished glassware in the factory; they, like the men whose payment schemes differed from the dominant skilled workers, believed they had little stake in the strike. The strike's contentious issues did not relate to their work organization. When I asked them why they did not join the picket line, one young, Catholic, female glass polisher explained, "The men would slag us, so why bother." After the first week, none of the female workers and few men in their job categories came to the picket line. Female workers did not participate in the three major trade union meetings that were held at the Roman Catholic parish hall, and relatively few unskilled male workers did either.

The picketers, who wanted to keep glassware from getting out the factory gates, spent much time in conversation, sitting or standing in circles to talk, rather than marching in a line. They discussed the problems they encountered, and their story lines articulated to the firm's public narrative—to community, to the family, to gender, and to skill.

The overarching theme in the glassworkers' conversations was relationships—how to make and unmake them. Their interactions with Dolan preoccupied them. They recalled that his daily visits to them on the shop floor gradually declined after the September one-day walkout until they had almost no interaction with him. In the process, the occasions for those speech acts that located them and Dolan at the same moral location dwindled, but some workers believed Dolan could be persuaded to their position in the first two weeks of the strike. They remembered him in ways analogous to those in which they memorialized Father Finbarr, as a man who did a lot for the community and a man who was metonymic for the glassworks. Dolan, too, stood for the whole.

Many believed, as Liam did, that Murphy, the production manager, precipitated the strike with his new timings. One glassblower said that he talked to Dolan once about the new prices, and Dolan confessed that he did not understand the piece rate and bonus systems. "Murphy has baffled him with science," this man said. Several workers remembered that they worked hard for Dolan when he saved the firm from NIDA, who they believed desired to shut it down.

As cited in the last chapter, one glasscutter recalled, "Everyone worked hard for him because we thought he was more or less like us. Now, he gets all the credit. We never get any, and we created the profit." Murphy, they said, never talked to them and Dolan was getting like him. One of the younger, unskilled workers interjected with an observation about social distance: "We give a good, natural hard time to Peter, Francie, and Adrian [the younger, white-collar male staff] as they drive through the gate, but we are quiet for Dolan, Murphy, and Mullally [the senior management team] because they have power over us and could get us back when we go back to work." He added, "It's like striking against God. They could make life tough for you."

Dolan had demonstrated his distance and his power that very morning, the end of the strike's third week. Workers with families and mortgages expressed anxiety over the strike's duration, and Liam had become frustrated with management's intransigence. During the strike, the union's area representative, Bernadette, a woman who was the shop steward at a poultry plant about one mile north of the glassworks, stopped at the picket line every day, teaching Liam about workers' rights and shop steward responsibilities. Meanwhile, Dolan offended Liam by talking at him, not with him, in their negotiating sessions. Their "we" was unraveling. This particular morning, it snapped.

Dolan and a salesman, O'Leary, a local man who was a white-collar union member, were loading up the trunk of O'Leary's car with glassware. Liam, having learned about the strategies and importance of trade union solidarity from Bernadette, walked through the gate to ask O'Leary about moving glass through the picket line. He warned O'Leary that he would report him to his salesman's union for crossing the glassworkers' picket. Dolan made a remark that no one could decipher, but it was read as provocative by the workers who watched. It angered Liam, who walked back to the gate. As O'Leary drove past him, Liam kicked the wheel of his car, punched the hood, and pounded the roof a few times. Dolan went to his office and phoned the police. They arrived minutes later and began to apprehend Liam but stopped when a passerby told the RUC men that they had no warrant. Liam was not causing a disturbance, so they could not arrest him, this man explained. The police let Liam go.

The passerby warned the picketing men to watch out for the police and informed them of their rights. Deeply skeptical of RUC action, like most nationalists, this man had performed a fairly routine act in this particular nationalist community where many Catholics believed the RUC was an illegitimate, sectarian force. Most of the workers believed that, and since Dolan had summoned the police he was now identified with them. After this event, the workers understood Dolan as distant from them and the narrative of the firm. Their conversations moved from questioning his distance to interpreting it, and his acts began to be emplotted in local narratives of the British state.

On the picket line, stories circulated that Dolan took down the photograph of Father Finbarr that overlooked the lobby when Protestant unionists visited the factory. The strikers remembered how many times they had seen newspaper photos of Dolan giving crystal glassware as prizes at unionist events. They represented Dolan as a character who participated in the state's exclusion of them. They made sense of his summoning the RUC in terms of the local Irish nationalist narrative.

The shop steward for the ancillary workers began a conversation with the themes of that narrative the next morning. This man, Kevin, had received permission from the union to cross the picket line to keep the furnaces burning in case the strike was settled because the furnaces took weeks to reignite and get back to working temperature. At the picket line, he offered his interpretation of the encounter between Liam, Dolan, and the RUC. Standing in a circle of six men, he expostulated themes he had voiced a few days before. On that previous occasion, no one paid much attention, but this time his discourse was determinate. The workers surrounding him took up the speech acts in which he connected the state of things on the picket line to the state of affairs in a variety of countries in the media—El Salvador, South Africa, Nicaragua.

Kevin said that England needed a revolution, and one of his interlocutors uttered, "Yeah, the problems would be solved if we burned all the Protestants." Immediately, another man exclaimed, "What?" The speaker changed his statement to "burn all the governments" while Kevin continued. He said, "The government in Russia is no worse than the government here." This engendered an immediate reply from the firm's youngest worker, who said, "No, that's not so!" Kevin asked him, "How is it different?" The sixteen-year-old replied, "We can move around here more," and one of the skilled workers in the circle shot back, "How many days can you leave your house and go up the town without being stopped?" The young fellow winced, shook his head in agreement, and sunk it in his shirt collar.

It was a point taken up by the group, and it signified not only the surveillance rampant in the town but also the gendering of public space. As discussed at various points throughout this book, Ballybogoin, located in the western, majority Catholic half of Northern Ireland, underwent much violence in the 1970s and 1980s. Ballybogoin itself had been one of the most bombed towns in Northern Ireland throughout the 1970s, and it was a prime site of assassination in the 1980s. The roads leading to and from Catholic working-class housing estates were often blocked off by RUC or British army patrols. The nationalist rural areas had SAS units camping out in fields and sometimes commanding country roads at night. The workers often spoke of their inability to move and talked about how free they felt when they crossed the nearby border to the Republic of Ireland. Sometimes workers arrived late to their jobs because they had been interrogated at roadblocks. This restriction of their space feminized them. It restricted their mobility. They feared certain neighborhoods in Ballybogoin and believed the police would not protect them there.

The young man who believed striking against Dolan was "like striking against God" told a story about an encounter with the RUC he had a few nights before. He had one pint of beer with other strikers before going home and was stopped by the RUC. They told him he had the smell of rum on his breath and took him to the inspection area near his border village, tore through his car, yelled at him for being an "Irish drunk," and, while waiting for a breath analyzer test, kept screaming at him, interrogating him as to the place he drank and whether it was a place they would be welcomed. He felt they named pubs where militant republicans gathered, and he told them he did not drink at any of them. He was one of the least political men in the factory and not sympathetic to the IRA. He finally got his breath analyzer test. There was so little sign of alcohol it was laughable. The RUC let him go. Being restricted of movement, being confined to domestic spaces, and feeling unsafe under the eyes of patriarchal authority were aspects of all nationalist Catholic workers' lives in this area, but as the story of the picket line shows, nationalist Catholic women were the objects of those practices within their own community as well.

Feminizing Problems

Ballybogoin started off the year 1984 with a male unemployment rate near 40 percent, and it remained over 30 percent for the next two years. Catholics were two and one-half times as likely to be unemployed as Protestants for the remainder of the decade.[8] The glassworkers feared job loss, and they had little hope of transferring their skills to another place of employment. During the fourth week of the strike management composed a letter that they sent to all workers' homes. The letter stated, "The industrial action, which has continued since 6 May 1985, has now caused a situation where the Company can no longer continue the recurring expense of firing the furnaces. Accordingly, these furnaces will be 'turned off' on Monday 3 June 1985." It concluded, "It is with deep regret that we take this course, since the Drumcoo Glassworks furnaces have never been turned off before."

Letters in hand, most of the male workers showed up at the picket line the next morning, even those who had not previously appeared. Again, the women did not participate. All but one of the Protestant blue-collar women had found other jobs, but none of the Catholics had. The workers interpreted the letter differently and argued vehemently over possible strategies of action. The following conversation, starting with a short discourse about Dolan, demonstrates this:

> *Worker 1:* That's his last card he can play. What else can he do, sure? Let him, I know, but he could've played that last, that was his last card. And everybody knew it that was his last card from day one that we came out on strike. Now he has played. It's up to the lads to stand their ground.

After twenty minutes of argument, the conversation turned to the topic of returning to work but continuing to resist.

> *Worker 1:* That's right. If you get the lads in there, you'll not get them back. You're finished. If the majority says to go back in I'll keep my 75 p. [This meant that he would not remain a member of the union, whose dues were 75 p per week.] Everybody's saying about Peter, Peter O'Higgins. Peter O'Higgins needs a fucking medal cause the last negotiations fucking broke down this road over a pay rise. Peter left the union. Yes, he was fucking right.

Worker 2: I'm gonna leave the union myself, Patrick.

Worker 1: Ah, fucking, if it's gonna be a union, stand together. Aye.

Worker 3: Well, that's what he's gonna get if you don't go in and stand together.

Worker 2: They can break the union if they want. Back on Monday, he's gonna close it down and not take anybody back.

Worker 4: Not if we all stand together.

Worker 3: How can we all stand together if we're all on the dole [on welfare] signing on.

Worker 1: If we stand together, then we don't go back.

Worker 3: How do you stand together when you? I have a wife and child up there, a fucking big mortgage. How do I stand together with that there? I go for money, that's what I'm fucking here for.

Worker 1: There. We should've, we shouldn't've held the strike on. We never should've asked for the strike. Yous should've said, "All right, forget about it. I can't afford to go on strike."

Worker 3: Before we were out on strike I was worried about taking an hour off to go to take the fucking car off for an MOT [motor vehicle inspection]. That's about all I was fucking worried about. We've been on strike now for four fucking weeks.

Worker 1: That's why we got to hold out now.

The narrative of family, the masculine provisioning of it, the story of the firm that Dolan had so wisely invested in dominated the discussions for the rest of that day and during the final union meeting when the workers decided to return to the two factory sites. Mortgages, wives, and children got the blame from the many men who realized that accepting management's terms meant losing the strike. They represented that position by invoking "the wife." Many men uttered, "The wife won't let me stay out," during that day and during the final trade union meeting.

This meeting occurred after the shop stewards, the union's area representative from the poultry plant, the regional trade union representative, and even the Northern Ireland leader of the union negotiated the terms of the workers' return. The only concession they got from management was a promise not to victimize any participants in the strike. Otherwise, the workers had to go back under the terms for which they struck.

When the ATGWU representative told the workers the news about no victimization, they all cheered. Everyone knew that meant Liam would keep his job, but it was announced that Liam would no longer be shop steward. The condition not to victimize depended on Liam's removal from his union post. New elections for shop steward would have to take place. After this announcement one of the ancillary workers stood up and said, "There's no better man than Liam McBride, and they made him loss the head off him. That's what happens when he gets no thanks for all that he's done." The workers cheered and took up a collection for Liam because of all he had done for them. Dolan had castrated his bull, and the workers wanted to compensate Liam.

Two days later the workers returned to work. That night I went to a local pub with several of them. As we sat there drinking beers, a pint was delivered to me by the barman. He pointed to a stool at the bar where O'Leary, the salesman whose car had been kicked and pummeled by Liam, sat. After a few minutes, I went to sit with him since the pint was a message to do just that. O'Leary, who obviously did not want to engage the workers, sidled up to me to tell me all that he knew.

O'Leary identified the four workers who voted against accepting management's "agreement." He then explained Liam's transformation during the strike. "That woman from the poultry plant, Bernadette, she led Liam astray," he said. He cast me another knowing look and presented his evidence. Liam, he heard, had gotten into a car with Bernadette one night as the picket line was under way, and the windows had steamed up. I pointed out to him that such an occurrence was not unusual on damp Irish nights when people talked in their cars and that Bernadette had been advising Liam on the workers' rights and trade union tactics during the first eleven days of the strike, when the workers could not get a response from either the regional office or the Northern Ireland office of the union. O'Leary, the white-collar union member, a middle-class man, did not recognize my emplotment of these events. His version circulated among his middle-class networks in Ballybogoin.

For many of the middle-class people in the Ballybogoin Catholic nationalist community, Liam's reputation as a family man was put into question. For his fellow workers, it never was, but the "we" that this model worker had established with management's network had dissolved. The workers' story line, that "no finer man" than Liam could be found and that "he lost the head" because management did not recognize either Liam or them, did not move beyond their social ties. The third-person references to Dolan that marked the first exchanges of the workers' conversations cited previously located Dolan as socially distant, not sharing the same moral order.

Patrick said that Dolan "played his last card," and he had no doubt that Dolan intended to win. It was a zero-sum game, and Dolan's "last card" had more power than any move the workers could muster. But it was not only his power that enabled Dolan to rule the results. The narratives through which both management and workers emplotted these events had profound effects. The narrative of masculine family provisioning in which Dolan had invested returned dividends for him and provided the rationale for most workers' acceptance of management's harsh terms. The hegemonic social order bolstered by the narrative that "real men" work hard for their families and ought to invest in housing had been naturalized and made immutable.

The rationality installed at the glassworks was a masculine one. At the end of the strike, most of the factory's men represented themselves through a nonagentive discourse: "the wives" wouldn't let them stay out. Women were assigned responsibility for the breakup of male, trade union solidarity. But this discursive practice articulated the wives to a valued accounting, the firm's public narrative of family/community viability and male provisioning. "The wives" subverted male class solidarity in the cause of the valued masculine practices of provisioning for families that the foundational narrative of the firm reinforced.

Management's gendered emplotment of the strike positioned a woman as the source of disorder, as antivalue. At the final union meeting, a second narrative emerged. The workers complained to the trade union officials that the media misrepresented them as violent and disorderly. Liam's outburst, featured in the media accounts, became a metonym for the strike as a whole among Ballybogoin's Irish nationalist citizens. The workers told of townspeople telling them, "The community owns that factory, and you have no business shutting it down. Get back to work." They attributed this interpretation to management's having "the media locked up." The media's narrative was management's, and the stories that circulated informally through the middle-class networks around the town after the strike plotted a woman as the cause of that perceived disorderliness. They narrated the transformation of Liam from model worker to disorderly strike leader as the pollution of a male ideal, as feminine. They disconnected Liam from the narrative of family reproduction that the firm so highly valued.

Liam lost his position at the center of the factory and became a marginal figure because he took advice from a woman who had the workers at her factory take up a collection for chicken, which they roasted and brought to the strikers on the picket line; a woman who fostered solidarity with her union members and the glassworkers; a woman who gave support when the trade union officials at headquarters did not respond to Liam's urgent requests for help; and a woman who won the respect of all the striking workers—Protestant and Catholic, men and women. Bernadette had helped to instigate a different social ordering, a new intersection of ties and accounts that functioned to mobilize workers around the category "class." Liam had reinforced that emergent ordering, but more powerful narrative and political networks halted those practices that were reconfiguring social ties and the bookkeeping and narrative accounts that mobilized them.

With the "agreement" between workers and management, workers became alienated from the union. No skilled worker would take up Liam's shop steward position. Seamus, the glassblowers' shop steward, resigned soon after, and no skilled worker assumed that post either. Masculine metaphors and themes permeated the emplotments that prevailed, and they indexed the terms of degradation. The shop stewards appeared disempowered and readily feminized. It was a position of questionable value. Maybe that young worker was right: striking against Dolan was "like striking against God," God in all his maleness.

8

Rendering Accounts

The true symbol of the British conquest is in Robinson Crusoe. The whole Anglo-Saxon spirit is in Crusoe; the manly independence and the unconscious cruelty; the persistence; the slow yet efficient intelligence; the sexual apathy; the practical, well-balanced, religiousness; the calculating taciturnity.

James Joyce, "Daniel Defoe"

Ballybogoin people, both Catholic and Protestant, but especially Catholic, share some of the same views of the English that Joyce does in the opening quote. In fact, this citation describes what Seamus meant by the term "workin' work." Seamus saw the merits, as Joyce did, of that "slow yet efficient intelligence" and that "taciturnity" that he saw in his unionist neighbors and workmates and that he perceived as the necessary, part-time personality of Catholics, but he was more at home with accelerated interaction, wit, *craic,* and the everyday practices entailed in "workin' moves." He lived by both "workin' work" and "workin' moves," and that doubleness, that split subjectivity, he believed, characterized Catholic difference within Northern Ireland and distinguished the Irish as a whole from the British. His "side of the house," he often repeated, had to both "work moves and work work" to get by.

This pair of signifiers represents a mixing of cultural practices. "Both sides of the house" participated in that mixing in their everyday lives, but to varying degrees. Starting with the four introductory tours of this book, those hybrid practices become apparent. Each tour took similar cultural form. Each person brought me to their significant places, each told stories with similar narrative structure, albeit different content, and each conducted the entire event in the same pattern. All the guides picked me up at my living place, took me to the sites that had meaning for them, and brought me back to their houses for tea before returning me to my apartment. All had a very similar mode of hospitality; each had an analogous way of making such an event meaningful. Northern Irish Protestant participation in such cultural forms rendered them a bit different than the English, from the Catholic perspective, and the Protestants recognized that difference as well.

The tours, however, indicated difference (understood here as a structure of power organized around a system of binaries) as they indexed a sharing of cultural forms.[1] In these tours, my guides moved through places that they perceived as opened or closed to them. They remembered the past as they traveled through these places and the binaries; planter and native, colonizer and colonized, Protestant and Catholic permeated the landscape. When they subjected their habitual bodily movements to discourse, they remembered the state and its practices: the Church of Ireland building to which Kathleen McDuffy brought me and its colonial reorganization by the British military, the unwillingness of Colm to put his body "out of place" in the territory of that church, the industrial sites and their identifications with the British modernity (one fostered strongly by the colonial state in Ireland) that Ian valued, the challenge to the state and its past that Ronan's bodily gestures constantly made.

All these signifiers indexed the fact that these people may have been hybrid and split subjects who shared two sides of the same house of cultural practices, but they were also subject to a state history and a set of state institutions that focused their cultural acts in ways that divided an "us" from a "them." Public spaces were marked by a binary in which the first terms of Britain/Ireland, unionist/Irish nationalist, Protestant/Catholic, valleys/hills, industry/agriculture, state/citizens, "the square"/"the OK corral," orange/green, and union jack/tricolor dominated decisively.

This book tries to show the dynamics of this dominant binary and the challenges to it at a variety of sites from the domestic to the public. It focuses on the level of everyday life and the location practices that occurred in a variety of spaces. The writing has not followed a linear trajectory dictated by theoretical argument. Instead, different episodes are juxtaposed to each other to demonstrate the density of contradictory relationships among people in Ballybogoin, the values they attribute to a variety of specific places, and the state's capacity to enter the events that people produced in the various place-worlds in which they dwelt.[2]

In a number of the stories and events represented, memories and perceptions of state practices or the actions of state agents entered the dialogic practices of persons with one another and with the landscape. These episodes demonstrated the power of the state to insinuate itself into the everyday practices that produce meaning. Conversations between Catholics and Protestants often stopped when the state was invoked. People who shared cultural practices and valued analogous methods of making meaningful relationships were divided when those acts articulated to the state's practices.[3] "Workin' work" dominated when citizens foregrounded identity with the state.

The first two chapters, for example, try to capture the power of the two firsts, the Ulster unionist (a version of a British nationalist narrative) and Irish nationalist stories, that legitimate so much division and violence in Ballybogoin. These narratives have epistemological and performative dimensions. They render knowledge of the social world to those who take them up, while they have the effect of dividing the relationships of persons and restricting their sociality no matter how many everyday cultural practices they share with those on the other side.

Such division occurred during the night out with the nailer and his Protestant mates, with the state narratives that the official from the ATGWU used in his attempt to persuade the glassworkers to continue their strike, and the entry of the police into management and worker relations at the strikers' picket line. All these episodes indicate how memories of state actions and practical consciousness articulate in the complex social field of the Ballybogoin region. They convey the processes through which subjects get fixed in their national identities as they repeatedly perform the British unionist and Irish nationalist repertoires that constitute everyday life.

This book shows that the British state worked to organize this opposition more powerfully than any group or institution. The very mapping of time and space and everyday bodily movements bore a marked sectarian division, one policed by the variety of state security services that permeated the area in the 1980s. Such actions enabled memory and history, particularly the history that signified war and the state's colonial division of territory, to exert force in and around Ballybogoin. People from "both sides of the house" drew upon memories and differing accounts of the state's history to produce a set of foundational skills that enabled them to move through social space, to create hypotheses for social action, and to justify both past and future acts of violence and exclusion.

E. Valentine Daniel alludes to the importance of such everyday skills and their ordering function in his consideration of another violent place, Sri Lanka. Daniel writes, "To be able to have some control over what would happen (future subjunctive) is to be part of the movement of signs in time, to be part of anthroposemeiosis, to be part of the project of being human. When the future is so uncertain as to be nonexistent, *semeiosis* is essentially choked off; so is 'human' life" (1996, 125). When such semiosis, the continuous production of meaning through signs, stops, then future prospects dim, as do recollections of a shared past. It is in such situations of uncertain knowledge and "epistemic murk" that death spaces proliferate (see Taussig 1987, 3–36, 127–38).

Telling and its function of focusing on the form of relationship, not the content, halt the production of meaning and disallow semiosis when bodies are read as other. Such daily encounters render future prospects uncertain and, in 1980s Ballybogoin, the practices of the state's agents, particularly the security forces, and the political violence of the IRA and the various loyalist paramilitaries fostered an environment for telling in everyday life that contributed to constraining the meaning making among all groups. This book tries to show that colonial legacies enter into these difference-making practices and that they form a significant part of the difficulties in fostering a shared politics, a common struggle over the future, or even the resources to debate them, at the start of the twenty-first century.

The British state, its history and memories of it as well as its contemporary actions, have abetted the construction of a powerful political and social boundary in Ballybogoin. The opposing poles pull culturally mixed persons to their different corners over and over again. Practices that created associative ties and unified group actions, such as the annual Orange Order marches that united Protestant British citizens while it divided them from Catholics, marked the events entailed in chapter 2. In 2001 and in their late twenties, Stevie and Patrick, the boys depicted in that chapter, talk again, and the fact that Stevie, a Protestant, has found a job with an Irish nationalist employer has much to do with that transformation of their relations. It is not, however, a relationship in which Patrick invests much. He still has no across-the-divide friendships, although he does have Protestant acquaintances, a situation that reproduces the norm in Ballybogoin.

Patrick and Mickey, it is argued in chapter 2, are racialized by the spatial strategies of the Orange Order and the state, as well as by the local classification of bodies. Unionist/loyalist political rituals are exclusionary ones that symbolically construct national identity for its participants, while those disallowed from partaking in them do not share the substance that renders the political rights of these British citizens as natural ones. Anthropologist Elliott Leyton, in his study of Protestant kinship practices, has recorded that Protestants in the village he studied referred to themselves as being of "one blood" (see Leyton 1975). The various Orange Order ceremonies and their logic institute such metaphors of race, colonizing and exclusionary processes, at this postcolonial moment. They marginalize Catholics by stimulating them to an exit from their home places in order to feel safe. Still, "postcolonial" seems the more apt phrase to characterize these Northern Ireland 1980s and 1990s cultural practices if we maintain the sense of postcolonial as the simultaneous operation of colonizing and decolonizing processes (Frankenberg and Mani 1996; Kiberd 1996). Catholic, Irish nationalist citizens resist these excursions into their neighborhoods, and, with the cessation of violence, these struggles have become the focus of political conflict and political difference throughout the 1990s and into the new century (see Bryan 2000).

Discourses are not innocent. The anthropological discourses on Ireland certainly are not. They have articulated to colonial discourses. The contrast between the anthropological discourse on rural Ireland, established by anthropologists from the United States, and the Ballybogoin emphasis on talk makes the point that cultural categories, national ones particularly, are not the best place to begin ethnographic discussion. Cultural practices whose effects are the naturalization of these categories seem a more suitable place to begin.

Talk, a valued practice in Ballybogoin, at least among nationalists (and, I think, for unionists in a somewhat different form), made relations in a society where subjectivities were difficult to assume due to the practice of telling. The practices entailed in talk, then, were a site of associative ties from which local and regional identities were constructed. They transformed subjects, joined them together, and were an important part of the challenge to institutional authority. We cannot assume that such challenges arise from an inherent quality of national character, as some of the anthropology of rural Ireland does. Ethnographers need to record such practices and trace their effects.

Ballybogoin's Irish nationalist cultural forms, *craic* in particular, enabled people to live on the edge, to perform their cultural differences by enacting mixed cultural forms through split selves. Protestants valued and produced *craic*, but Catholics often did not recognize this as they used it to mark their separate identity. Chapter 4 shows how this occurred and demonstrates the depth to which space was marked with division in Ballybogoin and how different temporalities coexisted. It depicts how people who negotiate the sharp edges of Ballybogoin's sectarian divide did so in the mid-1980s. The crucial element in forging or negating such relationships was negotiating with the state. Catholics, as the stories told in that chapter indicate, understood the state to consistently work against their "side of the house," and they had a tendency to perceive the state as metonymic for Protestants, a fact that could tear across-the-divide friendships apart.

There were many internal borders in Ballybogoin during the 1980s. The state was articulated to all of them, and its work had to be ignored to keep cross-community relations alive. When engaging the limits of Ballybogoin society, the nailer had to desaturate himself from the divided memories and the contradictory meanings that the state, among other institutions, helped to organize. The nailer attempted to transform his sociality and move it away from the nationalist identity people assumed for him, but transgressing the positions on which others placed him limited his desired networks of affiliation. When he remained silent with his nationalist friends during the many conversations that articulated to politics, he could not be read. He became "as deep as a well" to his mates who cared about him. They did not know what to say to him in particular conversational contexts.

As the story of our night out shows, the nailer encountered serious constraints in talking with his Protestant mates. He read their versions of social processes in South Africa differently than they did. When he provided his account of a black South African's foot dragging, he was positioned as other, not modern like the "natives" in South Africa. Talk stopped.

During my fieldwork, Catholics talked back to the state and its colonizing processes, including those that erased their history and still do. They understood that their history has been lost in space, as demonstrated by their imagination of the future archeology of the castle hill. They brought past and present together in their dreams of transforming O'Neill's fort into a tourist site. In doing so, they challenged, yet again, the hegemonic order. The past became theirs through these spatial stories, and the politics of memory was at work. The present affected the past (see Boyarin 1994). Such practices criticized modernity by offering a different temporality than the modern, lineal one so valued in the narrative of nation-states (see Bhabha 1994, 171–97, 236–56).

These critical practices may be labeled as resistance to a dominant hegemonic order and often are in social science accounts of conflict situations. This book is more concerned with these everyday acts in respect to the ways in which their practitioners draw on social orders in attempting to construct a coherent social world than it is with reading them as resistance. Irish nationalist practices that criticized the hegemonic social order occurred in each of the spaces depicted in this book, but they did not move out of those spaces into a series of articulations that peacefully challenged authority in the realm of civil society. The three chapters on organizing against colonial history, for a strike, and for retaining working men's masculinity evidence the dearth of organizational instruments available to Ballybogoin's Catholic citizens, both in the 1960s and in the 1980s.

At these moments, the state did little to extend accountability, that is, to embed "the decision making center in networks of autonomous political institutions that limit the arbitrariness of incumbents" (Stark and Bruszt 1998, 188). People in and around Ballybogoin had few institutions that they could put to use.[4] Spreading accountability across institutions and across the various groups in Ballybogoin might have enabled forms of civil society to develop, but this did not occur. The strike at the glassworks shows how difficult the creation of such networks was in Ballybogoin.

The strike and other struggles at the factory show how talk constituted a resource for Ballybogoin's Irish nationalist people. They relied on it as an instrument of persuasion and as a means to form group relations through the sharing of narratives. In the context of the strike, talk, speech acts, became an instrument to challenge and criticize the institutionalization of modernity through the internal labor markets that were established at the glassworks, a place that had fashioned itself as an alternative employer, "a community enterprise," but these performances did not find embodiment in institutions that were not saturated by the state and its meanings.

Many workers valued the mouth, not the eye, in the factory, and that bodily organization placed them outside the modern in the dominant discourses both inside and outside the factory. This became clear after the strike ended, when those who would not participate in the new internal labor market got labeled as other, as persons from "Wobland" who did not know how to navigate life outside their particular localities. This was reminiscent of colonial discourse, and it was easy to bring it to bear to marginalize recalcitrant workers.

In this failure to make an organized class grouping that stood united against management and used the trade union to fulfill its needs, talk unarticulated to organization showed its lack of social power. This replicated the situation that existed for Ballybogoin's working people in many areas of their lives. They had no space to come together and organize. The Roman Catholic parish hall was the only space the workers could find for their meetings, and it was not a space in which everyone felt comfortable. Several of the Protestant workers did not want to enter the Irish Street side of the town where the hall was located, and a few of them worried about the conspiratorial plans of the local Roman Catholic priests at a crucial moment during the strike.

One of the largest, most productive union meetings during the strike was broken up by one of the older, unskilled Protestant workers who came into the parish hall, huffing and puffing, after having rushed to the meeting from the picket line. He said management had found a way to ship glass through the factory gates. Upon hearing this, the workers charged out of the meeting to attend to the problem. It was their most unified moment of the entire struggle.

When they got to the factory gates, they found an old retired priest from the United States who was touring the area and wanted to buy a few items of glass to bring home. Management had arranged to let him into the retail shop. The Protestant workers who manned the picket line that day had not wanted to go to the Roman Catholic parish hall. Several feared going. When they saw this priest they believed he was conspiring with management to smuggle glass out to the firm's retail customers. The workers, whose crucial meeting was interrupted and ended when they rushed to support the picketers, did not hold the cessation of their organizational efforts against these Protestant men. They just rolled their eyes and lightly laughed at their conjuring up a conspiracy of priests.

Ballybogoin was a militarized space and a highly gendered one, as chapter 7 clearly indicates. The relations made through talk in public spaces, primarily pubs, were usually male ones. When women came to the picket line, they were "slagged" and felt unwelcome. Bernadette, the shop steward from the nearby poultry plant who had trade union savvy, tried to get the glassworks' women to join the picket line, but she could not persuade them. There was little space for women workers' voices in that male space. Talk, then, which was an instrument of empowerment for the exploited at certain moments, became an instrument of aggression and exclusion. That aggression remained after the strike in the rumors about Bernadette, who, loyal to the trade union movement, had put her quite substantial knowledge of labor struggles into the service of the inexperienced trade unionists at the glassworks. Management used her to feminize the workers who did not go along with the internal labor market. She got the blame for sending those workers "astray."

All these situations and the discourses that accompanied them articulated, in one form or another, to colonial discourses. Each episode, however, contains decolonizing moves directed against Northern Ireland's particular colonial modernity. They all index the difficult politics of location that Ballybogoin people, all of them, faced. Both the unionists and the Irish nationalists have been made subjects in relation to the colonial past and the meanings of it that get repeated today. Such positionings were not unrelated to the violence and the imagination of it that so permeated life in Ballybogoin in the 1980s.

Violence entered people's domestic spaces in a myriad of ways, but for Ballybogoin's Irish nationalists, who are the primary concern of this ethnography, the state saturated the social field and delivered the most powerful violence of representation and the physical violence of space patrolled and weapons deployed. This book shows that state practices rendered opposing positions as illegitimate in a variety of Ballybogoin's nationalist social spaces, from the workplace to the public square. Its agents, as well as other actors, instituted a politics of location, specifically one of class and nation, that positioned Irish nationalist working-class people as subaltern, as people whose knowledge and means of representing it were deemed less worthy if not illegitimate.

Since the Anglo-Irish Agreement of 1985, however, the United Kingdom of Great Britain and Northern Ireland, through the concerted actions of a variety of its agents, has directed itself to setting up new democratic organizations that extend the accountability of the state by widening the network of institutions in which it is embedded. This development has halted at times, but consultations between the Republic of Ireland and Great Britain have occurred regularly since 1985. The 1990s witnessed an intensifying of this relationship and an evolution of these organizations, and negotiations among the British and Irish governments and with Northern Ireland's nationalist parties led to the IRA cease-fire that began in August 1994. This cessation of violence was interrupted by several IRA military attacks, but since 1996 the cease-fire has stabilized.

The ending of IRA violence enabled multiparty negotiations to take place among Northern Ireland's main unionist party, the Ulster Unionist Party, several smaller unionist parties, the Northern Ireland Women's Coalition, the Alliance Party, the Labour Party, and the nationalist parties, the SDLP and Sinn Féin. Senator George Mitchell of the United States, General John de Chastelain of Canada, and ex-Prime Minister Harry Holkerri of Finland chaired these talks. This organization demonstrates the networks of accountability that were at work during the negotiations, and this embeddedness in a wider nexus of relationships helped the negotiations to succeed.

On April 10, 1998, an agreement, variously called the Good Friday Agreement or the Belfast Agreement, was reached, and it was endorsed in referenda that were held in both Northern Ireland and the Republic of Ireland. Its major innovation is a devolved Assembly for Northern Ireland that is organized around the parallel consent of British unionists and Irish nationalists. It pays heed to relations with the Republic of Ireland through the creation of a Ministerial Council that will operate across the Republic of Ireland Northern Ireland border, and it sets up modes of cooperation between the Republic of Ireland, Northern Ireland, Scotland, and Wales through a British-Irish Council.[5]

For Ballybogoin's Catholics, the major appeal of the agreement is its commitment to an equality agenda, whose fruits they are seeing as the security forces leave their streets. They are no longer under the acute surveillance of the 1980s, but the memory of their differential treatment by the police and army lingers. In fact, police reform and security concerns, such as the disarmament of the IRA, remain the biggest stumbling blocks in carrying out the promise of the Good Friday Agreement. For Irish nationalists who desire recognition of their cultural and national identity by the new bureaucratic bodies created by the British state in consultation with the Irish one, police reform and institutions that account for and make clear the nature of state violence during Northern Ireland's thirty-year "troubles" will serve as signs that the state apprehends their concerns. By the summer of 2001, these signs had not been produced. The ability of Irish nationalists to hold the state accountable to acts committed against their communities has not met their desires. The state's rendering of such accounting procedures will take much political work, and it needs to abandon its attempts to control and regulate these bodies and to extend accountability to its citizens (see Kelleher 2000).

As this book shows, decolonization in places like Ballybogoin, Northern Ireland, is a huge task. Past violence from all three sides—the British state, Ulster unionists and loyalists, and Irish nationalists—infiltrates a variety of social spaces through its political and cultural force and people's complex memories of it. The meanings of the colonizing state's production of itself and its Irish other endure. This weighs heavily on the people of Ballybogoin and its surrounds. The work of accounting for it and trying to make the state and civil society anew remains enormous.

Notes

⌐‾‾‾‾‾

Introduction

1. The names of all the people in this ethnography, other than my own, are pseudonyms. The name of the town and those of its surrounding villages are pseudonyms as well. Much of the fieldwork completed for this book was done in moments of extreme violence and danger. I promised those consulted for this book anonymity. As discussed in the preface, I am aware that more knowledge could be gleaned by contextualizing these events precisely in terms of statistical information and location, but such precision would be irresponsible in the Northern Ireland context. I have tried to protect the privacy of all the individuals represented in this book. I hope readers will honor their wishes to remain anonymous.

2. Throughout this book, "the British security forces" refers to the British army, the Northern Ireland police—the Royal Ulster Constabulary—and the Ulster Defense Regiment, a locally raised and mainly part-time unit of the British army that was created in 1970.

3. Scheper-Hughes includes this quote from one of her consultants in the second, paperback edition to her award-winning book. This inclusion, unusual in its time, was a very brave move, one that has helped subsequent field-workers of Ireland to reflect on their practices.

4. Although I use de Certeau's definitions of space and place here, I do not adhere to this notion of the differences between these terms in the remainder of the book. Conforming to anthropological understandings of place, I use place to represent the appropriation of physical space by social actors, particularly the attribution of meaning to physical space. De Certeau's depiction, however, provides an apt meaning for discussing the relationship I am trying to grasp here, so I use his categories to understand this situation.

5. In Ballybogoin, Irish nationalists and Irish republicans were distinguished from one another. Both groups aspire to a united Ireland, a nation-state that

would join the six of the nine counties of the Province of Ulster that make up Northern Ireland to the twenty-six counties of the Republic of Ireland, three of which are Ulster counties—Donegal, Monaghan, and Cavan. In Ballybogoin, the term "Irish nationalist" refers to people who desire this political entity but do not believe violence is a legitimate means to achieve it. Locally, Irish republicans are those people who think violence is justified, and those people form the support community of the IRA. On the distinction between Irish nationalists and republicans in Northern Ireland as a whole, see Ruane and Todd (1996, 71–72).

6. The metaphor of the house, a divided house, was often used by Ballybogoin's Catholics to describe their locality. "The two sides of the house," "our side of the house," and "the other side of the house" were invoked constantly to mark where people stood on a variety of issues. See Larsen (1982a).

7. Throughout this book I distinguish loyalist from unionist. Each term represents a different strand of unionist political culture. Ulster loyalists, although fervently unionist and desirous of the continued union with the United Kingdom of Great Britain and Northern Ireland, place their allegiances to Ulster (the six counties of Ulster that make up Northern Ireland) first and to the United Kingdom second. Ulster unionists identify themselves as British first and associate themselves with Ulster second. See Todd (1987) and Bruce (1994, 1–2).

8. The story of O'Neill is well known. Sources on his career in Ireland are plentiful. For useful summaries, see Bardon (1992, 87–118) and Foster (1988, 3–44).

9. For a historical consideration of the conflict up until 1996, see Coogan (1996). Coogan discusses the cease-fire and its 1996 interruption in the epilogue to this book (406–38).

10. Border areas often have a marked effect on social, cultural, and political life. For anthropological discussions of these borderland issues that give cause for reflection on Northern Ireland border issues, see Wilson and Donnan (1998) and Donnan and Wilson (1999).

11. Telling has been recorded extensively in ethnographic work in the city of Belfast, especially in those neighborhoods beset by political violence. See Aretxaga (1997, 35–36); Burton (1978, 47–67); and Feldman (1991, 56–59). Telling receives little attention in ethnographic work outside these urban areas. There is little mention of it as an organizing force in rural areas.

12. On matter out of place and its use in the classification of groups, see Douglas (1966) and Leach (1964). Allen Feldman (1991) has brilliantly dealt with questions of the body, dirt, formations of violence, and enactments of political classification.

13. On the contaminating touch and discussions on the interaction between discourses on dirt, high/low distinctions, and their relations to the domains of space, the body, the social formation, and psychic forms, see Stallybrass and White (1986, 125–90).

14. Feminizing discourses abound in colonial representations of Ireland, and images of women figure prominently in nationalist representations of themselves as well. For literary analyses of such representations, see Innes (1993) and Jones

and Stallybrass (1992). Begoña Aretxaga (1997) has linked these images to political organizing and the transformation of political subjectivity in Belfast.

15. George Marcus has engaged the problems of realist ethnography and the late-twentieth-century moment of experimentation that challenges them. See Marcus and Cushman (1982); Clifford and Marcus (1986); Marcus and Fischer, 2d ed. (1986); and Marcus (1998).

16. Feminist contributions to modernist experiments have been neglected by the major critics of realist ethnography. For criticisms of the critics see Gordon (1988). For feminist essays that demonstrate experimentation see Ginsburg and Tsing (1990). A number of full-length ethnographies demonstrate such feminist experimentations and innovative theorizations. For studies that address subject matter similar to that in this book, with silencing, colonialism, narrative, and spatial marginalization, see Aretxaga (1997); Steedly (1993); Stewart (1996); and Tsing (1993).

17. Richard Parmentier (1987, 1–19) discusses the use of historical signs in social action, but the mode of retrieving them in Belau, the society he studies, is different than the recovery of the past through fragments that Ballybogoin people use in social action. Sutton (1998) describes a European setting that more closely resembles the uses of memory in Ballybogoin.

18. For an interesting discussion of structure and its problems, one that addresses its social scientific aspects, not its relation to writing, but whose thrust reinforces some of the criticisms addressed in the writing culture debates, see Varela and Harré (1996).

19. See Scheper-Hughes (1982, v–xiv) for an extended discussion of the responses of villagers to her text.

20. On Rabelaisian laughter, see Bakhtin (1984, 59–144) and Stallybrass and White (1986, 6–26, 183–90).

21. Jean and John Comaroff (1991, 1–48) address the questions of fixed identities and their relation to power, culture, representation, ideology, and current theoretical debates. I have learned much from their discussions of culture, hegemony, and ideology, but I find their arguments and demonstrations for fixity less than convincing and adopt Hall's (1996b) notions of identity to better understand how the world appears fixed.

22. Joseph Ruane and Jennifer Todd (1996, 16–48) have discussed the cultural reverberations of these colonial oppositions and have provided an interesting genealogy of the contemporary cultural formation in which the meanings of these opposed categories live. The actual processes of settling the plantation are detailed in Robinson (1984).

23. For an important discussion of these two firsts and their ramifications for Northern Irish society today, especially the role of these narratives in reproducing stereotypes, see Deane (1990, 3–19).

24. This trope of modernity, resistance and accommodation, and Catholic foot dragging permeates much of the writing on the modernization of the island of Ireland. Both Beckett's (1966) and Foster's (1988) important works are organized around this powerful story line.

25. Stark and Bruszt (1998) are discussing the transformative processes in a

NOTES TO PAGES 24-34

changing Eastern Europe in the discussion cited here. I use their concepts and those of Stark throughout this book because they address the different transformations in Northern Ireland in productive ways.

Chapter 1

1. In 1983 the city council in Londonderry, with an Irish nationalist majority, changed the name of the council to the Derry City Council. This aroused consternation among some unionists. Ian Paisley led a march to Stormont to protest the council's name change. Neither the city nor the county had their name changed. On the politics of nomenclature introduced by the plantation, see Moody (1980).

2. See Beresford (1987) for a thorough discussion of this crucially important event for the recent history of Northern Ireland.

3. I lived in Belfast for nine months prior to moving to Ballybogoin to carry out ethnographic fieldwork.

4. Although I qualify the use of the term "colonial" to describe the Northern Ireland crisis, I am in agreement with Seamus Deane's (1990) analysis that the crisis is a colonial one. His discussions of colonial distinctions, stereotypes, and narrative are ones from which I have learned much. I follow several of his leads throughout this book. The understanding of the postcolonial that I adopt here enables the ethnographic articulation of everyday practices to the larger social formation. I want to question the binary division of Ballybogoin into the colonizer and colonized, but I want to examine colonizing processes in articulation to those that oppose them from "both sides of the house."

5. On the technologies of colonial rule see Cohn and Dirks (1988).

6. Although they do not advocate this category of the postcolonial per se, Ann Laura Stoler and Frederick Cooper (1997) outline a research agenda that the concept enables.

7. There are now many studies demonstrating this process, especially those that address colonial and anticolonial nationalisms. See Anderson (1983) and Chatterjee (1986, 1993).

8. Homi Bhabha has addressed these processes in a number of essays. See Bhabha (1994). For discussions of the time of the postcolonial and the mutual constitution of the colonized and colonizers, see Hall (1996b).

9. For a theoretical elaboration on this position see Frankenberg and Mani (1996, 287–92).

10. The chronology on Hugh O'Neill is derived from Bradshaw, Hadfield, and Maley (1993, xvii–xix). See Bardon (1992, 75–118) for information on Hugh O'Neill's career in Ulster.

11. This notion underlies the two major works that chronicle modern Ireland, Foster (1988) and Beckett (1966).

12. Feldman's (1991) earlier work on Belfast plots the symbolism of the body and the formation of political violence. It forms an important background to his more recent work on visualization and, indeed, to an understanding of the complex dynamics of "the troubles" as a whole.

13. See Said (1995) for a discussion of imperialism's "geographical element."

14. For a fictional account of this phenomena that smartly shows the operation of place, space, and identity in Belfast's terror, see McNamee (1995).

15. There were, of course, more bombings carried out in Northern Ireland's cities, Belfast and Londonderry, particularly.

16. For a discussion of the power of these narratives for historians (and the same applies, I believe, to Irish citizens and their narratives of everyday life), see Foster (1998).

17. Not long after this event, this story disappeared from the glass case. I never learned why, but there was speculation among Catholics that the truth of this story did not make the unionists look good when discussions about Northern Ireland's future governance were taking place. Many Catholics believed unionists removed it to keep that history forgotten, to keep it out of the considerations of politicians. For an interesting discussion of Irish politicians invoking the past in discussing present problems and on time and place, see MacDonagh (1983, 1–33).

18. On political subjectivity in Northern Ireland and transformations of it, see Aretxaga (1997). This book both accounts for women's political subjectivity in Northern Ireland and theorizes the transformations of it.

19. Nicholas Dirks (1992, 1–15) describes the processes of culture appearing as nature in the context of colonial situations.

20. In Northern Ireland, *craic*, pronounced "crack," is a much talked about practice that people relish engaging in. Henry Glassie writes: "Talk begins to entertain when it pushes past greetings and isolated comments, when it pulls people out of dangerous silence and brings everyone into conversation. Then it is 'chat.' Chat worth calling entertaining is informational or 'witty,' and when wit snaps dialogue forward it becomes 'crack'" (1982, 32).

21. For a discussion of the nonmodern and tradition that accords with the perspective offered here, see Nandy (1983).

22. For reflections on such processes of marginalization, see Boyarin (1994); Fabian (1983); Foucault (1980); and Lloyd (1987, 1997).

23. This position does not rule out the importance of different temporalities in postcolonial situations. On the importance of temporality and postcoloniality, see Bhabha (1994, 236–56).

24. For one view, among others, of practical consciousness, but the one Ingold cites, see Giddens (1984).

25. For important discussions, in a variety of forms, of iteration, see Bhabha (1994).

Chapter 2

1. The material enclosed by brackets attempts to represent the context of this episode with Patrick. It is culled from the fieldnotes I wrote during that time. The major narrative sequence and the arguments presented can be followed while omitting the bracketed sections.

2. These acts of cleanliness are considered Protestant ways of marking their difference in Northern Ireland. See Nelson (1984).

3. In Ireland "constitutional nationalist parties" refers to those parties that do not advocate violence to achieve their political ends.

4. This liberal philosophy and its importance to unionists have been commented upon by a variety of writers. See Aughey (1989) for an important discussion. See also Elliott (1985); Gibbon (1975); and McCartney (1985) for both historical and political considerations of liberalism.

5. For a chronological account of the hunger strikes, see Beresford (1987). For an important and insightful anthropological analysis, see Feldman (1991).

6. For an extended discussion of this material culture and its connection to the Orange Order "marching season" see Jarman (1997).

7. This phrase appeared on a banner erected near the Garvaghey Road housing estate in Portadown, Northern Ireland, during the summer of 1998, when the Orange Order and their supporters protested the government's prohibition on their marching through this nationalist housing estate on the first Sunday in July.

8. For accounts of such murals in a different context see Sluka (1992).

9. This statistical information comes from the Irish Information Partnership: Category C: Section Two: Quantitative Information, Political Affairs (London: IIP, 1984).

10. The Orange Order identifies its marches and parades as "tradition." They do not associate their activities with sectarian practices. I call them sectarian here because of the effects of these marches in Ballybogoin. They divide Protestant and Catholics and distance Catholics from the state and nation. For an accounting of the Orange Order from an insider perspective, see Dewar, Brown, and Long (1967).

11. For a discussion of seventeenth-century settlement patterns, see Robinson (1984).

12. For an extended discussion of this history, see Jarman (1997).

13. For studies of long-term struggles over language in colonial situations, see Hill and Hill (1986) and Mannheim (1991).

14. Accents and the pronunciation of specific words and letters constitute signs of, sometimes irreconcilable, difference in Ballybogoin, as they do in other areas polarized by issues of class, race, and ethnicity. For an interesting discussion of Puerto Ricans in New York, an analogous case in my view, see Urciuoli (1996).

15. Although their article deals with the reproduction of social classes, not cultures and cultural categories, Pierre Bourdieu and Luc Boltanski (1977, 61–69) address the question of classification struggles, "the permanence of the relation between words and things, between titles and jobs," in a way related to that presented here.

16. On this naturalizing filter and its presence in transition narratives, see Somers (1997). She does not write about racializing discourses, but her position is relevant to this distinction between racializing and ethnicizing discourses.

17. On the dynamic of this subordination and racialization at other locations, see Stanfield (1985); Urciuoli (1996); and Williams (1989, 1991).

18. I understand that this claim is a contested one in the academic work on

Northern Ireland. Historian Joseph J. Lee (1989), for example, made the claim that the unionist regime was a racist one. Graham Walker disagrees with Lee in a review essay (1992).

19. For elaborations on this view of structure, see Grossberg (1992).

20. This conjuncture of liberal philosophy in the British tradition of John Locke and John Stuart Mill and exclusion on the basis of natural law is not unknown in colonial situations. See Mehta (1997). For a discussion that addresses the articulation of religion and liberal strategies of exclusion, see Parekh (1997).

21. On mimicry in colonial situations, see the chapter "Mimicry and Man: The Ambivalence of Colonial Discourse," in Bhabha (1994, 85–92).

22. See Bryan (2000) for an extended discussion of the historical and political aspects of Orange marches.

Chapter 3

1. For an example of the disputes, usually not addressed, over ethnography in Northern Ireland, see Richard Jenkins's review (1992a), Allen Feldman's reply (1992), and the ensuing response from Jenkins (1992b).

2. Messenger's work (1969) is foundational in the ethnography of Ireland despite its troubling objectifications.

3. I am referring here to the group of authors whose work appears in Clifford and Marcus (1986).

4. Glassie's work, primarily folkloric, deserves praise and provides an important turning point in the ethnography of Ireland. This does not mean I read it uncritically. I think it suffers from some easy idealization and does not contextualize either social or economic division or violence sufficiently.

5. Prior to starting at the glassblowing shop, I had worked for four months in the glass-cutting factory that housed the administrative offices of the glassworks.

6. Subjectification is understood here as the product of practices and techniques. In this generic sense, it does not imply being dominated by others, although that is the context here. It designates "processes of being 'made up' as a subject of a certain type" (Rose 1996, 147). See Foucault (1986).

7. Unionist and loyalist working class people mark off their neighborhoods by flying British Union Jacks and by painting sidewalks red, white, and blue, the colors of the Union Jack. Stories circulated among some of the workers in the glassworks about fellow nationalists penetrating these places for sexual rendezvous after the pubs closed. These stories were often contextualized in terms of providing *craic*. On the night Brendan led the singing and storytelling, one of the workers said he had been in one of these dangerous loyalist places the night before. He named the woman he was with and said, "We have to provide all the *craic* around here. We even have to fuck their women."

Chapter 4

1. Both Protestants and Catholics refer to Roman Catholic places of worship as "chapels" in everyday speech. This usage originated in the seventeenth century

and became commonplace in the eighteenth century, when Roman Catholic services were outlawed and many Roman Catholic church buildings were usurped by the Established Church. At that time the Established Church buildings became differentiated from the "chapels" of Roman Catholics. This name stuck during later periods of Roman Catholic Church construction. See Corish (1981, 33).

2. On these events, see de Paor (1970) and Farrell (1976).

3. On the Ulster workers' strike, see Fisk (1975).

4. See Thomas 1986. I thank Jo Thomas for providing this information on the efforts of the dead man's family and the consequences of them.

5. For details of this shooting, see Thomas 1986. A useful article that lays out the controversy with "shoot to kill" is Thomas 1985.

6. The repetition of these acts and the legitimating processes that constitute them receive much comment among Irish nationalists.

7. See Rosaldo (1989) on subjectivity, social analysis, and the positions of the researcher and the researched.

8. On this process of sliding signifiers and the production of new meanings, ones that allow new subject positions to develop, see Cornell (1993, 170–94).

9. For a discussion on exclusion and usurpation, one that considers Northern Ireland, see Parkin (1979).

10. For a position on experience with which I am in agreement, see Scott (1992).

Chapter 5

1. For a comparison of the eastern area of Ulster to Ballybogoin's area, see Kennedy (1986). For the story of wealth accumulation in Ireland's northeast corner, see Rowthorn and Wayne (1988).

2. For insight into the divisions within Belfast in the early part of this century and its relation to these other United Kingdom cities, see Gray (1985).

3. On modernization and identity, a complex relational phenomenon in nineteenth-century Ireland, see Miller (1987). For a more thoroughly economic perspective see Rowthorn and Wayne (1988, 16–38).

4. On this development, see Garvin (1981).

5. On the governance of Northern Ireland and the devolved institutions of Stormont, see Arthur (1980).

6. All quotes from Brigid, a fictionalized name, are taken from transcripts of taped interviews held at the Oral History Archives, University of Ulster at Jordanstown.

7. There are many histories of the IRA. Useful ones for the post-1950s developments in the IRA and its affiliated organizations are Bell (1993) and Coogan (1995).

8. For a discussion of the relation of economy to political violence that considers this debate, see Feldman (1991, 18–21). I find Feldman's assessment of this debate and his position on the relation between economic circumstances and political violence persuasive.

9. For a general discussion of this unionist situation and the cultural losses suffered by the Protestant working class, see Nelson (1984).

10. The assorted statistics from these two paragraphs come from Rowthorn and Wayne's (1988) various tables and appendices.

Chapter 6

1. The local union did not have a meeting place. The workers got permission from the local Roman Catholic parish priest to have their strike meetings in his parish hall. The majority of Protestant workers told me they were afraid to go to that hall, located in the Catholic business district, for meetings. To show their solidarity with the strikers, Protestant workers who feared going to the parish hall maintained the picket line while the meetings went on. No female workers were at this decisive union meeting.

2. Discrimination in employment has been an ongoing concern in Northern Ireland since the civil rights marches in the mid-1960s. The Drumcoo Glassworks tried to recruit Protestant blue-collar workers but encountered difficulties. The firm had success recruiting blue-collar Protestant women and Protestant secretarial and management staff, but young Protestant men in the area told me they feared going to work in "a nationalist firm." On discrimination in Northern Ireland see Eversley (1989); Fair Employment Agency (1978); Gallagher, Osborn, and Cormack (1994); McCormack and O'Hara (1990); and Rowthorn and Wayne (1988). For ethnographically informed studies that explore unemployment and the networks at play in the labor market, see Howe (1990) and Maguire (1990). For general studies of the Northern Ireland troubles that relate employment discrimination to social, political, and religious factors, see McGarry and O'Leary (1995); Ruane and Todd (1996); and Whyte (1990).

3. Karl Marx develops the classic conceptualization of class in and for itself in Marx (1963) and Marx and Engels (1947). Harry Braverman has developed the concept in influential directions (1974), but see the discussion and criticism by Stark (1980) that I take up here.

4. For a criticism of this correspondence theory of class that makes the point about the complexity of class relations and criticizes class analyses that are mechanical, see Bourdieu (1993).

5. For relations between structure and practice see Bourdieu (1977) and Giddens (1984).

6. Bhabha does not address class categories specifically in this passage but rather the general working of categories.

7. Feldman (1991) has used narrative to relate contemporary history, spatiality, and violence in Belfast, Northern Ireland. Aretxaga (1997) has used narrative ethnography to discuss women's subjectivity and experience in Belfast. Stewart (1996) presents an interesting narrative ethnography that examines the narrative culture of marginalized people in rural West Virginia. Anagnost (1997) addresses issues of nation and narration implicit in this chapter. For narratives in psychology see Bruner (1986). For a discussion of narrative in the development of the physical sciences see Gould (1989).

8. These figures were based on informal surveys that the priests and several parishioners took on visits they made to the working-class housing estates in 1985.

9. This conceptualization of social order, developed in the context of examining the transformations in the Hungarian political and cultural economies, pays heed to the negotiation of ambiguities and to both economy and culture. It is particularly useful for making sense of conflicts within organizations and their articulation to accountings outside of them. Like agents in the transforming societies of Central and Eastern Europe, Northern Ireland citizens are accustomed to negotiating ambiguity and investing in social and cultural forms that provide a hedge against it.

10. Only four of the skilled workers in the factory had a parent who held lifelong, unionized industrial employment. The two Protestant men and one of the Catholic workers who voted against accepting management's ultimatum were among them.

11. This is not the precise name given to this housing estate, but it is a pseudonym that renders the sense of the name that Ballybogoin people living outside it have attached to it.

12. These games and the mimicry that followed made the workers into a class grouping, and these action signs were read as such. On bodies as a metaphor for class see Stallybrass and White (1986).

13. Masculine discourses and masculine performances permeated the shop floor struggles. Masculinity was crucial in shaping this conflict. See chapter 7.

14. I found this citation among Father Finbarr's papers, but it was also printed in the Ballybogoin weekly newspaper. I have deleted the county name from Father Finbarr's text for reproduction here.

15. This figure of the native as lack or absent of the modern is common in postcolonial transition narratives. It is at play in those narratives deployed to comprehend the relatively underdeveloped areas in the western regions of Northern Ireland. For a general discussion of these narratives see Chakrabarty (1992). There is a gendered and sexualized aspect to these narratives of lack as well, as discussed in Jones and Stallybrass (1992) and Aretxaga (1997).

16. Lawrence Taylor (1995) writes incisively on the power of priests in Donegal and attributes some of these perceived powers to status ambiguity within the Roman Catholic Church and in the unevenness of clerical performance. Father Finbarr resembles those priests studied by Taylor, although the ambiguities surrounding him are different.

17. Because of the high relative expenditures on state security in Northern Ireland, it was relatively advantaged in comparison with other peripheral areas of the United Kingdom during the Thatcher years. For discussions of changing regional policies and Thatcherism, see Gaffikin and Morrissey (1990, 41–49); Harris, Jefferson, and Spencer (1990, 86–121); and Rowthorn and Wayne (1988, 87–88).

18. Talk, as performed and represented by the workers, expresses a desire for intimacy and the making of intersubjective space-time. Michael Herzfeld links such practices of intimacy to state authority and nationalist social formations:

"Cultural intimacy may also reinforce the hand of power when its display becomes a sign of collective confidence" (1997, 3). Irish talk here may function as such a sign.

19. Only two of the twelve Protestant workers came to these union meetings that were held at the parish hall of the Ballybogoin Roman Catholic Church. Women workers came to the picket line on the first two days of the strike. They stayed in their cars for the most part and became alienated from the masculinist banter on the picket line. They did not go to the union meetings held at the parish hall. Five of the twelve Protestant production workers were women.

20. On talk's relation to making the future see Stewart (1996, 205–11).

21. On recognition and notions of the self see Taylor (1994) and Keane (1997, 14–28).

22. On indifference see Herzfeld (1992, 13) and Mills (1959, 11–14). I am following Herzfeld's use of it more closely here.

23. David Cannadine (1999, 175–84) attributes some of the 1980s and 1990s transformations in British class relations to Prime Minister Thatcher's persuasive powers and leadership skills.

24. For a discussion of usurpation and its links to Northern Ireland see Parkin (1979, 94–99).

Chapter 7

1. On this process, see Scott (1988, 63).

2. On temporality and ontological narratives, what he calls self-narration, see Gergen (1994, 185–209).

3. On the endorsement of some narratives over others and the justification for them, see Stark (1994, 31).

4. On determinate speech acts, see Davies and Harré (1990, 43–63) and Harré (1995, 124–25).

5. On indexicality see Silverstein (1976, 11–55). For an interesting discussion of indexicality and class, racial, and ethnic divisions, see Urciuoli (1996).

6. On qualisigns and their relation to value, see Munn (1986, 16).

7. On value and intersubjective relations, see Munn (1986, 9).

8. Data are taken from the Department of Economic Development Statistics, 1984; 1991 Northern Ireland Census of Population; and O'Dowd, (1995, 132–77). For a useful overview of the 1980s economy, see Rowthorn and Wayne (1988).

Chapter 8

1. For elaborations on this concept of difference, see Grossberg (1992, 38–43).

2. On the concept of place-worlds used here see Basso (1996).

3. This commonality of cultural practices encompassed by political division is discussed in Hughes (1991). See, especially, Ruane and Todd (1991, 27–44).

4. For a case study that delineates the difficulty of organizing in the post–Good Friday Agreement era see Kelleher (2000).

5. For an extended discussion on the agreement, see Ruane and Todd (1999).

Glossary

⟋

ATGWU	Amalgamated Trade and General Workers Union
DUP	Democratic Unionist Party. Founded in 1971 and led by the Reverend Ian Paisley.
INLA	Irish National Liberation Army, the military wing of the Irish Republican Socialist Party (IRSP) founded in 1974.
IRA	Irish Republican Army. In 1970 the IRA split into two factions, the Official IRA (OIRA) and the Provisional IRA (PIRA). The latter carried out the bulk of republican military activities in the 1970s and 1980s and is the group associated with Sinn Féin. The PIRA has become known as the IRA, and this group along with Sinn Féin has negotiated the disarmament attached to the Belfast or Good Friday Agreement.
NICRA	Northern Ireland Civil Rights Association. Founded in 1967, its leaders consisted of trade union and civil rights activists. It advocated nonviolence and led the civil rights protests of the late 1960s.
NIDA	Northern Ireland Development Association
NILRA	Northern Ireland Labor Relations Agency
RUC	Royal Ulster Constabulary. The police force of Northern Ireland whose legitimacy as a neutral force of law and order is questioned by Irish Republicans and many of Northern Ireland's Roman Catholics.
SAS	Special Air Service. The British state deployed the undercover SAS to South Armagh in 1976 in order to combat the PIRA. It has remained in Northern Ireland since and has been implicated in a variety of "shoot to kill" incidents.
SDLP	Social Democratic and Labor Party. Founded in 1970, the party was led by John Hume and represented the majority of nationalist Catholics for the remainder of the century. It advocates nonviolence.

UDA   Ulster Defense Association. Founded in 1971, this paramilitary organization served as the coordinator for the diverse loyalist military and vigilante groups.

UDR   Ulster Defense Regiment. A mainly part-time military force raised from the population of Northern Ireland. It lost legitimacy with Catholic citizens of Northern Ireland during the 1970s, its first decade of existence. Its Catholic membership was only 2 percent when it celebrated its tenth anniversary in 1980.

UUP   Ulster Unionist Party. Sometimes called the Official Unionist Party, it is the largest political entity in Northern Ireland. It is the largest party representing those Northern Ireland citizens who wish to remain part of the United Kingdom of Great Britain and Northern Ireland.

References

Amnesty International

    1983   *Amnesty International Report for 1983.* London: Amnesty International Publications.

    1988   *United Kingdom, Northern Ireland: Killings by Security Forces and "Supergrass" Trials.* London: Amnesty International Publications.

Anagnost, Ann

    1997   *National Past-Times: Narrative, Representation and Power in Modern China.* Durham, NC: Duke University Press.

Anderson, Benedict

    1983   *Imagined Communities: Reflections on the Origin and Spread of Nationalism.* London: Verso.

Appadurai, Arjun

    1990   Disjuncture and Difference in the Global Cultural Economy. *Public Culture* 2 (2): 1–4.

    1996   *Modernity at Large: Cultural Dimensions of Globalization.* Minneapolis: University of Minnesota Press.

Aretxaga, Begoña

    1997   *Shattering Silence: Women, Nationalism, and Political Subjectivity in Northern Ireland.* Princeton: Princeton University Press.

Arthur, Paul

    1980   *Government and Politics of Northern Ireland.* Essex: Longman.

Asmal, Kader, ed.

    1985   *Shoot to Kill: International Lawyers' Inquiry into the Lethal Use of Firearms by the Security Forces in Northern Ireland.* Dublin: Mercier.

Aughey, Arthur

    1989   *Under Siege: Ulster Unionism and the Anglo-Irish Agreement.* London: Hurst.

Baker, David J.
  1993   Off the Map: Charting Uncertainty in Renaissance Ireland. In *Repre-senting Ireland: Literature and the Origins of Conflict,* ed. Brendan Bradshaw, Andrew Hadfield, and Willy Maley, 76–92. Cambridge: Cambridge University Press.
Bakhtin, Mikhail
  1984   *Rabelais and His World.* Trans. Hélène Iswolsky. Bloomington: Indiana University Press.
Bardon, Jonathan
  1992   *A History of Ulster.* Belfast: Blackstaff.
Baron, Ava
  1991   Gender and Labor History: Learning from the Past, Looking to the Future. In *Work Engendered: Toward a New History of American Labor,* ed. Ava Baron, 1–46. Ithaca: Cornell University Press.
Basso, Keith H.
  1996   *Wisdom Sits in Places: Landscape and Language among the Western Apache.* Albuquerque: University of New Mexico Press.
Becker, Alton L.
  1979   Communication across Diversity. In *The Imagination of Reality: Essays in Southeast Asian Coherence Systems,* ed. Alton L. Becker and Aram A.Yengoyan, 1–5. Norwood, NJ: Ablex.
Beckett, J. C.
  1966   *The Making of Modern Ireland.* London: Faber and Faber.
———, ed.
  1983   *Belfast: The Making of the City.* Belfast: Appletree.
Bell, J. Bowyer
  1993   *The Irish Troubles.* New York: St. Martin's.
Berdahl, Daphne
  1999   *Where the World Ended: Re-Unification and Identity in the German Borderland.* Berkeley: University of California Press.
Beresford, David
  1987   *Ten Men Dead: The Story of the 1981 Irish Hunger Strike.* London: Grafton.
Berger, John
  1985   The Storyteller. In *The White Bird: Writings by John Berger,* 13–18. London: Chatto and Windus.
  1988   The Credible Word. *Harper's* (July) 277:35–37.
Bhabha, Homi
  1994   *The Location of Culture.* New York: Routledge.
  1995   The Commitment to Theory. In *Cultural Remix: Theories of Politics and the Popular,* ed. Erica Carter, James Donald, and Judith Squires, 3–27. London: Lawrence & Wishart.
  1996   Unpacking My Library . . . Again. In *The Post-Colonial Question,* ed. Iain Chambers and Lidia Curti, 199–211. London: Routledge.
Block, Fred, and Margaret R. Somers
  1984   Beyond the Economic Fallacy: The Holistic Social Science of Karl

Polanyi. In *Vision and Method in Historical Sociology,* ed. T. Skocpol, 47–84. Cambridge: Cambridge University Press.

Bourdieu, Pierre
1977   *Outline of a Theory of Practice.* Cambridge: Cambridge University Press.
1984   *Distinction: A Social Critique of the Judgement of Taste.* London: Routledge.
1985   The Social Space and the Genesis of Groups. *Theory and Society* 14:723–44.
1987   What Makes a Social Class? On the Theoretical and Practical Existence of Groups. *Berkeley Journal of Sociology* 32:1–18.
1989   Social Space and Symbolic Power. *Theoretical Sociology* 7 (1): 14–25.
1991   Social Space and the Genesis of "Classes." In *Language and Symbolic Power,* ed. John B. Thompson, 229–51. Cambridge: Harvard University Press.
1993   Concluding Remarks: For a Sociogenetic Understanding of Intellectual Works. In *Bourdieu: Critical Perspectives,* ed. Craig Calhoun, Edward LiPuma, and Moishe Postone, 263–75. Chicago: University of Chicago Press.

Bourdieu, Pierre, and Luc Boltanski
1977   Formal Qualifications and Occupational Hierarchies: The Relationships between the Production System and the Reproduction System. In *Reorganizing Education: Sage Annual Review of Social and Educational Change,* ed. E. King, 61–69. London: Sage.

Boyarin, Jonathan
1994   Space, Time, and the Politics of Memory. In *Remapping Memory: The Politics of Timespace.* ed. Jonathan Boyarin, 1–38. Minneapolis: University of Minnesota Press.

Bradshaw, Brendan, Andrew Hadfield, and Willy Maley, eds.
1993   *Representing Ireland: Literature and the Origins of Conflict, 1534–1660.* Cambridge: Cambridge University Press.

Braverman, Harry
1974   *Labor and Monopoly Capital: The Degradation of Work in the Twentieth Century.* New York: Monthly Review Press.

Bruce, Steve
1994   *The Edge of the Union: The Ulster Loyalist Political Vision.* Oxford: Oxford University Press.

Bruner, Jerome
1986   *Actual Minds, Possible Worlds.* Cambridge: Harvard University Press.

Bryan, Dominic
2000   *Orange Parades: The Politics of Ritual, Tradition and Control.* London: Pluto Press.

Buck-Morss, Susan
1987   Semiotic Boundaries and the Politics of Meaning: Modernity on Tour—A Village in Transition. In *New Ways of Knowing: The Sci-*

ences, Society, and Reconstructive Knowledge, ed. Marcus J. Raskin and Herbert J. Bernstein, 200–236. Totowa, NJ: Rowman and Littlefield.

Buckley, Anthony D., and Mary C. Kenney

    1995   *Negotiating Identity: Rhetoric, Metaphor, and Social Drama in Northern Ireland.* Washington, DC: Smithsonian.

Burton, Frank

    1978   *The Politics of Legitimacy: Struggles in a Belfast Community.* London: Routledge & Kegan Paul.

    1979   Ideological Social Relations in Northern Ireland. *British Journal of Sociology* 30:61–80.

Butler, Judith

    1992   Contingent Foundations: Feminism and the Questions of "Postmodernism." In *Feminists Theorize the Political,* ed. Judith Butler and Joan Wallach Scott, 3–21. New York: Routledge.

Cairns, David, and Shaun Richards

    1988   *Writing Ireland: Colonialism, Nationalism, and Culture.* Manchester: Manchester University Press.

Cannadine, David

    1999   *The Rise and Fall of Class in Britain.* New York: Columbia University Press.

Chakrabarty, Dipesh

    1989   *Rethinking Working-Class History: Bengal 1890–1940.* Princeton: Princeton University Press.

    1992   Postcoloniality and the Artifice of History: Who Speaks for "Indian Pasts"? *Representations* 37:1–26.

Chambers, Ross

    1979   *Meaning and Meaningfulness: Studies in the Analysis and Interpretation of Texts.* Lexington, KY: French Forum.

    1984   *Story and Situation: Narrative Seduction and the Power of Fiction.* Minneapolis: University of Minnesota Press.

Chatterjee, Partha

    1986   *Nationalist Thought and the Colonial World—A Derivative Discourse.* London: Zed Books.

    1993   *The Nation and Its Fragments: Colonial and Postcolonial Histories.* Princeton: Princeton University Press.

Clifford, James

    1988   *The Predicament of Culture: Twentieth-Century Ethnography, Literature, and Art.* Cambridge: Harvard University Press.

Clifford, James, and George E. Marcus, eds.

    1986   *Writing Culture: The Poetics and Politics of Ethnography.* Berkeley: University of California Press.

Cohn, Bernard S., and Nicholas B. Dirks

    1988   Beyond the Fringe: The Nation State, Colonialism, and the Technologies of Power. *Journal of Historical Sociology* 1 (2): 224–29.

References

Collins, Eamon, with Mick McGovern
  1997   *Killing Rage*. London: Granta Books.
Comaroff, Jean, and John Comaroff
  1991   *Of Revelation and Revolution: Christianity, Colonialism, and Consciousness in South Africa*. Chicago: University of Chicago Press.
Coogan, Tim Pat
  1995   *The IRA*. London: Harper Collins.
  1996   *The Troubles: Ireland's Ordeal, 1966–1996, and the Search for Peace*. Boulder, CO: Roberts Rinehart.
Corish, Patrick
  1981   *The Catholic Community in the Seventeenth and Eighteenth Centuries*. Dublin: Helicon.
Cornell, Drucilla
  1993   *Transformations: Recollective Imagination and Sexual Difference*. New York: Routledge.
Culler, Jonathan
  1988   Interpretations: Data or Goals. *Poetics Today* 9 (2): 275–90.
Curtis, L. P., Jr.
  1968   *The Anglo-Saxons and Celts: A Study of Anti-Irish Prejudice in Victorian England*. Bridgeport, CT: Conference on British Studies.
Daniel, E. Valentine
  1996   *Charred Lullabies: Chapters in an Anthropography of Violence*. Princeton: Princeton University Press.
Davies, Bronwyn, and Rom Harré
  1990   Positioning: The Discursive Production of Selves. *Journal for the Theory of Social Behavior* 20 (1): 43–63.
Deane, Seamus
  1985   Heroic Styles: The Tradition of an Idea. In *Ireland's Field Day*, ed. Field Day Theatre Company, 45–58. London: Hutchinson.
  1990   Introduction. In *Nationalism, Colonialism, and Literature*, ed. Seamus Deane, 3–19. Minneapolis: University of Minnesota Press.
de Certeau, Michel
  1984   *The Practice of Everyday Life*. Berkeley: University of California Press.
de Paor, Liam
  1970   *Divided Ulster*. London: Penguin.
Dewar, M. W., J. Brown, and S. E. Long
  1967   *Orangeism: A New Historical Interpretation*. Belfast: Grand Orange Lodge of Ireland.
Dirks, Nicholas B.
  1992   Introduction: Colonialism and Culture. In *Colonialism and Culture*, ed. Nicholas B. Dirks, 1–26. Ann Arbor: University of Michigan Press.
Donnan, Hastings, and Thomas J. Wilson
  1999   *Borders: Frontiers of Identity, Nation, and State*. Oxford: Berg.
Douglas, Mary
  1966   *Purity and Danger: An Analysis of Concepts of Pollution and Taboo*. London: Routledge & Kegan Paul.

DuBois, W. E. B.
  1903   *The Souls of Black Folk.* New York: Vintage.
Eley, Geoff
  1996   Is All the World a Text? From Social History to the History of Society Two Decades Later. In *The Historic Turn in the Human Sciences,* ed. Terrence J. McDonald, 193–243. Ann Arbor: University of Michigan Press.
Elliott, Marianne
  1985   *Watchmen in Sion: The Protestant Idea of Liberty.* Derry: Field Day Theatre Company.
Eversley, David
  1989   *Religion and Employment in Northern Ireland.* London: Sage.
Eversley, David, and Valerie Herr
  1985   *The Roman Catholic Population of Northern Ireland in 1981.* Belfast: Fair Employment Agency.
Fabian, Johannes
  1983   *Time and the Other: How Anthropology Makes Its Object.* New York: Columbia University Press.
Fair Employment Agency
  1978   *Industrial and Occupational Profile of the Two Sections of the Population in Northern Ireland: An Analysis of the 1971 Census.* Belfast: Fair Employment Agency.
Fanon, Frantz
  1967   *Black Skin/White Masks: The Experiences of a Black Man in a White World.* New York: Grove.
Farnell, Brenda
  1994   Ethno-graphics and the Moving Body. *Man* 29 (4): 929–74.
  1996   Metaphors We Move By. *Visual Anthropology* 8:311–35.
Farrell, Michael
  1976   *Northern Ireland: The Orange State.* London: Pluto.
Feldman, Allen
  1991   *Formations of Violence: The Narrative of the Body and Political Terror in Northern Ireland.* Chicago: University of Chicago Press.
  1992   On Formations of Violence. *Current Anthropology* 33 (5): 595–96.
  1997   Violence and Vision: The Prosthetics and Aesthetics of Terror. *Public Culture* 10 (1): 24–60.
Fernandez-Kelly, Maria
  1983   *For We Are Sold I and My People.* Albany: State University of New York Press.
Fisk, Robert
  1975   *The Point of No Return: The Strike Which Broke the British in Ulster.* London: Andre Deutsch.
Foster, R. F.
  1988   *Modern Ireland, 1600–1972.* London: Penguin.
  1998   Storylines: Narrative and Nationality in Nineteenth-Century Ireland.

In *Imagining Nations,* ed. Geoffrey Cubitt, 38–56. Manchester: Manchester University Press.

Foucault, Michel

1977 *Discipline and Punish: The Birth of the Prison.* New York: Vintage.

1978 *The History of Sexuality.* Vol. 1, *An Introduction.* Trans. Robert Hurley. New York: Random House.

1980 *Power/Knowledge: Selected Interviews and Other Writings, 1972–1977.* Ed. Colin Gordon. New York: Pantheon.

1986 *The History of Sexuality.* Vol. 3, *The Care of the Self.* Trans. Robert Hurley. New York: Pantheon.

Frankenberg, Ruth, and Lata Mani

1996 Crosscurrents, Crosstalk: Race, "Postcoloniality," and the Politics of Location. In *Displacement, Diaspora, and Geographies of Identity,* ed. Smadar Lavie and Ted Swedenburg, 273–93. Durham, NC: Duke University Press.

Frow, John, and Meaghan Morris, eds.

1993 Introduction. In *Australian Cultural Studies: A Reader,* ed. John Frow and Meaghan Morris, vii–xxxii. Urbana: University of Illinois Press.

Gaffikin, Frank, and Mike Morrissey

1990 *Northern Ireland: The Thatcher Years.* London: Zed Books.

Gallagher, Anthony M., R. D. Osborne, and R. J. Cormack

1994 *Fair Shares? Employment, Unemployment, and Economic Status.* Belfast: Fair Employment Commission.

Garvin, Tom

1981 *The Evolution of Irish Nationalist Politics.* Dublin: Gill and MacMillan.

Gates, Henry Louis, Jr.

1985 Editor's Introduction: Writing "Race" and the Difference It Makes. *Critical Inquiry* 12 (1): 1–20.

Geertz, Clifford

1968 Thinking as a Moral Act: Ethical Dimensions of Anthropological Fieldwork in the New States. *Antioch Review* 28:139–58.

1975 On the Nature of Anthropological Understanding. *American Scientist* 63:47–53.

Gergen, Kenneth

1994 *Realities and Relationships: Soundings in Social Construction.* Cambridge: Harvard University Press.

Gibbon, Peter

1975 *The Origins of Ulster Unionism.* Manchester: Manchester University Press.

Giddens, Anthony

1984 *The Constitution of Society.* Cambridge: Polity.

Ginsburg, Faye, and Anna Lowenhaupt Tsing, eds.

1990 *Uncertain Terms: Negotiating Gender in American Culture.* Boston: Beacon.

Glassie, Henry
  1982   *Passing the Time in Ballymenone.* Philadelphia: University of Penn-
         sylvania Press.
Gordon, Deborah A.
  1988   Writing Culture, Writing Feminism: The Poetics and Politics of
         Experimental Ethnography. *Inscriptions* 3/4:7–24.
Gould, Stephen Jay
  1989   *Wonderful Life: The Burgess Shale and the Nature of History.* New
         York: W. W. Norton.
Gramsci, Antonio
  1957   *The Modern Prince and Other Writings.* New York: International
         Publishers.
  1971   *Selections from the Prison Notebooks.* Ed. Quintin Hoare and Geof-
         frey Nowell-Smith. New York: International Publishers.
Gray, John
  1985   *City in Revolt: James Larkin and the Belfast Dock Strike of 1907.*
         Belfast: Blackstaff.
Greenblatt, Stephen, ed.
  1988   *Representing the English Renaissance.* Berkeley: University of Cali-
         fornia Press.
Grossberg, Lawrence
  1992   *We Gotta Get Out of This Place: Popular Conservatism and Post-
         modern Culture.* New York: Routledge.
Gupta, Akhil, and James Ferguson, eds.
  1997a *Culture, Power, and Place: Explorations in Critical Anthropology.*
         Durham, NC: Duke University Press.
  1997b *Anthropological Locations: Boundaries and Grounds of a Field Sci-
         ence.* Berkeley: University of California Press.
Hadfield, Andrew, and Willy Maley
  1993   Introduction: Irish Representations and English Alternatives. In *Rep-
         resenting Ireland: Literature and the Origins of Conflict,* ed. Brendan
         Bradshaw, Andrew Hadfield, and Willy Maley, 1–23. Cambridge:
         Cambridge University Press.
Hall, Stuart
  1983   The Problem of Ideology: Marxism without Guarantees. In *Marx: 100
         Years On,* ed. B. Matthews, 57–86. London: Lawrence & Wishart.
  1984   The Narrative Construction of Reality: An Interview with Stuart
         Hall. *Southern Review* 17 (1): 3–17.
  1986   On Postmodernism and Articulation: An Interview with Stuart Hall.
         Journal of Communication Inquiry 10 (2): 45–60.
  1988   *The Hard Road to Renewal: Thatcherism and the Crisis of the Left.*
         London: Verso.
  1991   Old and New Identities, Old and New Ethnicities. In *Culture, Glob-
         alization, and the World System,* ed. Anthony King, 41–68. Bingham-
         ton: State University of New York Press.

1996a Introduction: Who Needs Identity? In *Questions of Cultural Identity,* ed. Stuart Hall and Paul du Guy, 1–17. London: Sage.

1996b When Was "the Post-Colonial"? Thinking at the Limit. In *The Post-Colonial Question: Common Skies, Divided Horizons,* ed. Iain Chambers and Lidia Curti, 242–60. London: Routledge.

Hall, Stuart, and Martin Jacques, ed.

1990 *New Times: The Changing Face of Politics in the 1990s.* London: Verso.

Handler, Richard

1988 *Nationalism and the Politics of Culture in Quebec.* Madison: University of Wisconsin Press.

Harré, Rom

1995 Agentive Discourse. In *Discourse Psychology in Practices,* ed. Rom Harré and Peter Stearns, 121–36. London: Sage.

Harris, Richard, Clifford Jefferson, and John Spencer

1990 *The Northern Ireland Economy: A Comparative Study in the Economic Development of a Peripheral Region.* London: Longman.

Harris, Rosemary

1972 *Prejudice and Tolerance in Ulster: A Study of Neighbors and "Strangers" in a Border Community.* Manchester: Manchester University Press.

Hart, Janet

1992 Cracking the Code: Narrative and Political Mobilization in the Greek Resistance. *Journal of Social Science History* 16:631–68.

Hechter, Michael

1975 *Internal Colonialism: The Celtic Fringe in British National Development.* Berkeley: University of California Press.

Herzfeld, Michael

1992 *The Social Production of Indifference: Exploring the Symbolic Roots of Western Bureaucracy.* New York: Berg.

1997 *Cultural Intimacy: Social Poetics in the Nation-State.* New York: Routledge.

Hill, Jane, and Kenneth Hill

1986 *Speaking Mexicano: Dynamics of Syncretic Language in Central Mexico.* Tucson: University of Arizona Press.

Howe, Leo

1990 *Being Unemployed in Northern Ireland.* Cambridge: Cambridge University Press.

Hughes, Eamonn, ed.

1991 *Culture and Politics in Northern Ireland, 1960–1990.* London: Open University Press.

Hulme, Peter

1986 *Colonial Encounters: Europe and the Native Caribbean, 1492–1797.* London: Routledge.

Hurston, Zora Neale

1935 *Mules and Men.* Bloomington: Indiana University Press.

Ignatiev, Noel
   1995   *How the Irish Became White.* New York: Routledge.
Information on Ireland
   1984   *Nothing but the Same Old Story: The Roots of Anti-Irish Racism.* London: Information on Ireland.
Ingold, Tim
   1996   Introduction: The Past Is a Foreign Country. In *Debates in Anthropology,* ed. Tim Ingold, 201–5. New York: Routledge.
Innes, C. L.
   1993   *Woman and Nation in Irish Literature and Society.* Athens: University of Georgia Press.
Irish Information Partnership
   1984   *Political Affairs.* London: Irish Information Partnership.
Jarman, Neil
   1997   *Material Conflicts: Parades and Visual Display in Northern Ireland.* Oxford: Berg.
Jenkins, Richard
   1983   *Lads, Citizens, and Ordinary Kids: Working-Class Youth in Belfast.* London: Routledge & Kegan Paul.
   1992a Doing Violence to the Subject. *Current Anthropology* 33 (2): 233–35.
   1992b Reply to Feldman. *Current Anthropology* 33 (5): 596–97.
Jones, Ann Rosalind, and Peter Stallybrass
   1992   Dismantling Irena: The Sexualizing of Ireland in Early Modern England. In *Nationalisms and Sexualities,* ed. Andrew Parker, Mary Russo, Doris Sommer, and Patricia Yaeger, 157–71. New York: Routledge.
Jones, Jacqueline
   1998   *American Work: Four Centuries of Black and White Labor.* New York: Norton.
Joyce, Patrick
   1995   Introduction. In *Class,* ed. Patrick Joyce, 3–16. Oxford: Oxford University Press.
Joyce, Patrick, ed.
   1987   *Historical Meanings of Work.* Cambridge: Cambridge University Press.
   1995   *Class.* Oxford: Oxford University Press.
Keane, Webb
   1997   *Signs of Recognition: Powers and Hazards of Representation in an Indonesian Society.* Berkeley: University of California Press.
Kelleher, William
   1999   Putting Gender to Work on a Northern Ireland Shopfloor. In *Reclaiming Gender: Transgressive Identities in Modern Ireland,* ed. Marilyn Cohen and Nancy Curtin, 123–41. New York: St. Martin's.
   2000   Making Home in the Irish/British Borderlands: The Global and the Local in a Conflicted Social Space. *Identities* 7 (2): 139–72.

Kennedy, Liam
    1986   *The Two Ulsters: A Case for Repartition.* Belfast: Queens University Press.
Kennedy, Liam, and Phillip Ollerenshaw, eds.
    1986   *An Economic History of Ulster, 1820–1939.* Manchester: Manchester University Press.
Kiberd, Declan
    1996   *Inventing Ireland: The Literature of the Modern Nation.* Cambridge: Harvard University Press.
Larsen, Sidsel Saugestad
    1982a The Two Sides of the House: Identity and Social Organization in Kilbroney, Northern Ireland. In *Belonging: Identity and Social Organization in British Rural Cultures,* ed. Anthony P. Cohen, 131–64. Manchester: Manchester University Press.
    1982b The Glorious Twelfth: The Politics of Legitimation in Kilbroney. In *Belonging: Identity and Social Organization in British Rural Cultures,* ed. Anthony P. Cohen, 278–91. Manchester: Manchester University Press.
Lassalle, Yvonne M., and Maureen O'Dougherty
    1997   In Search of Weeping Worlds: Economies of Agency and the Politics of Representation in the Ethnography of Inequality. *Radical History Review* 69 (fall): 243–60.
Leach, Edmund R.
    1964   Anthropological Aspects of Language: Animal Categories and Verbal Abuse. In *New Directions in the Study of Language,* ed. Eric H. Lenneberg, 23–63. Cambridge: MIT Press.
Lee, Joseph J.
    1989   *Ireland, 1912–1985: Politics and Society.* Cambridge: Cambridge University Press.
Lees, Lynn Hollen
    1979   *Exiles of Erin: Irish Migrants in Victorian London.* Ithaca: Cornell University Press.
Leyton, Elliott
    1975   *The One Blood: Kinship and Class in an Irish Village.* St. John's, Newfoundland: Memorial University of Newfoundland.
Limon, José E.
    1994   *Dancing with the Devil: Society and Cultural Poetics in Mexican-American South Texas.* Madison: University of Wisconsin Press.
Lloyd, David
    1987   *Nationalism and Minor Literature: James Clarence Mangan and the Emergence of Irish Cultural Nationalism.* Berkeley: University of California Press.
    1993   *Anomalous States: Irish Writing and the Post-Colonial Moment.* Durham, NC: Duke University Press.
    1997   Nationalisms against the State. In *The Politics of Culture in the*

Shadow of Capital, ed. Lisa Lowe and David Lloyd, 173–97. Durham, NC: Duke University Press.

Lloyd, David, and Paul Thomas
    1998   *Culture and the State.* New York: Routledge.

Lowe, Lisa, and David Lloyd, eds.
    1997   *The Politics of Culture in the Shadow of Capital.* Durham, NC: Duke University Press.

Lüdtke, Alf
    1993   Polymorphus Synchrony: German Industrial Workers and the Politics of Everyday Life. *International Review of Social History* 38:39–84.
    1995   Introduction: What Is the History of Everyday Life and Who Are Its Practitioners? In *Reconstructing Historical Experiences and Ways of Life,* ed. Alf Lüdtke, 3–40. Princeton: Princeton University Press.

Lugo, Alejandro
    1990   Cultural Production and Reproduction in Ciudad Juarez, Mexico: Tropes at Play among Maquiladora Workers. *Cultural Anthropology* 5 (2): 173–96.
    1997   Reflections on Border Theory, Culture, and the Nation. In *Border Theory: The Limits of Cultural Politics,* ed. Scott Michaelson and David E. Johnson, 43–67. Minneapolis: University of Minnesota Press.
    1999   Destablizing the Masculine, Refocusing "Gender": Men and the Aura of Authority in Michelle Z. Rosaldo's Work. In *Gender Matters: Rereading Michelle Z. Rosaldo,* ed. Alejandro Lugo and Bill Maurer, 54–89. Ann Arbor: University of Michigan Press.

MacDonagh, Oliver
    1983   *States of Mind: Anglo-Irish Conflict, 1780–1980.* London: George Allen and Unwin.

Maguire, Michael
    1990   *Work, Employment, and New Technology: A Case Study of Multinational Investment in Northern Ireland.* Belfast: Policy Research Institute, Queens University.

Mannheim, Bruce
    1991   *The Language of the Inka since the European Invasion.* Austin: University of Texas Press.

Marcus, George E.
    1991   Past, Present, and Emergent Identities: Requirements for Ethnographies of Late Twentieth Century Modernity Worldwide. In *Modernity and Identity,* ed. Scott Lash and Jonathan Friedman, 309–30. London: Blackwell.
    1998   *Ethnography through Thick and Thin.* Princeton: Princeton University Press.

Marcus, George E., and Dick Cushman
    1982   Ethnographies as Texts. *Annual Review of Anthropology* 11:25–69.

Marcus, George, and M. F. K. Fischer
    1986   *Anthropology as Cultural Critique: An Experimental Moment in the Human Sciences,* 2d ed. Chicago: University of Chicago Press.

References

Marx, Karl
  1963 *The Eighteenth Brumaire of Louis Bonaparte.* New York: International Publishers.
  1967a *Capital.* Vol. 1, *A Critical Analysis of Capitalist Production,* ed. Frederick Engels. New York: International Publishers.
  1967b *Capital.* Vol. 2, *The Process of Circulation of Capital,* ed. Frederick Engels. New York: International Publishers.
Marx, Karl, and Frederick Engels
  1947 *The German Ideology.* New York: International Publishers.
Massey, Doreen, and Richard Meegan
  1982 *The Anatomy of Job Loss: The How, Why, and Where of Employment Decline.* London: Methuen.
McCabe, Herbert, O.P.
  1987 *God Matters.* London: Geoffrey Chapman.
McCartney, Robert L.
  1985 *Liberty and Authority in Ireland.* Derry: Field Day Theatre Company.
McCluskey, Conn
  1989 *Up off Their Knees.* Galway: Conn McCluskey & Associates.
McCormack, Vincent, and Joe O'Hara
  1990 *Enduring Inequality: Religious Discrimination in Employment in Northern Ireland.* London: National Council for Civil Liberties.
McEldowney, Eugene
  1984 The New Partition of Ireland. *Irish Times,* March 1, p. 13.
McGarry, John, and Brendan O'Leary
  1995 *Explaining Northern Ireland: Broken Images.* Oxford: Blackwell.
McNamee, Eoin
  1995 *Resurrection Man.* New York: Picador.
Mehta, Uday S.
  1997 Liberal Strategies of Exclusion. In *Tensions of Empire: Colonial Cultures in a Bourgeois World,* ed. Frederick Cooper and Ann Laura Stoler, 59–86. Berkeley: University of California Press.
Messenger, John C.
  1969 *Inis Beag: Isle of Ireland.* Prospect Heights, IL: Waveland.
Mills, C. Wright
  1959 *The Sociological Imagination.* New York: Oxford University Press.
Miller, David W.
  1978 *Queen's Rebels: Ulster Loyalism in Historical Perspective.* Dublin: Gill and MacMillan.
  1987 Presbyterianism and "Modernization" in Ulster. In *Nationalism and Popular Protest in Ireland,* ed. C. H. E. Philpin, 80–109. Cambridge: Cambridge University Press.
Moody, T. W.
  1980 *The Ulster Question, 1603–1973.* Cork: Mercier.
Morales, Alejandro
  1996 Dynamic Identities in Heterotopia. In *Alejandro Morales: Fiction*

Past, Present, Future Perfect, ed. José Antonio Gurpegui, 86–98. Tempe, AZ: Bilingual Review.

Mühlhäusler, Peter, and Rom Harré

1990 *Pronouns and People: The Linguistic Construction of Social and Personal Identity.* Oxford: Oxford University Press.

Munn, Nancy D.

1986 *The Fame of Gawa: A Symbolic Study of Value Transformation in a Massim (Papua New Guinea) Society.* Durham, NC: Duke University Press.

Nandy, Ashis

1983 *The Intimate Enemy: Loss and Recovery of Self under Colonialism.* Delhi: Oxford University Press.

Nelson, Sarah

1984 *Ulster's Uncertain Defenders: Protestant Political, Paramilitary, and Community Groups and the Northern Ireland Conflict.* Belfast: Appletree.

O'Dowd, Liam

1995 Development or Dependency? State, Economy, and Society in Northern Ireland. In *Irish Society: Sociological Perspectives,* ed. Patrick Clancy, Sheelagh Drudy, Kathleen Cynch, and Liam O'Dowd. 132–77. Dublin: Institute of Public Administration.

Omi, Michael, and Howard Winant

1994 *Racial Formation in the United States: From the 1960s to the 1990s.* 2d ed. New York: Routledge.

Ong, Aihwa

1987 *Spirits of Resistance and Capitalist Discipline: Factory Women in Malaysia.* Albany: State University of New York Press.

1991 The Gender and Labor Politics of Postmodernity. *Annual Review of Anthropology* 20:279–309.

Ó Tuathail, Gearóid

1996 *Critical Geopolitics: The Politics of Writing Global Space.* New York: Routledge.

Parekh, Bhikhu

1997 The West and Its Others. In *Cultural Readings of Imperialism: Edward Said and the Gravity of History,* ed. Keith Ansell Pearson, Benita Parry, and Judith Squires, 173–93. New York: St. Martin's.

Parkin, Frank

1979 *Marxism and Class Theory: A Bourgeois Critique.* London: Tavistock.

Parmentier, Richard J.

1987 *The Sacred Remains: Myth, History, and Polity in Belau.* Chicago: University of Chicago Press.

Peirce, C. S.

1956 Logic as Semiotic: The Theory of Signs. In *The Philosophy of Peirce: Selected Writings,* ed. J. Buchler, 98–119. London: Routledge & Kegan Paul.

Philpin, C. H. E., ed.
  1987   *Nationalism and Popular Protest in Ireland.* Cambridge: Cambridge University Press.
Polanyi, Karl
  1944   *The Great Transformation.* Boston: Beacon.
  1957   The Economy as Instituted Process. In *Trade and Market in the Early Empires,* ed. Karl Polanyi, Conrad M. Arensberg, and Harry W. Pearson, 243–69. New York: Free Press.
Robinson, Philip
  1984   *The Plantation of Ulster.* Dublin: Gill and MacMillan.
Roediger, David
  1991   *The Wages of Whiteness: Race and the Making of the American Working Class.* London: Verso.
Rosaldo, Renato
  1989   *Culture and Truth: The Remaking of Social Analysis.* Boston: Beacon.
Rose, Nikolas
  1996   Identity, Genealogy, History. In *Questions of Cultural Identity,* ed. Stuart Hall and Paul du Gay, 128–50. London: Sage.
Rouse, Roger
  1991   Mexican Migration and the Social Space of Postmodernism. *Diaspora* 1 (1): 8–23.
Rowthorn, Bob
  1981   Northern Ireland: An Economy in Crisis. *Cambridge Journal of Economics* 5 (1): 1–31.
Rowthorn, Bob, and Naomi Wayne
  1988   *Northern Ireland: The Political Economy of Conflict.* Cambridge: Polity.
Royal Irish Academy
  1979   *Atlas of Ireland.* Dublin: Royal Irish Academy.
Ruane, Joseph, and Jennifer Todd
  1991   "Why Can't You Get Along with Each Other?" Culture, Structure, and the Northern Ireland Conflict. In *Culture and Politics in Northern Ireland,* ed. Eamonn Hughes, 27–44. Milton Keynes: Open University Press.
  1996   *The Dynamics of Conflict in Northern Ireland: Power, Conflict, and Emancipation.* Cambridge: Cambridge University Press.
  1999   The Belfast Agreement: Context, Content, Consequences. In *After the Good Friday Agreement: Analysing Political Change in Northern Ireland,* ed. Joseph Ruane and Jennifer Todd, 1–29. Dublin: University College Dublin Press.
Said, Edward
  1989   Representing the Colonized: Anthropology's Interlocutors. *Critical Inquiry* 15 (2): 205–25.
  1995   Secular Interpretation, the Geographical Element, and the Methodology of Imperialism. In *After Colonialism: Imperial Histories and*

Postcolonial Displacements, ed. Gyan Prakash, 21–39. Princeton: Princeton University Press.

Scheper-Hughes, Nancy
    1982   *Saints, Scholars, and Schizophrenics: Mental Illness in Rural Ireland.* Berkeley: University of California Press.

Scott, Joan Wallach
    1988   *Gender and the Politics of History.* New York: Columbia University Press.
    1992   Experience. In *Feminists Theorize the Political,* ed. Judith Butler and Joan Wallach Scott, 22–40. New York: Routledge.

Segal, Daniel
    1998   The Hypervisible and the Masked: Some Thoughts on the Mutual Embeddedness of "Race" and "Class" in the United States Now. In *Democracy and Ethnography: Constructing Identities in Multicultural Liberal States,* ed. Carol J. Greenhouse, 50–60. Albany: State University of New York Press.

Sewell, William
    1980   *Work and Revolution in France.* New York: Cambridge University Press.
    1992   Introduction: Narratives and Social Identities. *Social Science History* 16:479–88.
    1996   Three Temporalities: Toward an Eventful Sociology. In *The Historic Turn in the Human Sciences,* ed. Terrence J. McDonald, 245–80. Ann Arbor: University of Michigan Press.
    1999   The Concept(s) of Culture. In *Beyond the Cultural Turn,* ed. Victoria E. Bonnell and Lynn Hunt, 35–61. Berkeley: University of California Press.

Silverstein, Michael
    1976   Shifters, Linguistic Categories, and Cultural Description. In *Meaning in Anthropology,* ed. Keith Basso and Henry Selby, 11–55. Albuquerque: University of New Mexico Press.

Sluka, Jeffrey A.
    1992   The Politics of Painting: Political Murals in Northern Ireland. In *Domination, Resistance, and Terror,* ed. Carolyn Nordstrom and JoAnn Martin, 190–216. Berkeley: University of California Press.

Somers, Margaret R.
    1992   Narrativity, Narrative Identity, and Social Action: Rethinking English Working-Class Formation. *Social Science History* 16:591–630.
    1994   The Narrative Constitution of Identity: A Relational and Network Approach. *Theory and Society* 23:605–50.
    1997   Deconstructing and Reconstructing Class Formation Theory: Narrativity, Relational Analysis, and Social Theory. In *Reworking Class,* ed. John R. Hall, 73–105. Ithaca: Cornell University Press.

Somers, Margaret R., and Gloria D. Gibson
    1994   Reclaiming the Epistemological "Other": Narrative and the Social Constitution of Identity. In *Social Theory and the Politics of Identity,* ed. Craig Calhoun, 37–99. Oxford: Basil Blackwell.

References

Stalker, John
    1988   *The Stalker Affair.* New York: Viking.
Stallybrass, Peter, and Allon White
    1986   *The Politics and Poetics of Transgression.* Ithaca: Cornell University Press.
Stanfield, John
    1985   Theoretical and Ideological Barriers to the Study of Race-Making. In *Research in Race and Ethnic Relations: A Research Annual,* ed. Cora Bagley Marrett and Ceryl Leggon, 161–81. Greenwich, CT: JAI Press.
Stark, David
    1980   Class Struggle and the Transformation of the Labor Process: A Relational Approach. *Theory and Society* 9:89–130.
    1986   Rethinking Internal Labor Markets: New Insights from a Comparative Perspective. *American Sociological Review* 51:492–504.
    1994   Recombinant Property in East European Capitalism. Working Papers on *Transitions from State Socialism,* no. 94–95, Cornell University, Ithaca, NY.
Stark, David, and László Bruszt
    1998   *Postsocialist Pathways: Transforming Politics and Property in East Central Europe.* Cambridge: Cambridge University Press.
Stedman Jones, Gareth
    1983   *Languages of Class: Studies in English Working-Class History, 1832–1982.* Cambridge: Cambridge University Press.
Steedly, Mary Margaret
    1993   *Hanging without a Rope: Narrative Experience in Colonial and Postcolonial Karoland.* Princeton: Princeton University Press.
Steinberg, Marc
    1996   "The Labour of the Country Is the Wealth of the Country": Class Identity, Consciousness, and the Role of Discourse in the Making of the English Working Class. *International Labor and Working-Class History* 49 (spring): 1–25.
Steinmetz, George
    1992   Reflections on the Role of Social Narratives in Working-Class Formation. *Social Science History* 16:489–516.
Stewart, A. T. Q.
    1977   *The Narrow Ground: Patterns of Ulster History.* London: Faber and Faber.
Stewart, Kathleen
    1996   *A Space on the Side of the Road: Cultural Poetics in an "Other" America.* Princeton: Princeton University Press.
Stoler, Ann Laura
    1989   Rethinking Colonial Categories: European Communities and the Boundaries of Rule. *Comparative Studies in Society and History* 13 (1): 134–61.
Stoler, Ann Laura, and Frederick Cooper
    1997   Between Metropole and Colony: Rethinking a Research Agenda. In

Tensions of Empire: Colonial Cultures in a Bourgeois World, ed. Frederick Cooper and Ann Laura Stoler, 1–56. Berkeley: University of California Press.

Strathern, Marilyn
1996   The Concept of Society Is Theoretically Obsolete: For the Motion. In *Key Debates in Anthropology,* ed. Tim Ingold, 60–66. New York: Routledge.

Sutton, David
1998   *Memories Cast in Stone: The Relevance of the Past in Everyday Life.* Oxford: Berg.

Taussig, Michael
1987   *Shamanism, Colonialism, and the Wild Man: A Study in Terror and Healing.* Chicago: University of Chicago Press.

Taylor, Charles
1994   The Politics of Recognition. In *Multiculturalism,* ed. Amy Gutmann, 25–73. Princeton: Princeton University Press.

Taylor, Lawrence J.
1995   *Occasions of Faith: An Anthropology of Irish Catholics.* Philadelphia: University of Pennsylvania Press.

Teague, Paul
1993   Discrimination and Fair Employment in Northern Ireland. In *The Economy of Northern Ireland,* ed. Paul Teague, 141–69. London: Lawrence & Wishart.

Thevenot, Laurent
1985   Rules and Implements: Investment in Forms. *Social Science Information* 23 (1): 1–45.

Thomas, Jo
1985   "Shoot to Kill" Policy in Ulster: The Debate Rages. *New York Times,* April 12.
1986   "Shoot to Kill" Rumors Will Not Die. *New York Times,* March 17.
1988   Bloody Ireland. *Columbia Journalism Review* (May/June): 31–37.

Thompson, E. P.
1978   Eighteenth-Century English Society: Class Struggle without Class? *Social History* 3 (2): 133–65.

Todd, Jennifer
1987   Two Traditions in Unionist Political Culture. *Irish Political Studies* 2:1–26.

Tsing, Anna
1993   *In the Realm of the Diamond Queen.* Princeton: Princeton University Press.

Tyler, Stephen
1986   Post-Modern Ethnography: From Document of the Occult to Occult Document. In *Writing Culture: The Poetics and Politics of Ethnography,* ed. James Clifford and George E. Marcus, 122–40. Berkeley: University of California Press.

References

Urciuoli, Bonnie
:   1996 *Exposing Prejudice: Puerto Rican Experiences of Language, Race, and Class.* Boulder: Westview.

Varela, Charles R., and Rom Harré
:   1996 Conflicting Varieties of Realism: Causal Powers and the Problems of Social Structure. *Journal for the Theory of Social Behaviour* 26 (3): 275–325.

Viney, Michael
:   1983 The Yank in the Corner: Why the Ethics of Anthropology Are a Worry for Rural Ireland. *Irish Times,* August 6, p. 9.

Walker, Graham
:   1992 Old History: Protestant Ulster in Lee's *Ireland. The Irish Review* 12 (spring/summer): 65–71.

Watzlawack, Paul, Janet H. Beavin, and Don D. Jackson, eds.
:   1967 *Pragmatics of Human Communication: A Study of Interactional Patterns, Pathologies and Paradoxes.* New York: W. W. Norton.

White, Harrison C.
:   1993 Values Come in Styles, Which Mate to Change. In *The Origin of Values,* ed. Michael Hechter and Richard E. Michod, 63–91. New York: Aldine De Gruyter.

White, Hayden
:   1987 *The Content in the Form: Narrative Discourse and Historical Representation.* Baltimore: Johns Hopkins University Press.

Whyte, John
:   1988 Interpretations of the Northern Ireland Problem. In *Consensus in Ireland: Approaches and Recessions,* ed. Charles Townshend, 24–46. Oxford: Oxford University Press.
:   1990 *Interpreting Northern Ireland.* Oxford: Oxford University Press.

Williams, Brackette
:   1989 A Class Act: Anthropology and the Race to Nation across Ethnic Terrain. *Annual Review of Anthropology* 18:401–44.
:   1991 *Stains on My Name, War in My Veins: Guyana and the Politics of Cultural Struggle.* Durham, NC: Duke University Press.
:   1995 Classification Systems Revisited: Kinship, Caste, Race, and Nationality as the Flow of Blood and the Spread of Rights. In *Naturalizing Power: Essays in Feminist Cultural Analysis,* ed. Sylvia Yanagisako and Carol Delaney, 201–36. New York: Routledge.

Williams, Raymond
:   1980 Base and Superstructure in Marxist Theory. In *Problems in Materialism and Culture,* ed. 31–49. London: Verso.
:   1981 *The Sociology of Culture.* New York: Schocken.

Willis, Paul
:   1977 *Learning to Labor: How Working-Class Kids Get Working-Class Jobs.* New York: Columbia University Press.

Wilson, Thomas, ed.
:   1955 *Ulster under Home Rule.* Oxford: Oxford University Press.

Wilson, Thomas M.

    1988   Culture and Class among the "Large" Farmers of Eastern Ireland. *American Ethnologist* 15 (4): 678–93.

Wilson, Thomas M., and Hastings Donnan, eds.

    1998   *Border Identities: Nation and State at International Frontiers.* Cambridge: Cambridge University Press.

Yanagisako, Sylvia, and Carol Delaney

    1995   Naturalizing Power. In *Naturalizing Power: Essays in Feminist Cultural Analysis,* ed. Sylvia Yanagisako and Carol Delaney, 1–22. New York: Routledge.

Yelvington, Kevin A.

    1995   *Producing Power: Ethnicity, Gender, and Class in a Caribbean Workplace.* Philadelphia: Temple University Press.

Index

economy
    effects of violence on, 143–44
    global transformations of, 150
Eley, Geoff, 151, 152
Elizabethan Conquest, 31, 32, 39, 56
Elliott, Marianne, 220n. 4
embodiment, 13–14, 162
emigration rates, 163–64
Engels, Friedrich, 223n. 3
ethical discourses, 79
ethnography, 14–16
    fieldwork and moral ambiguity,
        69–70
    fieldwork engagements, x
    position of ethnographer, 56
    postmodern, 92
    writing of, 74
European Parliament elections, 68
Eversley, David, 223n. 23

Fabian, Johannes, 219n. 22
Fair Employment Agency, 223n. 2
Fanon, Frantz, 83
Farrell, Michael, 78, 222n. 2
Feldman, Allen, 33–36, 43, 100, 216n.
    11, 218n. 12, 220n. 5, 221n. 1,
    222n. 8, 223n. 7
feminist anthropology, 15
feminist theory, 128, 151, 183–84
Ferguson, James, 88
Fernandez-Kelly, Maria, 152
fieldwork engagements, x
Finbarr, Father, 150, 162–69, 188, 191,
    224n. 14
Fischer, Michael F. K., 15, 217n. 15
Fisk, Robert, 222n. 3
Foster, R. F., 32, 217n. 24, 218n. 11,
    219n. 16
Foucault, Michel, 17, 32, 219n. 22,
    221n. 6
Frankenberg, Ruth, 29, 30, 57, 76, 207,
    218n. 9
Frow, John, 155

Gaffikin, Frank, 224n. 17
Gallagher, Anthony M., 223n. 2

Garvaghy Road housing estate,
    220n. 7
Garvin, Tom, 222n. 4
Gates, Henry Louis, Jr., 61
gender, 183–202, 211
geography, 23–60
Gergen, Kenneth, 225n. 2
Gibbon, Peter, 220n. 4
Gibson, Gloria D., 184
Giddens, Anthony, 219n. 24, 223n. 5
Ginsburg, Faye, 217n. 16
Glassie, Henry, 93–94, 100, 102, 219n.
    20, 221n. 4
Geertz, Clifford, 71
Good Friday Agreement, 212–13
Gordon, Deborah A., 217n. 16
Gould, Stephen Jay, 223n. 7
Gramsci, Antonio, 175
Gray, John, 222n. 2
Greenblatt, Stephen, 115
Grossberg, Lawrence, 154, 175,
    225n. 1
Gupta, Akhil, 88

Hadfield, Andrew, 3, 218n. 10
Hall, Stuart, 19, 150, 154, 175, 180,
    217n. 21, 218n. 8
Harré, Rom, 187, 225n. 4
Harris, Richard, 224n. 17
Hart, Janet, 155
H-Blocks, 48, 76
Hechter, Michael, 144
Herzfeld, Michael, 181, 224n. 18,
    225n. 22
Hill, Jane, 220n. 13
Hill, Kenneth, 220n. 13
historical consciousness, 56
"historiography of excuse," 42–43
history as division, 115
Holkerri, Prime Minister Harry,
    212
Howe, Leo, 223n. 2
Hughes, Eamonn, 225n. 3
Hume, John, 68
hunger strike, 167, 176, 220n. 5
Hurston, Zora Neale, 3, 61

space
  and time, 55–56
  and value, 31
Special Air Services (SAS), 49, 50, 227
speech acts, 186–94, 196
Spencer, John, 224n. 17
split subjectivity, 88, 127, 203
Stallybrass, Peter, 153, 216n. 13,
    216–17n. 14, 224n. 12
Stanfield, John, 220n. 17
Stark, David, 155, 157–58, 176,
    223n. 3, 225n. 3
state, 19–20, 32, 53, 57, 63, 81, 123,
    131, 204–6, 208–13
  accounts of, 206
  and security force misinformation,
    116–18
  terror, 49
  and violence, 197, 206, 211–12
Stedman Jones, Gareth, 152–53
Steedly, Mary, 217n. 16
Steinberg, Marc, 156
Steinmetz, George, 156
Stewart, Kathleen, 217n. 16, 223n. 7,
    225n. 20
St. Marys Star (Kansas), 183
Stormont, 139
Strathern, Marilyn, 180
strike, 161–82
structures, 153–54, 217n. 18
subjectivities, 79–80, 207–8
  fixity of subjects, 205
  subjectification, 221n. 6
Sutton, David, 217n. 17

talk, 2–3, 11–12
  as an index of identity, 157–59
  and moral community, 94–103
  as a social practice, 172–74, 177,
    224n. 18
  and striking workers, 210
  as value, 167–71
Taylor, Charles, 225n. 21
Taylor, Lawrence, 224n. 16
telling, 11–17, 34, 58, 73–85
  dual meaning of, 54–55

and ethnographic issues, 12–16
as everyday practice, 54–60
eye as an organ of, 34, 43
interpretation by, 159
middle-class form, 72
as a producer of silence, 157
state and, 58
Thatcher, Prime Minister Margaret,
    64–65, 166, 175–76, 180, 224n. 17,
    225n. 23
  economic policies of, 166, 175–77
Thevenot, Laurent, 158
Thomas, Jo, 36, 222n. 4
Thompson, E. P., 152
Todd, Jennifer, 215–16n. 5, 216n. 7,
    223n. 2, 225n. 3
truth, 2–3, 18
Tsing, Anna Lowenhaupt, 217n. 16
Twelfth of July (holiday), 62, 66,
    120–23

Ulster Defense Regiment (UDR), 36,
    37, 40–41, 46–47, 71, 105, 228
Ulster Unionist Party (UUP), 67, 228
Ulster Volunteer Force (UVF), 34, 62
unemployment, comparative rates in
    Northern Ireland, 147
unionist(s), ix, 9
  discourse of, 82
  vs. loyalist, 216n. 7
  neighborhood markings, 62–68,
    221n. 7
United Kingdom of Great Britain and
    Northern Ireland, 10, 20
University of Ulster at Jordanstown,
    222n. 6
Urciuoli, Bonnie, 73–74, 78, 80, 220n.
    17, 225n. 5

Varela, Charles, 217n. 18
Viney, Michael, 88–90
violence, 9, 17
  as collective memory, 35–36

Walker, Graham, 220–21n. 18
Watzlawack, Paul, 75